Norman Geras's Political Thought from Marxism to Human Rights

"Cowling's book is the first comprehensive study of the works of a major mid-century Marxist intellectual. While sympathetically recounted, Geras's views are subjected here to discerning critique. Geras is best known for his contributions to the debates on Marx and human nature, and morality and justice. In further compact chapters, Cowling also explores the wider reaches of his controversial thought, covering the Holocaust, a 'contract of mutual indifference', Israel/Palestine and the 2003 invasion of Iraq. The Marx revival is underway, and the Geras revival is long overdue."

—Professor Terrell Carver, *University of Bristol, UK*

Mark Cowling

Norman Geras's Political Thought from Marxism to Human Rights

Controversy and Analysis

palgrave
macmillan

Mark Cowling
Teesside University [retired]
Middlesborough, UK

ISBN 978-3-030-08906-1 ISBN 978-3-319-74048-5 (eBook)
https://doi.org/10.1007/978-3-319-74048-5

Cover illustration: weiXx

Printed on acid-free paper

This Palgrave Macmillan imprint is published by Springer Nature
The registered company is Springer International Publishing AG
The registered company address is: Gewerbestrasse 11, 6330 Cham, Switzerland

To: Camillia, Sophie and Ralph.

Preface

This book originated in a variety of papers given at Political Studies Association Annual Conferences and in the Marxism Stream of the Manchester Workshops in Political Theory. I had always found the work of Norman Geras both extremely impressive and invariably provoking me and others who read it to want to engage in a critical discussion of the issues raised. Those, like me, who were privileged to know Norman had the same experience when talking with him. The project developed into a more systematic discussion of the wide-ranging areas on which Geras wrote. I am very grateful to everybody who debated the issues with me. Special mention should be made of John Kelly, who made helpful comments on an early draft of the chapter on Trotsky, Eve Garrard, who has been helpful on some issues to do with the Holocaust and with normblog, Adèle Geras, Paul Raekstad and David Bates. Also, I would like to thank my editor at Palgrave, Imogen Gordon Clark, who has been extremely helpful, and the Palgrave production team, headed by Mathivanan SenthilKumar, who have been very efficient and courteous.

I have had support of another kind from my family. I have particular difficulties because of being disabled with multiple sclerosis, and my wife Amani, and my children, Camillia, Sophie and Ralph have all made my life whilst writing this much easier and more interesting than it would otherwise have been. The book is dedicated to my dear children.

Finally, some comments about the writing of the book. The opinions expressed in the book and the errors it contains are my responsibility. As is conventional in philosophical writing I refer to myself as 'I' rather than 'we'; if you imagine discussing, for example, personal identity using the authorial 'we', it should become obvious why. Many of the quotations are taken from the wonderful website www.Marxists.org, which is an excellent source of Marxist and other writing, which is all available under a Creative Commons License. It will be obvious from the references where I have used this website. The websites used are all well established, so that putting the date on which they were accessed is unnecessary.

Middlesborough, UK Mark Cowling

Contents

CHAPTER 1

Introduction

Norman Geras sadly died in October 2013 from cancer of the prostate. He was born in 1943 in what is now Zimbabwe, but would have been Rhodesia at the time, and went to school there. He never spoke about this to me, but I would imagine that being part of a Jewish family in Rhodesia would have presented various challenges given that the white population tended to be racist. Geras subsequently became a student at Pembroke College and Nuffield College at the University of Oxford. In 1967 he was appointed as a lecturer at the University of Manchester, and eventually became a professor there. He was famous for his view that Manchester was the centre of the universe! I am not sure at what stage he became a Marxist, but he was certainly a Marxist by the time that I first encountered him as an undergraduate student when I was at the University of Manchester. I recall him lecturing on Lenin's 'What Is to Be Done?'. At that stage he must have been only three or four years older than the students he was teaching. Subsequently I was lucky enough to be able to do a PhD at Manchester University. My supervisor, Mike Evans, had an unrivalled knowledge of Marx's work, but was reluctant to debate general perspectives, and Norman was extremely helpful in this respect.

A personal recollection from my student years is that there were widespread protests against the apartheid regime in South Africa, and British students planned to disrupt the series of test matches between England and the visiting South African cricket team. Norman said that he supported these protests rather reluctantly, as he was extremely fond of watching

M. Cowling, *Norman Geras's Political Thought from Marxism to Human Rights*, https://doi.org/10.1007/978-3-319-74048-5_1

cricket, and one of the highlights of his year when living in Rhodesia had been the visit of the South African cricket team. He loved the team with a real passion: 'For this South African team, the South Africa of the mid-1950s, is my team. It is the team of my life, the one launched in the deepest recesses of my consciousness' (Holliday 2012, p. 251). His love of cricket was indeed remarkable. He possessed a library of some 2500 books about cricket (Holliday 2012, p. 252). Geras co-wrote two short books about cricket with the Ian Holliday. Each describes a test match in great detail. One feature of both books is that Geras had a phenomenal grasp of cricketing statistics that enabled him to puzzle even a very knowledgeable fellow cricket lover. As we will see, the title of one of his books, much of which is based upon a study of the Holocaust, came to him as he was on his way to Headingley cricket ground.

For the last few years of his life Geras posted extensively to his prize-winning political blog, normblog. Some good general appreciations of this have been written by no less than four authors in Garrard and de Wijze (2012). Apart from adding my enthusiastic agreement to the generally appreciative comments of these authors I shall not be discussing normblog in general terms in this book. I shall, however, make reference to it from time to time in order to amplify the discussion.

The Plan of the Book

Apart from the above I shall have very little to say about Geras's personal life. Instead, I shall focus on the main books and articles that he wrote. In each case I shall give an exposition of what he said, together with a more or less critical commentary. On some issues I regard his work as extremely thorough and very well argued, and there will be little by way of criticism. Other chapters are more critical. It is only a shame that Geras himself is not available to respond to critical comments, as I am certain that his replies would have been very interesting.

The chapters of the book basically follow the order of publication of Geras's writings, although certain issues are run together—for example, earlier articles that linked to his discussion of Marx and human nature are run together with the book that he wrote on this theme.

Chapter 2 discusses Geras's first book, which comprises of four essays on Rosa Luxemburg, discussing barbarism and the collapse of capitalism; the debate that occurred between socialists following the 1905 revolution in Russia about the nature of the forthcoming Russian revolution; the role of the mass strike; and the issue of the extent to which day-to-day socialist struggles should be linked to the ultimate goal of socialist revolution. This chapter largely comprises exposition, but in the course of Geras's book on Luxemburg he asserts that both she and Lenin came to agree with Trotsky's theory of permanent revolution. I take issue with this in Chapter 3. I also have reservations about his treatment of the economic aspects of Luxemburg's theories. Geras is to be commended particularly for his emphasis that Luxemburg did not advocate spontaneity for its own sake.

Chapter 3 deals with Geras's early Trotskyism. I consider his writings in this area one of the least satisfactory parts of his overall work. I go carefully through Geras's discussion of permanent revolution, politics, the use of terror and the rise of fascism, and argue that he failed to apply his usual rigorous approach to Trotsky's work and theories. If Geras had been more careful in his assessment of Trotsky, he might well have adopted the liberal Marxist position that characterizes his later work at a much earlier stage. Indeed, in the conclusion, Chap. 13, there is a section where this theme is further considered, because even in his later writings, Geras arguably never really comes to terms with his views about Trotsky.

Chapter 4 is discussion of Geras's work on the issue of Marx and human nature. In his book: *Marx and Human Nature: Refutation of a Legend* (Geras 1983), Geras is widely held to have demonstrated that there is a theory of human nature in the older Marx, and thus to have vindicated the position taken by the majority of British commentators on Marx that there is an overall continuity between Marx's writings on alienation between 1843 and 1845, and the older Marx. I disagree with this position. I show that the account of human nature that Geras legitimately finds in the older Marx is a very thin one, which basically does not support the alienation theory. I also go on to show that the appearance of the alienation theory in the older Marx that Geras to some extent and others very enthusiastically see as demonstrating continuity in Marx fails to do this. I agree with him that we require a theory of human nature today as part of a theory of justice which we need as part of our arguments for socialism, but do not agree that such a theory is readily available throughout Marx's work.

Chapter 5 is a discussion of Geras's critique of Althusser. In Chap. 4 I had already identified that Geras has criticized Althusser's assertion that the older Marx's theories are not based on a theory of human nature. In Chap. 5 Geras takes issue with Althusser's conception of science. In particular, he asserts that Althusser's conception of science is on the borderlines of idealism, of a picture of science as something neutral outside the social formation. Instead, Geras wants to emphasize that all the most famous Marxists learned from the practice of the working class, Marx learning the necessity of destroying the bourgeois state from the Paris commune, Rosa Luxemburg learning the value of the mass strike, Trotsky learning the value of permanent revolution from the experience of the revolution of 1905, and Lenin learning the importance of the Soviets. He also takes issue with Althusser's idea that ideology continues under communism.

I offer a limited defence to Althusser on the grounds that Geras is selective in the political practice from which his Marxists learned.

Chapter 6 considers Geras's work on Marx's theory of justice. Most authors in this area have their own view of whether or not Marx has a theory of justice, and therefore there is widespread disagreement on Geras's conclusion that Marx had a theory of justice but did not think that he had a theory of justice. However, for a succinct summary of what Marx says in this area and the possible positions available in the considerable literature up to the time of Geras's articles on Marx and justice there is no one to equal Geras. If you are looking for his finest writing in the sense that everyone would agree that it makes a valuable contribution, this is it.

Geras concludes that Marx has a theory of justice, but, particularly as it is stated in a contradictory way, it is quite limited and a theory of justice based on Marxism requires considerable fleshing out. Geras's attempts to do this are discussed in Chap. 7, which examine a series of pieces in which Geras produces a more substantive approach to questions of justice. These include the relationship between Marxism and moral advocacy, and a discussion of whether, if violent revolution is required, there are moral limits to revolutionary violence. In 2006 Geras was the lead author of the Euston Manifesto, a manifesto for leftist bloggers. This contains a very strong commitment to human rights and parliamentary democracy. The last part of Chap. 7 deals with Geras's discussion of Marx's economics, which argues that it is not sustainable as economic theory but, by looking at its inadequacies, many worthwhile issues for an egalitarian theory of justice may be developed.

Chapters 8 and 9 deal with Geras's critique of various forms of postmodernism. Chapter 8 comprises of his assault on Laclau and Mouffe, who contended that there were such a lot of problems with Marxism that it was necessary to move on to a struggle for radical democracy.

Chapter 9 comprises of an account of Geras's critique of Richard Rorty's *Contingency, Irony and Solidarity* (Rorty 1989), which advocates a form of ironic liberalism based on pragmatism. Rorty contends that there is no such thing as human nature. As might be expected, Geras takes him to task at some length on this issue. Rorty also asserts that people are most naturally sympathetic to those with whom they have something in common. While this might sound plausible in the abstract, Geras brings forward extensive evidence to show that people's motivation was invariably to do with human decency in one way or other rather than prior acquaintance. Geras also takes issue with what might be seen as the foundations of Rorty's anti-foundationalism, namely his advocacy of pragmatism.

I am generally sympathetic to Geras's critique of Rorty, but suggest some additions, particularly based on analyzing Rorty's pragmatism in greater philosophical depth.

Chapter 10 is largely the exposition of an edited collection on the Enlightenment. Geras was one of the editors. I provide a brief exposition of this excellent collection.

Chapter 11 comprises a departure from the Marxist-inspired themes of previous chapters. It is based on Geras's very extensive reading of the secondary literature on the Holocaust. Here Geras plumbs the depths of human iniquity. His main interest is in the question of why bystanders simply got on with their daily life rather than attempting to intervene. He comments that the same basic situation applies to most people in the advanced countries. There are horrors in the world—starvation, lack of shelter and care, various forms of state repression including torture and mass extermination—and yet most of us carry on with our daily enjoyments and do very little about it. Geras says that it is as if there was a contract of mutual indifference, meaning that we agree with each other not to give mutual aid. He finds this to be a deeply pessimistic conclusion, and explores ways in which we might escape the contract of mutual indifference. If it is accepted that there is a duty to bring aid, and a corresponding right to assistance in extreme distress, then we have the beginnings of a way out of the contract of mutual indifference. He goes on to discuss Ralph Miliband's views about the possibility of socialism given that there have been such dreadful events as the Holocaust. Geras concludes that there is a basic human capacity for doing evil, and that this needs to be factored into any plans for a socialist future. One Marxist who discussed the Holocaust from time to time was Ernest Mandel. Geras considers that his analysis of the Holocaust is inadequate, in a way that raises questions about whether any Marxist explanation of the Holocaust could be satisfactory. In a fine piece of applied analytical philosophy, Geras discusses the question of whether or not the Holocaust was unique, and manages to show both that no other historical events quite matches it, but that it shares common features with other events. In the last two sections of Chap. 10 two related issues are discussed. One is Geras's attitude to the state of Israel and the Palestinians—was he willing to accept conduct from Israel that amounted to ethnic cleansing? I conclude that he can be defended on this score. I then briefly consider some things that he said about anti-Semitism, arguing that this is an important but extremely complex and fraught issue.

Chapter 12 deals with Geras on the issue of human rights and humanitarian intervention. In his book *Crimes against Humanity* (2011) Geras starts by identifying crimes against humanity. He then puts forward a strong case for humanitarian intervention to avoid human suffering. In the book the main example he uses is a very limited case of intervention, the use of Israeli special forces to rescue hijacked airline passengers at Entebbe airport. This was actually a brilliant success, but even if it had gone wrong it is unlikely that the results would have been catastrophic. Subsequently Geras supported the US's invasion of Iraq, complete with regime change. I agreed with majority of the rest of the left in regarding this as potentially disastrous, and history has proved us right. In the second half of Chap. 12 this issue is discussed at some length, the argument being that Geras advocates the invasion on grounds of humanitarian intervention, but fails to consider the lies that were told to justify the invasion, and the very long record of indifference, displayed by the USA and Britain, to the suffering of Iraqi people. This leads on to a more extensive discussion of situations in which humanitarian intervention might be considered.

Chapter 13 is the conclusion. After praising Geras's lifetime achievements, the chapter goes on to discuss three areas of possible criticism. First, there is the ongoing curiosity that the later Geras continued, so far as can be seen, to admire Trotsky, and yet, as seen in Chap. 3, Trotsky's affiliation to human rights and pluralist democracy was very much open to debate, and his perfectionist assumptions about human nature are out of line with Geras's conclusions about the Holocaust and other horrors that people inflict on one another. A second issue is the very limited amount that Geras had to say about party politics, about the actual ways of getting into power and implementing socialist policies in liberal democracies. This, in turn, may be linked to the third area, which is that, by the time he had finished, Geras seems to have had hardly any faith in Marxism as a way of analyzing societies, as opposed to providing ideas about the egalitarian measures.

References

Garrard, E., & de Wijze, S. (Eds.). (2012). *Thinking Towards Humanity*. Manchester: Manchester University Press.

Geras, N. (1983). *Marx and Human Nature: Refutation of a Legend*. London: Verso.

Geras, N. (2011). *Crimes Against Humanity*. Manchester: Manchester University Press.

Holliday, I. (2012). Cricket, the Best-Loved Game. In E. Garrard & S. de Wijze (Eds.), *Thinking Towards Humanity*. Manchester: Manchester University Press.

Rorty, R. (1989). *Contingency, Irony and Solidarity*. New York: Cambridge University Press.

CHAPTER 2

The Legacy of Rosa Luxemburg

Geras's first major work was *The Legacy of Rosa Luxemburg* (Geras 1983, originally published in 1976). Geras describes this as a collection of essays, and this is a very common pattern in his other books, which tend to be collections of essays on closely related themes. The first essay in this book looks at the relationship between Luxemburg's economic theory of capitalist breakdown and her political ideas, particularly disputing the idea that she had a 'spontaneist' conception of class struggle. The second essay deals with her ideas about the nature of the Russian Revolution following the abortive Revolution of 1905, together with her ideas about democracy. The third essay discusses her ideas about the mass strike, which Geras argues she sees as an element in the preconditions of successful proletarian revolution. The final essay discusses Luxemburg's criticisms of the Bolsheviks in 1918 and the insistence on democratic rights and freedoms both in the course of revolution and after it. For each essay I shall follow the procedure that will be followed throughout the book, namely offering an exposition of Geras's ideas, followed by a more or less extended commentary.

Barbarism and the Collapse of Capitalism

Geras makes it clear that Luxemburg did subscribe to the idea of a collapse of capitalism. In contrast to revisionists such as Bernstein she argued that Marxism is distinguishable from reformism because it believes in a breakdown of capitalism, a catastrophe (Geras 1983, p. 14). The reason for this

M. Cowling, *Norman Geras's Political Thought from Marxism to Human Rights*, https://doi.org/10.1007/978-3-319-74048-5_2

was that capitalist accumulation must come to a stop when capitalism dominates production in all countries. At that point it will be impossible to realize surplus value (Geras 1983, p. 15). A simplistic version of Luxemburg would thus argue that the coming of socialism is pretty much automatic—with capitalist collapse there will be mass actions that lead to socialism (Geras 1983, p. 16). This is, as will be imagined, too simplistic. Geras points out that Luxemburg said that a purely spontaneous development from the collapse of capitalism would merely lead to a crisis of civilization, to a new Dark Age (Geras 1983, p. 18). However, Luxemburg makes it clear that the collapse of capitalism is a precondition of socialism, but that socialism depends upon 'conscious interference' and working-class 'political struggle' (Geras 1983, p. 19). In the famous *Junius Pamphlet*, (1915) Geras points out that Luxemburg talks of the proletariat being under the leadership of Social Democracy (Geras 1983, p. 21). Practice divorced from theory is a 'sad caricature' of Marxism (Geras 1983, p. 37). What emerges from this brief summary is that Luxemburg thought that the development of capitalism would inevitably lead to its collapse, but that, although this is the precondition of the emergence of socialism, socialism does not emerge automatically. Socialism will only emerge if the working class engages in political struggle under the leadership of a social democratic party. If there is a collapse without these preconditions of socialism being present the result will be barbarism.

What did Luxemburg mean by barbarism? She makes it clear that she regards the First World War as a reversion to barbarism, and thinks that under imperialism, militarism and war will become permanent unless there is a socialist revolution (Geras 1983, p. 33).

Geras comments that Luxemburg's economic analysis is almost certainly flawed, and also that, short of nuclear warfare, a society characterized by barbarism and imperialism would have its own social forms. He insists however, that the socialism or barbarism formulation is an extreme version of that which separates Marxism from philosophies of progress: the idea that capitalism is 'profoundly and inescapably contradictory' (Geras 1983, p. 39). Capitalist scientific developments provide new forces of production that can be beneficial, as well as such things as gas chambers, nuclear weapons, napalm, 'scientific' methods of torture, free-fire zones and strategic hamlets (Geras 1983, p. 41).

At this point it is worth summarizing some obvious problems and ambiguities in Luxemburg's perspective as presented by Geras so far. One obvious issue, which will be discussed later, is the nature of the Social

Democratic party as understood by Luxemburg, its internal functioning, and the relationship between the Social Democratic party and the working class more generally. All of these are likely to be different depending on the circumstances of the relevant country. For example, Germany had a mass Social Democratic Party with a sophisticated and at least notionally Marxist leadership, a relatively well-educated working class, which was economically very important to the country and which lived in a country where it was possible to meet and discuss politics relatively freely. In contrast, of course, in Russia political organization was very difficult, free discussion was dangerous, and very many workers had until recently been peasants, and, indeed, might wish to go back to the countryside in the right circumstances, or to help get the harvest in. Rates of literacy are difficult to measure as they depend on the standard used, but in 1917 some 60% of the population of the Czar's Empire were illiterate (Eklof 2008, cited in Berendt 2012). Although strategically important, the working class was a minority in a country where the majority constituted peasants.

A second issue concerns the economic logic of the idea of collapse. Rosa Luxemburg's economic view about collapse is premised on the idea that it would be impossible to realize surplus value in a world that had become entirely capitalist. This view is brilliantly argued in her book *The Accumulation of Capital* (Luxemburg 1951). The book displays an impressive grasp both of Marx's economic theory and of that found in a wide range of critics of Marx. As an economist Luxemburg was clearly on a par with contemporaries such as Hilferding or Lenin. That said, her theory is based on an analysis of expanded capitalist reproduction. She argues that this depends on the expansion of the market into areas not dominated by capitalism. Hence the conclusion that once the entire world has become capitalist, capitalist expansion would grind to a halt. In the edition above, Luxemburg's book is introduced by the Cambridge Marxist economist Joan Robinson. She points out a series of logical flaws in Luxemburg's economic analysis.

Contemporary readers of Luxemburg are likely to be sceptical about her analysis on the basis that it just doesn't seem to fit with the real world. The capitalist economy carried on expanding from the end of the Second World War through to 1989 in spite of the general ending of colonialism, and of communist economies being basically removed from the capitalist sphere for much of the period. Sub Saharan African countries, particularly, were largely marginalized by the main flows of trade. Since 1989 many of the biggest and most successful capitalist enterprises have been very heavily based on knowledge rather than physical resources—consider Apple, Microsoft, Google and related companies, Facebook, and, by and large, companies traded on the NASDAQ stock market. According to Marx, discontent with capitalism arises when capitalist relations of production turn into fetters on the forces of production. However, massive advances are occurring. The power and scope of computers and related devices has expanded enormously. Robots are increasingly used in industry. People can increasingly control their domestic environment using smart phones. Driverless cars are a real prospect. A range of medical advances is occurring, many of them based on use of computers.

Thus, there does not seem to be anything based on reproduction conditions to stop a purely capitalist world economy from carrying on expanding. Also, if it became impossible to realize surplus value, the standard result is a capitalist crisis in which the value of goods goes down, or, indeed, the goods are physically destroyed until profitability is restored. Episodes of this sort are liable to lead to political instability, but there is nothing to stop them being resolved without some kind of catastrophe. Economic crises up to Rosa Luxemburg's day had been resolved in the way described above without resulting in collapse, socialist revolution or barbarism.

Geras's point that scientific advances can be put to evil uses is interesting in the light of his subsequent discussion of the Holocaust. The Holocaust was made much easier by a variety of innovations driven forward by capitalist advance, such as the development of railways, poison gas and so forth. However, Geras himself, as we will see, came to think in terms of a category of evil that is not purely explained by capitalism.

Between the Russian Revolutions

This second essay in the book essentially concerns the debate that followed the Russian Revolution of 1905 between Lenin, the Mensheviks, and, of course, Rosa Luxemburg. Geras argues plausibly that Stalin took an opportunistic approach to Rosa Luxemburg, altering his account of her theories according to the convenience of the moment. (Geras may well have had in mind Trotsky [1932], where this case is plausibly made.) He says that in assessing the significance of the Russian Revolution she adopted 'a perspective essentially identical with Trotsky's theory of permanent revolution' (Geras 1983, p. 46). After arguing that commentators have made a nasty mess of interpreting Rosa Luxemburg's theory in this area, Geras goes on to give his view of her intentions.

He says that two important themes emerged well before 1905: that a proletarian conquest of power would be inherently premature, and that bourgeois democracy and liberalism are inherently bankrupt (Geras 1983, p. 51). The rights of organization available to the working class under bourgeois democracy are vital as part of preparations to attain power. However, the bourgeoisie itself was progressively abandoning bourgeois democracy (Geras 1983, p. 54). She thought that through long struggles the German working class would in due course be sufficiently mature to achieve 'the definitive victory of the revolution' (Geras 1983, p. 52). Obviously, says Geras, bourgeois democracy has remained useful to the bourgeoisie for much longer than Luxemburg anticipated (Geras 1983, p. 55). He points out that consent is achieved through democratic rights, elections and so forth, behind which the bourgeois state apparatus is concealed, so that the working class does not understand that actually they are being exploited and dominated. He also, interestingly, claims that Trotsky understood this. He also points out that the bourgeoisie are willing if unduly threatened to turn to outright repression as, for example, in Chile in 1973 (Geras 1983, pp. 59–63).

Democracy in Germany had basically been a gift from above and could easily be revoked if it suited the bourgeoisie, and in this respect Rosa Luxemburg turned out to be surprisingly prophetic (Geras 1983, p. 57).

Geras says that the bourgeoisie supports bourgeois democracy not because it is a progressive force but because bourgeois democracy helps to arrest revolutionary progress towards the emancipation of 'the working masses from exploitation' (Geras 1983, p. 63). One possible implication of this would be that the collapse of bourgeois democracy might actually be desirable, revealing the iron fist in the velvet glove, but this is definitely not an implication that Geras talks about or accepts.

The view of Germany in both Luxemburg and Geras is unduly crude. Manhood suffrage was indeed a gift from above, meaning from the Prussian state under Bismarck. However, to simply regard this as a gift from the bourgeoisie ignores important features of German history. To start with, there was a thoroughly justified dread of instability, and an accompanying love of order based on the religious disruptions that accompanied the Reformation. Lutherans challenged a corrupt religious order based on Catholicism. Luther himself came down on the side of authority, but Anabaptists had a role in Germany's peasant war, and followers of Zwingli advocated a version of Protestantism based much more on the community of believers than on Princes. The community of the faithful, rather than a secular ruler, would thus be in charge. A period of turmoil was resolved by the Peace of Augsburg (1555). This was based on the principle that the secular ruler could determine the religion of the area he governed, but that subjects who felt oppressed could leave for an area where their religious beliefs were more acceptable. From 1615 to 1645 this settlement broke down completely in the Thirty Years War. This was by no means a purely religious conflict, but religion played a substantial part in it. The effects on parts of Germany were devastating, and exacerbated in the 1640s by extreme weather conditions. The War was eventually basically resolved by the important Peace of Westphalia (1648). This reaffirmed the main principles of the Peace of Augsburg, but with the important additional principle that sovereign states should not interfere with the internal affairs of other states, an important principle of international relations subsequently (for details see, for example, Greengrass 2014, pp. 440, 643). The memory of this time and also of the French invasion during the Napoleonic wars left Germans with an understandable desire for peace and order.

A second part of German political culture was the issue of national unity. Germany was divided between many small city states and princely states, of which Prussia and Bavaria were the largest. A greater degree of unity was obviously desirable. The basic necessity was for a unity of custom's tariffs. This customs union (Zollverein) was agreed in 1834, but still greater union was generally felt desirable. Marx and Engels and socialists and liberals generally hoped that this would be based on the southern German states, but it was actually achieved under Prussian leadership. This also raised the issue of which geographic places should be included. Germans lived in parts of Poland, indeed Königsburg was so far east that it has now become Kaliningrad, part of Russia. There was also the question of Austria and of the Sudetenland. Divided loyalties were therefore to be expected. In contrast, English, French and Spanish identities were generally more straightforward. Thinking about a British as opposed to an English identity, the only land frontier of the UK as it stands today is in Northern Ireland, where there is, of course, considerable contention about national identity. Ambiguities and rivalries of this sort applied to many areas where Germans lived mingled with other peoples.

Third, more needs to be said about the Junkers, which were the legacy of Bismarck and the Kaiser. The Prussian government and upper civil service, together with the army, were essentially run by the Junkers. The Junkers were landowners from East Prussia. A characteristic pattern was for the oldest son of the estate owner to run the estate, while his younger brothers joined the Army or the civil service. Prussia had universal conscription, so that members of the government, civil servants and soldiers all enjoyed a common background of military service at some point. So far, this sounds like a description of a reactionary military caste. Officers were encouraged to develop a strong sense of honour, and to defend this through duelling, which was frequent. However, there was a very strong tradition, fostered by Prussian kings, and subsequently, with German unification, the Kaiser, who was also the king of Prussia, of public service, and of a strong sense of duty. The Kaiser was a constitutional monarch. His laws operated through the courts. The civil service had a very good reputation for efficient and neutral administration. Germany had excellent universities, and the ruling caste had a respect for higher education, including scientific education, which was put to use with good effect in their country estates.

Bismarck, described by Engels as a 'backwoods Prussian Junker' (Marx and Engels 1975, vol. 26, p. 475), dominated Prussian and subsequently German politics for some 30 years up to 1890. He had no political principles other than Prussian and personal aggrandizement. In many ways his policies were extremely successful. From 1864 through to 1870 Prussia fought three wars, first against Denmark over Schleswig Holstein, then against Austria, and finally against France in 1870. In all of these the Prussian army was highly successful. Bismarck managed to manipulate the other states into attacking Prussia at a time of Prussian choosing, in a superb and complex diplomatic game of chess. Prussian victory in the war against Austria ensured that German unification would be carried out under Prussian leadership, and Wilhelm I became not merely King of Prussia but Kaiser of the German Empire. The war against France ended with Louis Napoleon Bonaparte III being taken prisoner, the end of the Second Empire in France, and with France paying very substantial reparations to Prussia, which caused a boom followed by a bubble in Germany. Bismarck's use of 'blood and iron' to dominate Prussia's neighbours obviously increased the prestige of the Prussian army.

Bismarck also introduced manhood suffrage for the lower houses of both the Reichstag and the Prussian parliament. This may have been a gift from above, but remember that in comparison Britain only achieved manhood suffrage in 1918, and the power of the Lords was only broken in 1911. This in turn led to the growth of both the SPD (Sozialdemokratische Partei Deutschlands) and the Catholic Centre party, both of which consequences Bismarck deplored. Bismarck responded to the growth of the

SPD by banning it, which was not very effective at all. However, he also introduced the basics of a welfare state, including the best public education system in Europe, pensions and sickness insurance (The above account of Germany under Bismarck is a matter of straightforward historical record, but for an excellent account see Steinberg 2012).

This is obviously very different indeed from the situation in czarist Russia. The czars regarded the acceptance of a constitution as betraying their divine right and duty to rule. Russian military adventures depended on an ill-equipped steam roller of peasants, and the Russian state was not, in the remotest, a welfare state. The mass strike, therefore, was carried out in Russia by people with much less to lose than in Germany, and with no real reason to be loyal to the government.

Turning specifically to Rosa Luxemburg and the Russian revolution, Geras says that she concluded that the proletariat would have to struggle to bring about bourgeois democracy against the opposition of a bourgeoisie that was too tied up with the czarist regime and too fearful of proletarian revolution (Geras 1983, p. 64). She continued with this view up to 1917 (Geras 1983, p. 68). Geras points out that there is much in common between Luxemburg's views and Lenin's—Lenin talked about bourgeois revolution being achieved by the proletariat in combination with the peasantry (Geras 1983, p. 71). He says that Luxemburg, along with Trotsky, was not as explicit as Lenin in emphasizing the role of the peasantry—for Trotsky in particular it had a much more subordinate role (Geras 1983, p. 73). Geras supports the general idea of permanent revolution, by which he means that there was no hard and fast distinction between the bourgeois and proletarian revolutions (Geras 1983, p. 77). However, he makes clear that the fact that socialist revolution came to be possible in 1917 was thanks to Lenin's leadership of the Bolshevik Party, and that without this the October Revolution would not have occurred (Geras 1983, p. 81).

There are a variety of issues in the above paragraph, some of which will be discussed later. One is whether it was realistic to expect that a staple bourgeois democracy could be established in Russia. A second issue, which will be dealt with more fully in Chap. 3, concerns a fairly complicated relationship between Geras, Luxemburg, Trotsky, Lenin and Stalin. Within this there are several topics that will need to be discussed, including: the question about the relationship between the proletariat and the peasantry in either a bourgeois revolution or a socialist revolution in Russia, as mentioned briefly in the previous paragraph. Related to this is the fraught issue of permanent revolution.

Geras identifies Lenin's conception of imperialism as a crucial turning point because the bourgeois democratic development required by backward countries took on an anti-imperialist, and hence anti-capitalist trajectory (Geras 1983, pp. 98–99). He says that in 1917 Luxemburg agreed with Lenin that the proletariat should make a revolution, but Luxemburg thought that this would necessarily be followed by a period of bourgeois democratic rule (Geras 1983, p. 101). For this reason it should not be assumed that she simply agreed with Trotsky's theory of permanent revolution (Geras 1983, p. 103). However, Geras argues, by the time of her imprisonment in 1917 Luxemburg had come round to the view that a socialist revolution in Russia was possible, but that it depended upon developments elsewhere, and in this sense her ideas, like Lenin's, had converged with those of Trotsky (Geras 1983, p. 109). If we assume that this is true, it remains important to analyze the extent to which the three revolutionaries agreed with each other prior to 1917, and, of course, whether this harmony continued over the next few years. In addition there is the question of democracy. To what extent is it possible to maintain freedom of expression, freedom of assembly, multiparty democracy and so on in a post-revolutionary society, particularly, of course, one where these freedoms had been only sporadically available under the czars? The obverse of this is the question of terror: to what extent is the use of terror justified in achieving a revolution, and in maintaining a post-revolutionary regime? This in turn relates to the question of means and ends. The question of means and ends is obviously tied up with the question, much subsequently discussed by Geras, of whether Marx had a theory of justice, and whether this theory is fundamental to the justification for revolution. Finally, there is the question of the extent to which Geras was a Trotskyist when writing his book on Rosa Luxemburg, and the extent to which he retained this orientation. All of these will be discussed later.

Luxemburg and the Mass Strike

Geras says that in order to make sense of Luxemburg's conception of the mass strike one should disregard notions that Luxemburg had a metaphysical belief in the virtues of spontaneity. The best way to make sense of it is to think in terms of the distinction made by the German Social Democratic Party between minimum and maximum demands, and emphasize that it was necessary in some way to link the daily struggles of the masses and the achievement of socialism. She was particularly concerned that the party was concentrating exclusively upon the minimum programme (Geras 1983, pp. 113–115). From 1905 onwards, impressed by events in Russia, she came to regard the mass strike as the way of proceeding from one programme to the other (Geras 1983, p. 117). However, she agreed with Lenin that mass strikes and revolutionary situations were not something that could be called forth by parties or political leaderships (Geras 1983, p. 118. Geras's account is strongly supported by a reading of Luxemburg's work and of two major biographies—see Luxemburg 2014, locations 148, 202, 345, 722, 757; Nettl 1966, pp. 502–504; Fröhlich 1966, p. 109). In the past, groups influenced by Trotsky and Luxemburg such as the British International Socialists/Socialist Workers Party were prone to calling mass strikes in very unpromising situations—they could be criticized for taking from Luxemburg the value of the mass strike, but not her reservations about calling mass strikes for little reason.

Luxemburg certainly thought that the mass strike had an educational effect—a year of revolt had a greater effect than 30 years of Parliamentary and trade union struggle. Crude versions of this were popular in the 1960s, such as 'a kick in the balls from a policeman is worth a year of seminars'. On the other hand she said that a mass strike would simply lead to demoralization and confusion if the strike was not taken forward by a determined revolutionary leadership (Geras 1983, p. 129). Geras concludes on the issue of the mass strike that Rosa Luxemburg is part of the tradition of revolutionary Marxism along with Lenin and Trotsky (Geras 1983, p. 131). David McLellan is quite right to say that Geras rescues 'Luxemburg from some rather patronising characterisations of her as entertaining an irrational faith in mass spontaneity' (McLellan 2012, p. 32). Much of Luxemburg's discussion of mass strikes dates from the years after the Russian revolution of 1905 where political strikes played such a large role. Mass strikes also broke out in Germany, and Luxemburg was keen to see them taken forward as far as possible. However, obviously, none of them came really close to triggering a revolution.

Luxemburg was also very much concerned with mass strikes during the failed attempt at revolution that lasted from November 1918 through to the failure that also resulted in her murder in January 1918.

At this point we come back to the discussion of Bismarck and his legacy above. Even in the situation of defeat at the end of 1918, the Kaiser and the German regime had much more political credit then did the czars. Germany had been defeated in the First World War, but, famously, German soldiers were still on foreign territory. There was less reason to see the war as a completely irresponsible military adventure. The legacy of legality, constitutionalism, and general care for the welfare of German citizens contrasted dramatically with the situation in Russia in October 1917. Willingness to engage in a mass strike in Germany was less of an indication of willingness to support revolutionary objectives than it had been in Russia.

This becomes particularly important in the failed revolutionary attempt of 1918–1919. Luxemburg was personally tremendously popular, and if it was known that she was scheduled to speak at meetings it would guarantee a large audience. However, she and the other leaders of the Spartacists failed to pay sufficient attention to the question of which masses they were leading. Many of their followers seemed to be particularly attracted by the higher wages they awarded themselves out of public funds, and there was a strong suggestion that the Berlin police chief that they were committed to defending was guilty of serious corruption. Other German workers regarded many of the Spartacists as layabouts interested in what they could get out of revolutionary activity.

This rendered Luxemburg, Liebknecht and their followers very vulnerable when the SDP union leader Ebert, who became president of the provisional government following the abdication of the Kaiser, ended up calling on Noske to organize military intervention against the Spartacists. They were fairly easily defeated by soldiers loyal to the government. A subsequent demonstration of support for what the government had done was very widely supported by members of all social classes including the working class. The unattractive features of the description of the Spartacist uprising come from an interesting contemporary history written by an US journalist who was present in Germany throughout the First World War and the events immediately after it. He was unsympathetic to socialism, but his overall account of the events of 1918–1919 looks generally honest, so that his allegations are worth considering (Bouton 1921).

A more sympathetic portrayal of the events leading to Luxemburg's death from Chris Harman reinforces the above view that Luxemburg was hoist with her own petard. Luxemburg, he says, regarded the demand for the overthrow of the SDP government as 'a propaganda slogan to rally the revolutionary proletariat rather than a tangible object of revolutionary action'—an immediate rising would chiefly be confined to Berlin. It would be a small-scale version of the Paris Commune (Harman 1997, p. 74). However, such slogans could easily be misinterpreted. There was also the possibility of a figure such as Liebknecht getting swept away and demanding the actual seizure of power. As Luxemburg put it 'Karl, how could you!', (e.g. Harman 1997, p. 77). Effectively she was a victim of her own rhetoric. But she also thought that if the Spartacists showed that they were the most resolute fighters for the revolution it would stand them in good stead for subsequent revolutionary attempts (Harman 1997, p. 87). Defeat in revolution tends to be anything from extremely unpleasant to fatal for those involved, which suggests Luxemburg's strategy might be flawed.

Thus, Geras's account of the mass strike is generally fine so far as it goes, but could usefully have been extended to a discussion of the role of the 'masses' in the failure of the revolutionary attempt of 1918–1919.

On the Relation of Ends and Means

The burden of this fourth essay is the idea that day-to-day revolutionary struggles should be informed by the revolutionary socialist goal. It is this which distinguishes revolutionary socialists such as Luxemburg from anarchists on the one hand and social democrats on the other (Geras 1983, p. 154). Luxemburg was insistent that socialist democracy characterizes the revolutionary process itself, and is not simply something to be postponed until a future socialist society (Geras 1983, pp. 160, 178). Something of Geras's own attitudes at this stage in his development may be seen from a footnote critical of the Communist Party of Great Britain's Road to Socialism, which looked to the winning of political power without armed struggle, on which Geras comments that armed struggle could possibly itself be democratic (Geras 1983, pp. 167, f. 47). Luxemburg emerges from Geras's pages as more of a democratic figure than, for example, Lenin—she expresses reservations about the Bolshevik dissolution of the Constituent Assembly (Geras 1983, p. 186). She insisted that the proletarian dictatorship must include a full set of democratic freedoms—elections, press freedom, freedom of assembly, freedom of dissent (Geras 1983, p. 188). More extensive reading about Luxemburg thoroughly vindicates Geras's views. Luxemburg's image of post-revolutionary society was plainly one in which there would be a plurality of (at least) socialist parties, and a high degree of free speech, and, presumably, most of the other standard accompaniments of liberal democracy (she basically made this point in opposition to Trotsky—see Fröhlich 1966, pp. 248 et seq.; Nettl 1966, pp. 701–703). Luxemburg was also consistently opposed to terror, both in Germany and in Russia (see, for example, Nettl 1966,

p. 732). When Luxemburg presented a proposed general programme of the KPD (Kommunistische Partei Deutschlands) to its inaugural Congress, one of its clauses was:

> The Spartakusbund will never take over governmental power except in accordance with the clear and explicit will of the great majority of the proletarian masses throughout Germany, except in accordance with their conscious approval of its views, aims, and fighting methods. (quoted in Fröhlich 1966, p. 270)

Another indication of Luxemburg's views was the revolutionary programme that she drafted for the Social Democracy of the Kingdom of Poland and Lithuania during the Russian Revolution of 1905. Soviets featured only as a means to revolution, not as a goal. A full range of liberal freedoms was included, together with the election of officials at all levels and the replacement of the standing army by a popular militia (see Nettl 1966, p. 340).

It is, of course, arguable how realistic this was in the desperate circumstances faced by the Bolsheviks in the early years of the revolution.

At the conclusion of the book Geras defends Luxemburg against a whole series of misinterpretations from an assortment of commentators. The overall picture that emerges is of someone who wanted to retain democratic freedoms as part of a socialist revolution, and thought that this could best be done through the instrument of the mass strike. One of the themes of the book is that there is some kind of interrelationship between a satisfactory revolutionary process and the preservation of democratic rights. As we will see, this concern is a major theme in Geras's work, and in particular he became interested in the question of whether there is an ethical basis to revolution. So far as I can see, the overall conclusion of Geras's book on Rosa Luxemburg on the issue of socialist democracy is that he basically concurs with her. I shall argue in the next chapter that this position is not compatible with his admiration for Trotsky at this stage in his intellectual development. Geras's account of Luxemburg on the inclusion of democratic rights in the process of bringing about revolution, and maintaining them afterwards, is strongly supported by more detailed reading about her. She had great faith in the wisdom of the masses, and for that reason was critical of Lenin's stance at the Second Congress of the RSDLP (Russian Social Democratic Labour Party) (see Fröhlich 1966, p. 86). However, the Spartacists proposed to suppress the bourgeois press;

a stance that does not point in the same direction as most of the rest of Luxemburg's thinking on democratic rights. Indeed, in the course or immediate aftermath of a revolution achieved by force of arms, it is open to question as to the extent to which it is realistic to expect non-economic liberal freedoms to be preserved.

References

Berendt, M. (2012, March). Education, Literacy, and the Russian Revolution: A Look at the Struggle for a Liberatory Education in Revolutionary Russia. In *International Socialist Review*. Retrieved from http://isreview.org/issue/82/education-literacy-and-russian-revolution.

Bouton, S. M. (1921). *And the Kaiser Abdicates: The German Revolution November 1918–August 1919*. New Haven: Yale University Press.

Eklof, B. (2008). Russian Literacy Campaigns 1861–1939. In R. F. Arnove & H. J. Graff (Eds.), *National Literacy Campaigns and Movements: Historical and Comparative Perspectives* (pp. 128–129). New Brunswick, NJ: Transaction Publishers.

Fröhlich, P. (1966). *Rosa Luxemburg: Ideas in Action*. London: Pluto Press.

Geras. (1983). *The Legacy of Rosa Luxemburg*. London: New Left Books, 1976/Verso, 1983.

Greengrass, M. (2014). *Christendom Destroyed: Europe 1517–1648*. London: Allen Lane Penguin.

Harman, C. (1997). *The Lost Revolution: Germany 1918–23*. London: Bookmarks.

Luxemburg, R. (1951). *The Accumulation of Capital* (A. Schwarzchild, Trans. & J. Robinson, Introd.). New Haven: Yale University Press.

Luxemburg, R. (2014 [1906]). *The Mass Strike, the Political Party and the Trade Unions*. Anarco Communist Institute e-book.

Marx, K., & Engels, F. (1975). *Collected Works*. London: Lawrence and Wishart.

McLellan, D. (2012). The Marxism of Norman Geras. In E. Garrard & S. de Wijze (Eds.), *Thinking Towards Humanity* (pp. 27–42). Manchester: Manchester University Press.

Nettl, J. P. (1966) *Rosa Luxemburg* (in two volumes). London: Oxford University Press.

Steinberg, J. (2012), *Bismarck, A Life* (Kindle ed.). Oxford: Oxford University Press.

Trotsky, L. (1932). Hands Off Rosa Luxemburg! Retrieved from https://www.marxists.org/archive/trotsky/1932/06/luxemberg.htm.

CHAPTER 3

Geras and Trotskyism

In this chapter Geras's attitude to Trotskyism will be discussed. The obvious starting place is his specific discussions of Trotsky and Trotskyist themes. In addition to this we have, of course, the earlier discussion of the interrelationship between Rosa Luxemburg, Lenin and Trotsky. The discussion will involve revisiting the acrimonious debate between Trotsky and Stalin.

The way in which the issues will be approached is as follows. I shall start by very briefly recapping the major differences between the situation in which Geras admired Trotsky and was a member of the International Marxist Group, the British section of the Trotskyist Fourth International, whose most famous member was Tariq Ali, and the situation today. I shall then go on to discuss four areas of Trotsky's thought relevant to Geras's concerns—the issue of permanent revolution, the question of Trotsky's politics, Trotsky's positions on democracy and terror, and Trotsky's sounding of the alarm about the rise of fascism. My argument will be that each of these areas would have benefited from the thorough analytical rigour with which Geras had approached Rosa Luxemburg, and with which he would subsequently approach some central issues in Marx. If he had worked through these more thoroughly, he might well have arrived at the liberal Marxist views, which he eventually developed, much sooner.

M. Cowling, *Norman Geras's Political Thought from Marxism to Human Rights*, https://doi.org/10.1007/978-3-319-74048-5_3

Then and Now

One of the pleasures of discussing Marxism following the fall of the Soviet Union is that the antagonism between people taking a broadly Stalinist or post-Stalinist approach, notably members of the British Communist Party, and those taking a Trotskyist approach, be they members of the International Marxist Group or members of the International Socialists (now the Socialist Workers Party) is basically at an end. The British Communist Party dissolved itself. Supporters of violent revolution have become much less enthusiastic. What is the point, it is widely thought, although not necessarily spelled out, of achieving a revolution in the course of which people are inevitably killed and injured, there is widespread deprivation, very likely intervention from the capitalist states, leading to further loss of life and devastation, when the eventual consequence is a badly managed reversion to capitalism, as in the Soviet Union, or a communist government presiding over a highly dynamic capitalist economy as in China? Exactly what conclusions Marxists should draw from these stories has obviously been much debated, but straightforward enthusiasm for a revolution with the post-revolutionary state presided over by Trotskyists, Maoists or Stalinists has much diminished. As a consequence relations between previously hostile Marxists of various persuasions have become much more friendly, given that Marxists tend to be regarded as harmless eccentrics. The role of a major threat to the Western way of life has largely been taken over by varieties of Islamic terrorists.

The review of Geras's writings on Trotsky and Trotskyism, which follows, will be one of the more critical sections of the book. It needs to be borne in mind that the world of the early 1970s, from which some of these writings date, was very different from that of today, so that we have the benefit of a considerable amount of hindsight.

The Britain of the 1970s experienced persistent problems in which the trade unions were in a position to successfully demand inflationary pay increases, which were damaging to the economy, resulting in balance of payments problems as British exports became less competitive. The Conservative Prime Minister Edward Heath attempted to legally regulate industrial relations, but climbed down when faced with the prospect of imprisoning trade unionists. Subsequently he was confronted by a highly successful miners' strike, which resulted in serious power cuts and a three-day working week. He called a general election in February 1974 on the theme of 'Who Rules Britain?', and his electoral defeat by a narrow margin suggested that the trade unions did, and he didn't. In Northern Ireland, the Provisional IRA was mounting a bitter and effective armed struggle, which also spilled over onto the British mainland. Some sections of the left gave the IRA conditional or unconditional support on the basis that they were Marxists, or that they were conducting an anti-imperialist struggle.

Globally, Communism was approaching its historical peak of success. The expansion of Soviet communism into Eastern Europe at the end of the Second World War, combined with the Russian development of nuclear weapons gave Stalin's successors a much expanded and apparently stable community of communist nations. They had been joined by China in 1949 and Cuba in 1959. There had nearly been a revolution in France in May 1968. The Vietnam War was won by the North Vietnamese and their allies in the south, defeating the world's most powerful nation. The Portuguese revolution against the Salazar regime nearly turned into a communist revolution; former Portuguese and Spanish colonies in Africa—Mozambique, Angola and Guinea-Bissau—turned Communist, as did Ethiopia. Whilst there was much to criticize in particular communist states, and there was a lurking problem of stagnation in the Soviet Union, the overall picture suggested that communism might well advance further. Trotskyists could obviously hope for some sort of further transformation in communist countries and expansion elsewhere.

The standard Trotskyist view, held, for example, by the International Marxist Group, of which Geras was a member, was that the Soviet Union was a degenerated workers' state. The International Socialists adopted the view proposed by Tony Cliff that the Soviet Union was state capitalist, so that the ruling bureaucracy had become an exploiting class, and a revolution would be needed to convert it into a socialist state. The degree to which it fitted either of these descriptions is, of course, a matter for extensive debate.

We are plainly living in a very different world. In Britain the triumph of Mrs Thatcher weakened trade unions significantly and they have as yet to recover. Along with the collapse of the Soviet Union other former communist states have reverted to capitalism, with the notable exceptions of Cuba and North Korea, which are best seen as anomalies rather than harbingers of a glorious future. The process of globalization has devastated industry in many first world countries. It survives in Britain as a mainly technologically advanced niche production rather than a mass employer. Pay for working people has tended to stagnate, and inequality has greatly increased. The process is only tolerable because of the combined effect of computerization and cheap labour in places such as Mexico and much of Asia has greatly cheapened a wide range of products. The prospects for socialist advance do not currently look particularly good.

To reiterate, we are approaching Geras's ideas about Trotskyism from the early 1970s with the benefit of a considerable degree of hindsight.

Geras on Trotsky

The time has now come to summarize what Geras has to say about Trotsky. So far we have his assertion that Lenin came to agree with Trotsky's theory of permanent revolution in 1917, and that Rosa Luxemburg also came to agree with it by the time of her imprisonment.

In a brief overall assessment of Trotsky, he praises him for three things: 'one of the best examples of the creative application of Marxism … between the time of Lenin's death and his own'; second, a standard of literary excellence rarely achieved by Marxists since the days of Marx himself; and thirdly, that he rejected both the gradualism of West European socialism and the authoritarian Stalinism, and instead favoured combining 'proletarian revolution and workers democracy' (Geras 1986, p. 147).

In an essay from 1970 on political participation Geras quotes Trotsky's famous critique of what he saw as Lenin's over-emphasis on the role of the party subsequent to the Second Congress of the Russian Social, Labour and Democratic Party (RSDLP): 'the party organisation … at first substitutes itself for the party as a whole; and finally, a single 'dictator' substitutes himself for the Central Committee' (Trotsky, quoted in Geras 1986, p. 158). He then says that this critique of Lenin is 'strikingly similar' to Rosa Luxemburg's critique of Lenin, but that both of them could accept a role for the party in leading the revolution. He then goes on to say that it is 'more than doubtful' that this was an 'organic part' of Trotsky's political thought in subsequent years (Geras 1986, p. 158). This leaves the question of substitutionism rather up in the air. In his writings up to 1917 Trotsky seems to have felt that it was not a worry because he thought that in any subsequent revolutionary outbreak the masses would at least initially sweep the party along in a revolutionary upsurge, as happened in 1905. For this reason he stood above the constant bickering between the Bolsheviks and the Mensheviks, and sought for party unity. His theory of permanent revolution led him to believe that because the Russian revolution would bring the proletariat to power it would be impelled forward to take socialist measures. This distinguished him from both the Mensheviks and the Bolsheviks.

A little later, Geras states that with the reorientation of the Bolshevik Party in 1917 to Lenin's position in his *April Theses*, its political approach was now 'in all essential respects, identical to Trotsky's own perspective of permanent revolution'. However, of course, Trotsky's earlier idea that a revolutionary crisis would bring the Bolsheviks and Mensheviks closer together was shown to be definitely and conclusively false (Geras 1986, p. 162).

Trotsky's commitment to democracy wavered in 1921, says Geras, when he attacked the Workers' Opposition for demanding the right to elect representatives, claiming that the party had a right to assert its dictatorship even if that dictatorship 'temporarily clashed with the passing moods of the workers' democracy' (Geras 1986, p. 164, referring to Deutscher 2003, pp. 508–509). Geras comments that Trotsky was making a virtue of necessity, and thus playing his part in erecting Stalin's eventual dictatorship, a point also made by Rosa Luxemburg (Geras 1986, p. 164). Thus Geras's version of Trotsky presents him as a democrat, temporarily led astray around 1921.

Geras moves on to discuss Trotsky's writings from 1929 to 1933 on the rise of the Nazis. He rightly castigates the policy of class against class put forward by Stalin in the Third Period of the Comintern. The idea of this was that there was no essential difference between fascism and Social Democracy, combined with the view that it did not particularly matter if Hitler came to power. In contrast, Trotsky argued that a Nazi victory would lead to the destruction of all workers' organizations, and that it was vital to form a united front between the communists and Social Democrats (Geras 1986, p. 167). Thus, for Geras, one of Trotsky's strong points was his sound appreciation of the dangers of Nazism, and proposals to fight it.

Geras gave a brief but interesting talk on Lenin, Trotsky and the revolutionary party at a symposium organized by the International Marxist Group in 1977. He was concerned with Lenin's formula that socialist consciousness is brought to the working class from outside. Geras objects to Lenin's adoption of the idea, originally derived from Kautsky, that socialist consciousness is introduced to the working class by bourgeois intellectuals. Geras's criticism is that this is too vague—one needs to know which intelligentsia we are dealing with and under what conditions (Geras 1986, p. 182). The central proposition in Lenin's theory of the party, says Geras, is that the party is a necessary instrument of political centralization (Geras 1986, p. 183). Trotsky and Luxemburg accused Lenin of wanting to replace the self-emancipation of the working class by the actions of an elite. In this, Geras argues, they were wrong because a revolution cannot be made without a proletarian vanguard (Geras 1986, p. 184). On the other hand, Trotsky and Luxemburg realized, unlike Lenin, that there is a danger of an organizational apparatus developing its own interests and conservatism (Geras 1986, p. 185). They saw, sooner than Lenin, that a successful revolution depends not just on a vanguard but on the upsurge of the masses, which at least in the first instance is spontaneous (Geras 1986, p. 186).

Geras then proceeds to discuss stick bending. It is possible to see his overall intention, which is to stress the importance of internal democracy in a working-class party, but the detail is unsatisfactory. He says that it was not justified for Lenin in *What is to be Done?* to say that an emphasis on professional revolutionaries—strict selection of members, dedication, confidence in each other is better than 'democratism'. He says that this is an unjustified example of stick bending because it led to a reluctance in 1905 to open up the party to masses of workers, and was also used by Stalin to justify 'crimes and horrors'. Apparently contradicting this, he continues: 'I am *not* saying, in any form or shape, that there is a germ of Stalinism in the work of Lenin' (Geras 1986, pp. 188–189). Linked to this, he says that the older Trotsky came to recognize that it was a mistake, in 1921, to ban factions in the Bolshevik Party and to ban the legal Soviet opposition (Geras 1986, p. 190). Geras then goes on to assert that vigorous internal debate was essential to any party worthy of the name, and quotes Lenin to this effect (Geras 1986, p. 191).

In a further essay: *Classical Marxism and Proletarian Representation*, Geras argues that Trotsky in *Our Political Tasks* takes a position very similar to those of Luxemburg. They are both critical of what in an earlier report Trotsky had described as Lenin's 'sterile formalism'. They both say that opportunism is something that arises naturally from the labour movement in the difficult conditions of czarist Russia, and that Lenin was wrong to eliminate opportunism from the Party by means of manipulating its constitution. The failure of many Bolsheviks was that they were unable to link the day-to-day and trade union interests felt by many working-class people with revolutionary politics (Geras 1986, pp. 201–202). Trotsky argued that, while Lenin was, of course right to value Marxist doctrine, he was over-reliant on it—it did not fully and permanently prevent political error (Geras 1986, p. 203).

Geras moves on in the essay to extrapolate from Trotsky and Luxemburg a pluralist principle, which is well defended in moral and political philosophy.

He says that actual Communist societies speak 'eloquently enough on its behalf as a negative example', and asks what institutional proposals Trotsky and Luxemburg have for implementing it. To start with, he argues, they say that what Geras calls 'Social-Democratic centralism'—is there any reason for him using this term rather than the more usual 'democratic centralism'?—is founded on the 'will and initiative' of the party's rank and file, and not just on 'dictates' from the centre (Geras 1986, p. 206).

The Trotsky of *Our Political Tasks* extends this to the work of post-revolutionary socialist construction: there are bound to be debates thrown up by new problems for which there are no ready-made solutions. Rosa Luxemburg expresses essentially the same idea in criticizing what she described as the Lenin-Trotsky dictatorship (Geras 1986, p. 207).

However, both Trotsky and Luxemburg assume that there is a single party representing the working class. Geras comments that, while there is nothing in classical Marxism that entirely rules out the notion of a single party state, there is also a general assumption that there will be just one party that properly represents the interests of the working class. He makes it plain that this is not an acceptable assumption today. He argues for pluralism on the basis not just of Trotsky and Luxemburg in the texts he discusses, but also of the work of John Stuart Mill (Geras 1986, pp. 208–212).

The direction in which this argument is heading should be clear: 'the norms of socialist democracy must allow, in unambiguous terms, for organisational pluralism.' Under socialism 'there must be room for any organisation that will respect a properly constituted socialist legality' (Geras 1986, p. 215). This conclusion is clear and unambiguous. It plainly raises the question of to what extent Trotsky was a democrat. Also, given the purported agreement between Trotsky and Lenin on the question of permanent revolution by the time we get to 1917, and the view that Lenin was generally favourable to inner-party democracy, there is obviously also the same set of issues when it comes to Lenin: is there clear evidence that he really did favour inner-party democracy, let alone a socialist society with a plurality of parties and a high degree of public freedom of debate?

Geras's final major essay on Trotsky, *Literature of Revolution*, discusses, as the title implies, the relationship between literary excellence and political substance. It contains many examples of extremely striking descriptions from Trotsky's pen. A particular strength, which Geras pinpoints in the essay, is the way in which Trotsky links major historical events such as the development of the Soviets in 1905 and speeches or actions of ordinary individuals: the woman who passionately argues for the continuation of a strike; and the sailor who shoots an officer, refuses to say it is an accident, and has to be released because of the feelings expressed by his comrades (Geras 1986, pp. 216–267). Trotsky's literary merit cannot be doubted, but does not, of itself, warrant lengthy discussion here. There is a question as to whether sometimes Trotsky uses literary flourishes as a substitute for proper analysis, as in the following quotation: 'Everything that happens in the world happens for the purpose of war. War is now no longer an instrument of the bourgeois regime; the bourgeois regime is an instrument of war.' What could this really mean? Nations can be taken over by war fever, as in the run-up to the First World War, but unless Trotsky had something like that in mind the quotation does not make any sense—war is something that people, or, if you like, social classes make. Another example could be drawn from his analysis of German National Socialism. Having said a little about Nazi racism he continues:

> Everything that should have been eliminated from the National organism in the course of the normal development of society has now come gushing out from the throat; capitalist society is puking up the undigested barbarism. Such is the physiology of National Socialism. (Trotsky 1975, p. 413)

This certainly tells us that Trotsky deplored National Socialism, but what extent is it Marxist analysis? This minor excursion into criticism rather than exposition concludes my account of Geras on Trotsky.

Assessment of Geras on Trotsky

From the above it is clear that by the 1970s Geras was in favour of genuine inner-party democracy, although the mechanisms for this are not spelled out. He is also in favour of a pluralist, socialist democracy for post-revolutionary society. He assumed that this commitment was in line with Trotsky's views.

The accuracy and comprehensiveness of his account of Trotsky is, however, open to dispute. The comments that follow will be divided into four sections. The first will comprise of an account and assessment of the theory of permanent revolution. The argument will be that we are dealing not so much with a developed theory but with a set of possible examples to which Trotsky adds speculation. Geras does not seriously consider the case for socialism in one country. He disparages Stalin and Stalinism without a single reference to anything that Stalin wrote or to a biography of Stalin. Second comes a short section on the question of politics. It will be argued that Trotsky was not actually politically very effective. Geras does not assert that he was, and does not discuss this issue, but if neither Trotsky himself nor Trotskyists have been effective in actual political debate and struggle, this is surely very important. The third will be a discussion of Trotsky the democrat. Geras picks out the more attractive democratic aspects of Trotsky. The argument will be that Trotsky's commitment to democracy as Geras would understand it is questionable. Moreover, both Lenin and Trotsky approved of the use of terror in such a way as to make the flourishing of democracy difficult. I have not entirely stuck to the order of exposition above, which follows the order of Geras's writings. Trotsky's theories about the rise of Nazism are somewhat separate from the other issues, and I have therefore left them to the final part of the critical discussion.

Permanent Revolution

The theory that is, above all, associated with Trotsky is the theory of permanent revolution. Because, once he had developed it, Trotsky adhered to this theory for the rest of his life; this can be taken from a variety of sources. The theory essentially has three strands. A revolution in Russia, but probably also a revolution anywhere else, would not be able to stop at the bourgeois phase. The bourgeoisie in Russia, but also elsewhere, have become too threatened by the prospect of socialist revolution to feel at all happy about overthrowing czarism. Therefore any revolution would have to be led by the proletariat, which would mean that it would take the leading role in introducing democratic reform. Any problems in post-revolutionary society between the owners of the means of production and the workers would lead to the necessity of adopting socialist measures, and thus ultimately introducing a socialist economy. The second strand is that the onward development of post-revolutionary society would involve continuing major changes. The third strand would then come into play. A socialist revolution in Russia would be unable to survive on its own, and would therefore have to strive, using propaganda, and perhaps even military assistance, to bring about revolutions in the leading capitalist societies. A straightforward exposition of these ideas is given in the Introduction to the first Russian edition of *The Permanent Revolution* (Trotsky 1931).

In order to assess the merits of the theory of permanent revolution, it is necessary to consider it in more depth, which I shall do using *Results and Prospects*, which Trotsky wrote in 1906, and *The Permanent Revolution*, (Trotsky 1931) which he wrote in 1928. He starts by stressing that capitalism in Russia was introduced by the state much more than growing up autonomously. Thanks to its geographical situation, the economic development of Russia was behind that in Western Europe, but the Russian state was potentially threatened by other European states. For this reason it built up its military capacity. In order to pay for this capacity it was impelled, from the end of the seventeenth century onwards, to accelerate Russia's economic development (Trotsky 1906, location 232). The absolutist system developed a colossal army and railways that would enable it to move its forces rapidly from one end of the country to another as well as a telegraph system to facilitate communication and command (Trotsky 1906, location 260). Trotsky notes that the development of towns occurred rapidly in the late-nineteenth and early-twentieth centuries, with the urban population numbering just over 16 million or about 13% by 1897 (Trotsky 1906, location 311). Manufacturing developed rapidly, but was largely a government-facilitated import from the West. The bourgeoisie was therefore more closely aligned with the czarist government than the Western bourgeoisie had been with pre-capitalist regimes. Moreover, the czarist government was very dependent on Western money markets, which meant that the Western capitalists were also supporters of the czarist regime in order to make sure that they received their interest (Trotsky 1906, location 370). (The exposition in all of the above account of Russian development is very similar to that in Trotsky 1973, pp. 1–26.)

The proletariat became concentrated in enormous masses, while, as we have seen, the bourgeoisie was numerically small and isolated from the people (Trotsky 1906, location 394). In Western Europe revolution had historically very much been bound up with the petty-bourgeoisie, but in Russia this class was numerically small and was tending to be wiped out by the development of light industry. The role of the revolutionary class was taken instead by the urban proletariat (Trotsky 1906, location 565).

Capitalist industry was relatively small in Russia compared to, for example, the USA. In Russia about 5 million people were involved in capitalist industry, some 16% of the employed population, as against 6 million, or 22% of the working population of the USA. However, the overall population of Russia was twice that of the USA (Trotsky 1906, location 616). Nonetheless, Trotsky emphasizes that the towns have a strategic importance greater than one would imagine from the above because of the concentration of industry and commerce there and the way that they are linked to the provinces by railways (Trotsky 1906, location 1095). Trotsky emphasizes a point made by Kautsky that, thanks to the above, the Russian industrial proletariat is the only class that is really effective against absolutism; 'the peasants may render considerable support but cannot play a leading role' (Trotsky 1906, doc 645).

In Russia 'the proletariat, on taking power, must, by the very logic of its position, inevitably be urged toward the introduction of state or management of industry' (Trotsky 1906, location 661). The proletariat would not be well advised to participate in a bourgeois democratic government, hedged in as it would be by a treacherous capitalist bourgeoisie and the wavering of the urban petty bourgeoisie, the diverse and primitive peasantry, and the variegated intelligentsia (Trotsky 1906, location 694). However a post-revolutionary government is described, the hegemony must belong to the working class (Trotsky 1906, location 704). The proletariat will 'stand before the peasants as the class which has emancipated it' (Trotsky 1906, location 723). 'Historical experience shows that the peasantry are absolutely incapable of taking up an independent political role' (Trotsky 1906, location 733). A 'proletarian and peasant dictatorship' is 'unrealisable—at least in the direct immediate sense' (Trotsky 1906, location 752). He says that as the workers' government defines itself so 'the antagonism between the component sections [of the peasantry] will grow' (Trotsky 1906, location 791). He sees the proletarian government gaining some support from the poor peasants, but appears to envisage a situation in which the government becomes opposed by the bulk of the peasantry 'the more definite and determined the policy of the proletariat in power becomes, the narrower and more shaky does the ground beneath its feet become' (Trotsky 1906, location 806). Later, he modifies this somewhat: he envisages the socialization of production on expropriated large estates, followed, once it is properly established, by the prohibition of hired labour. Small capitalist farming would be impossible, but there would still be room for subsistence holdings, which would not be forcibly expropriated (Trotsky 1906, location. 1256). Nonetheless, he was obviously expecting considerable resistance. In particular, collectivism and internationalism would meet with opposition (Trotsky 1906, location 812). While Marxists generally assumed that socialist revolution in one country would lead to a series of such revolutions elsewhere, Trotsky's view that the peasantry would in the main not support moves to socialism commits him to this view particularly strongly.

In 1905 and again in 1917 the Mensheviks and, initially in 1917 most of the Bolshevik leadership, assumed that the revolution would essentially stop at the bourgeois stage, with the abolition of the czarist monarchy, the introduction of a constitution, and with socialists remaining as a party of opposition to the bourgeois government. Trotsky disagreed strongly with this:

> 'But do you really believe,' the Stalins, Rykovs and all the other Molotovs objected dozens of times between 1905 and 1917, 'that Russia is ripe for the socialist revolution?' To that I always answered: No, I do not. But world economy as a whole, and European economy in the first place, is fully ripe for the socialist revolution. Whether the dictatorship of the proletariat in Russia leads to socialism or not, and at what tempo and through what stages, will depend upon the fate of European and world capitalism. (Trotsky 1931)

The above passage has an obvious immediate application: for a proletarian revolution to succeed in Russia in introducing socialism, revolution elsewhere is necessary. But further than this it is quite vague: people in, say, the Belgian Congo were linked to the world economy in the sense that some of what they produced ended up traded in Europe and the USA, but it hardly means the Congo itself was ready to become a socialist utopia. And the idea of the USA becoming a socialist society does not look plausible in either those years or subsequently. A socialist Germany would be more plausible, but exactly what relationship it would have with Russia is not immediately apparent. What quantities of free technology would become available? (see Thatcher 2003, p. 135). And would a German revolution in turn be dependent upon revolutions in France and Britain—and could Spain, Italy and Holland be regarded as more marginal and inessential? A line of thinking typical of Trotsky follows from this: if the revolution was not going well in any one particular country the explanation was most likely the failure of revolution to develop somewhere else, and the most obvious explanation of such failures would be the revolutionary leadership given by established communist states.

By the late 1920s, when Trotsky was writing *The Permanent Revolution*, the Soviet Union was plainly not going to be immediately joined by other socialist states. Stalin's response to this was to proclaim the construction of socialism in one country. Trotsky argues at some length that 'National Socialism' as he calls it, will not work in complete isolation from the capitalist world. He argues that what should be done is:

> A realistic program for an isolated workers' state cannot set itself the goal of achieving 'independence' from world economy, much less of constructing a national socialist society 'in the shortest time.' The task is not to attain the abstract maximum tempo, but the optimum tempo, that is, the best, that which follows from both internal and world economic conditions, strengthens the position of the proletariat, prepares the national elements of the future international socialist society, and at the same time, and above all, systematically improves the living standards of the proletariat and strengthens its alliance with the non-exploiting masses of the countryside. This prospect must remain in force for the whole preparatory period, that is, until the victorious revolution in the advanced countries liberates the Soviet Union from its present isolated position. (Trotsky 1931)

While this formula sounds sensible, it doesn't really have much by way of concrete content. For example, would it be possible to collectivize just some of the peasantry? What if the peasantry were not in a mood to supply the towns with agricultural produce? How long would the Soviet Union have to wait until the victorious revolution in the advanced countries actually happened?

Seen in the above light, the idea of attempting to develop socialism in one country has its attractions. There was some truth in the Stalinist criticism of Trotsky, but which would also apply to Luxemburg, that of the neglect of the peasantry. From Lenin's *The Development of Capitalism in Russia* (Lenin 1899) onwards, Lenin took the view that the bourgeois revolution in Russia would be achieved by the democratic dictatorship of the proletariat and the peasantry, and that a subsequent socialist revolution would be achieved by the poor peasantry in alliance with the proletariat. The peasantry is thus very important in Lenin's thinking on revolution, and remained so subsequently. Their numerical preponderance in the population has already been noted above. The famous slogan of the Bolsheviks in 1917, 'Bread, Peace and Land', reflects the view that land should be immediately redistributed in the countryside. The obvious socialist aspiration would be for some form of collective farming, but Lenin supported immediate land redistribution doubtless for practical reasons, but also because he wanted to indicate that the Bolsheviks were offering the peasants a genuine partnership by adopting the central policy of the Socialist Revolutionary Party. For this reason, insisting on the thorough subordination of the peasantry to the leadership of the proletariat, as argued by Trotsky, was potentially damaging to the development of the revolution.

What actually happened in the Soviet Union did not entirely vindicate either Trotsky or Lenin. Land was redistributed in the immediate aftermath of the October Revolution, so that peasant holdings became much more equal than they had been. This equality was reinforced by the policy of War Communism, in which committees of small peasants were formed in the villages with a view to removing grain from kulaks who were allegedly hoarding it. With the introduction in 1921 of the New Economic Policy (NEP) the Bolsheviks tacitly encouraged the differentiation of the peasantry. However, this had not advanced very much by the time of collectivization at the end of the 1920s. The peasantry as a whole was reluctant to be collectivized. Peasants who resisted tended to be described as kulaks and shot, sent to labour camps, or packed into adapted cattle trucks and transported to Siberia, where they were expected to engage in farming despite a lack of proper implements or accommodation. This somewhat fits in with Trotsky's theory that the peasantry would resist a proletarian government as a whole, but the corollary on which he insisted, namely that the proletarian government would require support from abroad, was not pursued. Nonetheless, the Soviet government survived, and the rapid development of industry in the five-year plans enabled the Soviet Union to field what was essentially a properly equipped modern army against the German invasion.

Trotsky continues his 1906 exposition of the theory of permanent revolution with a series of thought experiments. The first of these is the issue of the eight-hour day, which was part of the minimum programme of social democracy. However, he says, in 'a period of intensified class passion' the capitalists would resist, for example, through lockouts and the closing down of factories (Trotsky 1906, location 828). This would lead to the expropriation of the closed factories (Trotsky 1906, location 837). The next example he considers is the question of unemployment—a proletarian government would take energetic measures to solve this question (Trotsky 1906, location 847). This would again lead to capitalist resistance and the introduction of communal production (Trotsky 1906, location 857). So, problems with the peasantry, the issue of the eight-hour day, and unemployment, all lead in the direction of the implementation of a maximum programme and the introduction collective forms of production:

> For this reason there can be no talk of any sort of special form of proletarian dictatorship in the bourgeois revolution, of democratic proletarian dictatorship (or dictatorship of the proletariat and the peasantry). The working class

> cannot preserve the democratic character of its dictatorship without refraining from overstepping the limits of its democratic programme (Trotsky 1906, location 866). [There seems to be a problem with the translation of this passage—the last sentence says the opposite of what Trotsky plainly means.]

Was it the case, as argued by Trotsky, that revolution in Russia would either fail or would go beyond the achievement of bourgeois freedoms, and would move on to socialist revolution, which in turn would become international? Given what actually happened under the NEP from 1921 up to the late 1920s, another possibility would be for a proletarian government to do some kind of a deal with the capitalists. It was not forced to proceed immediately to the implementation of its maximum programme. Did Lenin simply come to agree with Trotsky about this in 1917, or was this some sort of temporary agreement, more apparent than real?

Given that Lenin could quite frequently be scathing about Trotsky this degree of happy harmony would seem to be exaggerated. There had been quite a lot of bad blood between them in the years before the Revolution. It will be recalled that Trotsky denounced Lenin's 'substitutionism' following the Second Congress in 1902. Trotsky then stood outside the Bolshevik and Menshevik factions, attempting to bring them together. In 1910 Lenin commented that Trotsky had joined forces with the liquidationists: 'we agree with Plekhanov that it is impossible to do anything with Trotsky' (Thatcher 2003, p. 52). Geras's picture of a fair degree of harmony between Trotsky and Rosa Luxemburg is rather undermined by the letter she sent to Karl Kautsky's wife in which she comments that Trotsky was accusing the Bolsheviks of being splitters, but saying nothing about Martov's pamphlet against Lenin, which was worse than anything Lenin had written about him, and was obviously aimed at splitting the party, 'The good Trotsky is more and more exposed as a rotten fellow' (Thatcher 2003, p. 56). Trotsky and the Bolsheviks fell out over attempts to unite the anti-war left, leading Trotsky to describe Lenin as 'a terribly egocentric person' and Trotsky's thought to be described by the Bolsheviks as the most 'vacuous and unprincipled ever to have existed in Russian Social Democracy' (Thatcher 2003, p. 75).

It is worth unpicking this a bit further. There is a view that Lenin engaged in a piece of revolutionary opportunism (as opposed to the sort of opportunism that Lenin deplored) in 1917, and that the logic of his position prior to that point was that what was possible in Russia was a bourgeois democratic revolution, which would be followed by a period of capitalist development presided over by a government that represented 'the democratic dictatorship of the proletariat and peasantry', with a subsequent socialist revolution based on the poor peasantry and working class. He reverted to a view on these lines in 1921 with the introduction of the New Economic Policy, in which capitalist development would be encouraged both in the towns and countryside with a view to developing the forces of production sufficiently to make a socialist revolution possible. This is distinct from the happy harmony between Lenin, Luxemburg and Trotsky, in which they all came to believe in something on the lines of the theory of permanent revolution by 1917. In particular, prior to 1917, all Marxists including Marx and Engels had taken the view that a revolution in one country would be followed by of revolutions in the leading capitalist countries. In point of fact the only successful socialist revolution up to the Second World War was that in Mongolia, which was by no stretch of the imagination a leading capitalist country.

The Soviet Union, as it became, emerged in the course of the bitter Civil War in which the Bolsheviks fought off counter-revolutionary Whites, who were aided by forces sent by a variety of capitalist countries. There was certainly instability in several capitalist countries, such as Germany in 1921 and 1923, a temporary socialist government in Hungary, the General Strike in Britain, and so forth, but not the hoped-for series of revolutions. This in turn led to the issue of what the Russian leadership should do. Trotsky took the view that the Stalinist leadership had become bureaucratized, and was no longer seriously interested in revolution elsewhere. Whenever there was something that looked like a revolutionary opportunity abroad, Trotsky argued that it was not developed properly because of the failure of the Stalinist leadership. The extent to which this was true has been much debated. Several of these 'opportunities' are not particularly plausible. The one with which British people are obviously most familiar is the General Strike. During this event the Communist Party of Great Britain numbered about 5000, and the strikers famously arranged football matches with the police. Trotsky was surely fantasizing.

Ian Thatcher makes several judicious comments on this theme of over-optimism: 'Trotsky does not seem to have been a particularly sagacious commentator on the likely spread of proletarian revolution. His prognoses were consistently over-optimistic'. Thatcher mentions Trotsky's belief that the murder of Rosa Luxemburg showed that Germany's October was soon at hand, and his idea that Bolshevism could be readily exported to India in 1919 (Thatcher 2003, p. 111).

If it is accepted that there were not serious revolutionary opportunities, the question obviously arises as to what the Soviet leadership should do. There would plainly be a need for stabilizing relationships with the Western capitalist countries. This might not mean permanent stabilization in either direction, but something sufficient to allow a modicum of trade, and for both sides to feel that there was no immediate danger of war to spread the revolution, or, on the Soviet side, invasion or major destabilization. The other very important activity was to build up the forces of production in the Soviet Union, notably, of course, through industrialization.

At this point it is appropriate to take a closer look at *The Permanent Revolution*. One would think that, given Stalin's increasing dominance in the late 1920s, an obvious text to go through and carefully critique would be Stalin's *Problems of Leninism*. However, Trotsky basically insults this text and then moves on to spend a great deal of time discussing work by Radek:

> Stalin's *Problems of Leninism* constitutes a codification of this ideological garbage, an official manual of narrow-mindedness, an anthology of enumerated banalities (I am doing my best to find the most moderate designations possible). (Trotsky 1931)

He is keen, of course, to emphasize the degree to which he and Lenin were in agreement, and it is obviously particularly proud of the following:

> Still more noteworthy in this respect is Lenin's speech at the November 1 (14), 1917, session of the Petrograd Committee. There the question was discussed, whether to make an agreement with the Mensheviks and the Socialist-Revolutionaries. The supporters of a coalition endeavoured even there—very timidly, to be sure—to hint at 'Trotskyism'. What did Lenin reply?
>
> 'Agreement? I cannot even speak seriously about that. Trotsky has long ago said that unity is impossible. Trotsky understood this—and since then there has been no better Bolshevik.' (Trotsky 1931)

Obviously, following the death of Lenin, all the Soviet leaders were keen to emphasize the Leninist pedigree of their theories and their politics, and the above quotation is one of the strongest ones in Trotsky's favour. It needs to be borne in mind that Trotsky had a long history in the years leading up to the revolution of working in exile to try to unite the

Bolshevik and Menshevik factions of the RSDLP, while others such as Stalin had been risking their lives and freedom working in the Bolshevik underground inside the Russian Empire. Lenin was happy to support Trotsky for his outstanding organizational abilities and his ability to inspire the masses.

Just because there was 'no better Bolshevik' it does not follow that Lenin subsequently always agreed with Trotsky. Trotsky himself felt that every minor disagreement he had had with Lenin was being raked up by Stalin and others in order to discredit him. In the period that led up to the NEP, Trotsky had proposed the absorption of the trade unions into the apparatus of the Soviet state, once his earlier proposal for something on the lines of the NEP had been rejected. Lenin commented on Trotsky's pamphlet:

> My principal material is Comrade Trotsky's pamphlet, *The Role and Tasks of the Trade Unions*. When I compare it with the theses he submitted to the Central Committee, and go over it very carefully, I am amazed at the number of theoretical mistakes and glaring blunders it contains. How could anyone starting a big Party discussion on this question produce such a sorry excuse for a carefully thought out statement? Let me go over the main points which, I think, contain the original fundamental theoretical errors. (Lenin 1920)

However, once Lenin had died, Trotsky came to be seen as possibly less reliable than other figures. All the Russian revolutionaries looked back to the great French Revolution of 1789 for precedents. In particular, the Bolsheviks were anxious about the possible emergence of a figure equivalent to Napoleon, a dictator who would encapsulate some of the original aims of the revolution, but would dramatically alter its character. Of the various leaders Trotsky looked to others to be the one most likely to fit the bill.

Trotsky expresses another point of agreement with Lenin, which he obviously felt was a trump card, as follows:

> Lenin did not confine himself to hope for 'pressure' by the proletariat, but repeatedly asserted that without revolution in Germany we should certainly perish. This was correct in essence, although a greater period of time has intervened. Let there be no illusions; we have received an undated moratorium. We live, as before, under the conditions of a 'breathing-space'. (Trotsky 1931)

The above is a sample quotation—Trotsky refers to Lenin making this point repeatedly. Trotsky also expresses agreement with Lenin in counselling against coups d'état by supporters in the West that had little chance of success, but which were intended to give support to the Russian revolution. But after seven years of 'breathing space', the idea of remaining indefinitely in an ill-defined moratorium must really have been losing its appeal.

Assuming that the Soviet Union was indeed attempting to build socialism in one country, the support of the peasantry, or significant parts of it, would be particularly important.

We now return to the issue of the peasantry. *Problems of Leninism* was part of Stalin's attempt to present himself as an orthodox follower of Lenin. It seems to me to present many of the central features of Lenin's ideas in a relatively pedestrian but very clear fashion. In particular, Stalin is keen to emphasize that the peasantry should be seen as the 'first reserves' of the proletariat, and he generally echoes Lenin's approach as outlined above.

In *The Permanent Revolution*, Trotsky quotes Lenin as follows:

> In 1907, Lenin wrote:
>
> 'It is possible ... that the objective difficulties of a political unification of the petty bourgeoisie will check the formation of such a party and leave the peasant democracy for a long time in the present state of a spongy, shapeless, pulpy, Trudoviki-like mass.' (VIII, 484 [6])
>
> In 1909, Lenin expressed himself on the same theme in a different way:
>
> 'There is not the slightest doubt that a revolution which reaches ... so high a degree of development as the revolutionary dictatorship will create a more firmly-formed and more powerful revolutionary peasant party. To judge the matter otherwise would mean to assume that in a grown-up man, the size, form and degree of development of certain essential organs could remain in a childish state.' (XI, Part 1, 230 [7])

The obvious interpretation of the above is that Lenin is forecasting the increasingly better organization of the Socialist Revolutionary Party as the representative of the peasants. Trotsky immediately states that the assumptions in the above quotation were not borne out. His point is that the Socialist Revolutionary Party became for a time the party of the overwhelming majority of the peasants, but then betrayed them by siding with the bourgeoisie against the peasantry in 1917.

Trotsky is able to find quotations from his own work that are more similar to the idea of Lenin, such as the following, but this seems to me to go against the general run of the theory of permanent revolution, which sees the proletariat in power as forced to turn to socialist measures and to revolution overseas. Here is the quotation:

> The proletariat will find itself compelled to carry the class struggle into the villages and in this manner destroy the community of interest which is undoubtedly to be found among all peasants, although within comparatively narrow limits. From the very first moment after its taking power, the proletariat will have to find support in the antagonisms between the village poor and the village rich, between the agricultural proletariat and the agricultural bourgeoisie. (Our Revolution, 1906, p. 255 [3]) (Trotsky 1931)

While this passage bears some similarities to Lenin, it very much lacks the depth, variety and complexity of Lenin's *The Development of Capitalism in Russia*, and the strategies that he developed from this over the ensuing years.

Much of the discussion in *The Permanent Revolution* is taken up with the disaster that occurred in China in 1927. Trotsky attributes the disaster to Chinese adherence to Stalinist advice from Moscow aimed at encouraging a 'democratic dictatorship of the proletariat and peasantry', and thus the subordination of the Communist Party to the treachery of Chiang Kai-shek. There is no doubt that Stalin's policies were disastrous. What is less clear is whether Trotsky's would have worked any better, or whether Chiang was in such a powerful position that he could have purged communists however they were organized and whatever slogans they adopted. It is open to question to what extent any of the Russian leadership fully grasped Chinese realities. Part of Trotsky's contribution reads as follows:

> But in the words just quoted there was nevertheless a kernel of truth: there is almost no estate of landlords in China, the landowners are much more intimately bound up with the capitalists than in Tsarist Russia, and the specific weight of the agrarian question in China is therefore much lighter than in Tsarist Russia; but on the other hand, the question of national liberation bulks very large. (Trotsky 1931)

Based on what actually happened in 1949, the Chinese Revolution basically comprised a very effective peasant-based revolution. The issue of national liberation was, of course, very important. However, in a peasant revolution, the idea that 'the agrarian question China is ... much lighter than in czarist Russia' is very wide of the mark. The theory of permanent revolution does not seem to offer much of an advance on its Stalinist rival where China was concerned.

It is therefore not at all clear that Trotsky, Lenin and Rosa Luxemburg straightforwardly agreed with each other about the theory of permanent revolution. The theory of permanent revolution is not very precisely formulated. It is debatable as a guide to action, in the sense that, by placing such a very strong emphasis on the need for revolution abroad, it is prone to lead to exaggerated hopes being placed on situations that are not realistically revolutionary and to then blame a failure of leadership locally and in Moscow. If Geras had approached the question of permanent revolution with the thoroughness he subsequently applied to Marx, he would not necessarily have agreed with the above criticisms of Trotsky, but it would have surely been more critical.

Trotsky and Politics

Geras fails to consider this question, and, thinking of his subsequent work generally, was not tremendously interested in it, but it is surely important to consider a revolutionary leader's political abilities, in the narrow sense of his ability to succeed in day-to-day struggles. He needs to have an appreciation of his standing with other leading members of his party, and of how this relates to the way the party makes decisions. Trotsky's talents in this area were limited, which was very important in the situation immediately following Lenin's death. The other Bolsheviks, following the analogy of the French revolution, became worried about who might become Napoleon, and Trotsky seemed the most likely candidate. Given his history of standing outside the Bolshevik party only to join in 1917 he should have realized his vulnerability, and spent more time reassuring others that he simply wanted to be part of a collective leadership. He also does not seem to have realized the importance of the internal organization of the party, meaning, particularly, that Stalin was in a position to make sure that his supporters occupied important positions. His arrogance must also have been an issue—he was famous for getting out a French novel and reading it during what he deemed to be over-lengthy reports to meetings he was chairing. This must have conveyed the idea that he has a high sense of his own importance, and left whoever was giving the report feeling embittered and humiliated.

More generally, his subsequent political judgements did not stand him in good stead, be it wild over-optimism about the prospects of revolutions in an assortment of countries, or the possibilities of the opposition inside the Soviet Union following the complete triumph of Stalin, at a time when Trotsky's followers had been executed or were in labour camps.

Democracy and Terror

As we saw the above, Geras, following Rosa Luxemburg, was committed to the idea of multiparty democracy under socialism. The argument here will be that neither Trotsky nor Lenin was committed to this. Czarist Russia was not fertile ground for the growth of democracy. There was no real prospect of replacing the regime peacefully. Political parties tended to be made illegal. Thus virtually all political parties were in some sense revolutionary. There was general agreement in socialist circles with Lenin's judgement in *What is to be Done?* that an effective party would have to be centralized, and that straightforward open elections to party offices on the Western model would simply be a gift to the secret police. This background was hardly conducive to the flowering of multiparty democracy after the October Revolution. There was no tradition of loyal opposition, of stable constitutional government, of freedom of the press, of free and open elections, or, in the case of the Bolshevik party, of what is normally understood as internal party democracy.

The crucial year where the issue of democracy is concerned is 1921. With the ending of the Civil War the peasantry, who had now got their land, had less reason to be loyal to the Bolshevik party, as the Whites generally wanted to reappropriate landlord land, but they had now departed from the scene. The direct appropriation of peasant produce on the pattern of war communism was increasingly seen as intolerable: why grow things only to have them taken away? The most class conscious parts of the working class tended to have disappeared, either by being killed during the Civil War or by becoming part of the new administrative apparatus. Thus there was a communist government lacking the strong working-class base on which it had come to power, facing a mutinous peasantry. This was a very dangerous situation.

The danger was made particularly clear by the Kronstadt uprising of March 1921. The Kronstadt sailors had been a mainstay of the October Revolution, but now, sympathizing with fairly similar demands put forward by workers in Petrograd, they advanced a series of demands to the Soviet government:

(1) In view of the fact that the present Soviets do not express the will of the workers and peasants, immediately to hold new elections by secret ballot, the pre-election campaign to have full freedom of agitation among the workers and peasants; (2) To establish freedom of speech and press for workers and peasants, for Anarchists and left Socialist parties; (3) To secure freedom of assembly for labour unions and peasant organisations; (4) To call a nonpartisan Conference of the workers, Red Army soldiers and sailors of Petrograd, Kronstadt, and of Petrograd Province, no later than March 10, 1921; (5) To liberate all political prisoners of Socialist parties, as well as all workers, peasants, soldiers, and sailors imprisoned in connection with the labour and peasant movements; (6) To elect a Commission to review the eases of those held in prisons and concentration camps; (7) To abolish all politotdeli (political bureaus) because no party should be given special privileges in the propagation of its ideas or receive the financial support of the government for such purposes. Instead there should be established educational and cultural commissions, locally elected and financed by the government; (8) To abolish immediately all zagryaditelniye otryadi; (* Armed units organised by the Bolsheviki for the purpose of suppressing traffic and confiscating foodstuffs and other products. The irresponsibility and arbitrariness of their methods were proverbial throughout the country. The government abolished them in the Petrograd Province on the eve of its attack against Kronstadt—a bribe to the Petrograd proletariat. A. B.) (9) To equalise the rations of all who work, with the exception of those employed in trades detrimental to health; (10) To abolish the Communist fighting detachments in all branches of the Army, as well as the Communist guards kept on duty in mills and factories. Should such guards or military detachments be found necessary, they are to be appointed in the Army from the ranks, and in the factories according to the judgment of the workers; (11) To give the peasants full freedom of action in regard to their land, and also the right to keep cattle, on condition that the peasants manage with their own means; that is, without employing hired labour; (12) To request all branches of the Army, as well as our comrades the military kursanti, to concur in our resolutions; (13) To demand that the press give the fullest publicity to our resolutions; (14) To appoint a Travelling Commission of Control; (15) To permit free kustarnoye (individual small-scale) production by one's own efforts. (Berkman 1922, Chapter 2)

Berkman, from whose *The Kronstadt Rebellion* this quotation is taken, was an US anarchist who had served a lengthy prison sentence for a political assassination. He came to Russia as a sympathizer of the October revolution, but became disillusioned by the requisitioning of peasant produce by force, the imprisonment and execution of socialists and anarchists who sympathized with the revolution but disagreed with the Bolsheviks, the reintroduction of capitalism under the NEP, and the use of terror against the working class, the bolshevization of the Soviets and trade unions, the use of intimidation at election times et cetera. The Kronstadt sailors were expressing a set of demands that would have been generally pretty popular across Russia, particularly amongst the more politically conscious supporters of the revolution. Alarmingly for the Bolsheviks they talked in terms of a third revolution against the Bolshevik tyranny.

Lenin and Trotsky denounced the Kronstadt sailors as tools of former czarist generals and the Socialist Revolutionaries (Berkman 1922). Petrograd was 'cleaned up'—strikes were prohibited, there were numerous arrests, and the families of Kronstadt sailors were taken into custody as hostages (Berkman 1922). According to Berkman Zinoviev was given the task of making a series of lying speeches in which he denounced the Kronstadt sailors in libellous and inaccurate terms (Berkman 1922). Trotsky and Kamenev issued a proclamation denouncing the Kronstadt sailors as counter-revolutionary mutineers and threatening them with military action. As Trotsky puts it 'I'll shoot you like pheasants' (Berkman, ibid.). The Communist forces attacked across the ice and with an artillery bombardment. When they were successful an extensive massacre of the Kronstadt population, including women and even children followed. Numerous sailors were imprisoned and systematically shot; the remainder was dispatched to particularly nasty labour camps.

While the Kronstadt mutiny was actually taking place, Trotsky gave an interview to foreign correspondents in which he stated that the original Kronstadt garrison, which had been instrumental in bringing about the October Revolution, had largely been replaced by less committed personnel. The rebellion had been called, like others, at the behest of the agents of imperialism (Trotsky 1921). Trotsky did not subsequently refer to this episode at all frequently, but gave an account of his actions in 1938 (Trotsky 1938). In essence, his response is a sociological one. He says that the original Kronstadt sailors who were the mainstay of the revolution in 1917 had largely been called upon to deal with a variety of crises during the Civil War. They had been replaced by petty bourgeois and peasant elements, whose main interest was in increasing their rations in a situation of hardship. Particularly during a civil war, says Trotsky, the characteristics of a party are determined considerably more by its social composition than by its oral and written declarations. In the Kronstadt revolt, as in some other episodes during the Civil War, such as the revolt led by Makno, it was a matter of the petty bourgeoisie being ground between big capital and the dictatorship of the proletariat. The Kronstadt rebels could not simply have been left alone because they would have needed supplies, which could only come from the bourgeoisie externally, which would have meant that the revolt came under the leadership of the most reactionary elements. The Petrograd workers, says Trotsky, though hungry and discontented, did not sympathize with the mutineers. Although the revolt was one factor that stimulated the introduction of the NEP, simply telling the mutineers about the policy would not have been sufficient, because, as members of the petty bourgeoisie, they were not able to produce a coherent account of their own interests. What is happening is that the petty bourgeois blunderers and eclectics are trying to use the events of Kronstadt 17 years previously against the Fourth International, the party of revolution.

Thus for Trotsky, what the mutineers actually said and demanded can be disregarded. What actually matters is that they were objectively counter-revolutionary. From his position anything that an anarchist says may be disregarded, again on grounds of class position. Groups of workers critical of aspects of the revolution would almost certainly receive the same sociological treatment. This seriously does not look like a good basis for either genuine inner-party democracy, or for the sort of multiparty socialist democracy that Geras was advocating.

The Tenth Party Congress was held against the background of the Kronstadt revolt. Concessions were made to popular discontent in the form of the introduction of the NEP, involving a limited reversion to capitalism. There was a recognition within the party that it faced a very dangerous situation, and that internal divisions could lead to disaster. Trotsky supported Lenin in his call for a ban on factions. Groups were allowed—however, one gets the impression that you are part of a faction whereas I am part of a group. Members of the Central Committee could be expelled for factionalism. Indeed, two-thirds of the Central Committee could expel the other one-third for factionalism. The first purge was instituted and just under one-quarter of the party was expelled. Geras denies that Lenin's political practice was a precursor of Stalinism. Although Lenin's day-to-day conduct was less Draconian than his proposals at the Tenth Party Congress would suggest, let alone the evidence I detail later, much of his conduct was certainly conducive neither to freewheeling discussion inside the party, nor to socialist pluralism outside it.

At the Eleventh Party Congress, held in 1922, Lenin pursued the same theme that unity and discipline are particularly important in a situation of retreat, and had this to say about relationships with Mensheviks:

> And the Mensheviks and Socialist-Revolutionaries, all of whom preach this sort of thing, are astonished when we declare that we shall shoot people for such things. They are amazed; but surely it is clear. When an army is in retreat a hundred times more discipline is required than when it is advancing, because during an advance everybody presses forward. If everybody started rushing back now, it would spell immediate and inevitable disaster.
>
> The most important thing at such a moment is to retreat in good order, to fix the precise limits of the retreat, and not to give way to panic. And when a Menshevik says, 'You are now retreating; I have been advocating retreat all the time, I agree with you, I am your man, let us retreat together,' we say in reply, 'For the public manifestations of Menshevism our revolutionary courts must pass the death sentence, otherwise they are not our courts, but God knows what.'
>
> They cannot understand this and exclaim: 'What dictatorial manners these people have!' They still think we are persecuting the Mensheviks because they fought us in Geneva. But had we done that we should have been unable to hold power even for two months. Indeed, the sermons which Otto Bauer, the leaders of the Second and Two-and-a Half Internationals, the Mensheviks and Socialist-Revolutionaries preach express their true nature—' The revolution has gone too far. What you are saying now we have been saying all the time, permit us to say it again.' But we say in reply: 'Permit us to put you before a firing squad for saying that. Either you refrain from expressing your views, or, if you insist on expressing your political views publicly in the present circumstances, when our position is far more difficult than it was when the whiteguards were directly attacking us, then you will have only yourselves to blame if we treat you as the worst and most pernicious whiteguard elements.' (Lenin 1922)

This is not exactly multiparty socialism. Another worry about the dangers of retreat was expressed as follows:

> The deviations towards the bad side are the abuses committed by former government officials, landowners, bourgeois and other scum who play up to the Communists and who sometimes commit abominable outrages and acts of tyranny against the peasantry. This calls for a terrorist purge, summary trial and the firing squad. (Lenin 1921)

Lenin's concern with the dangers of retreat was also reflected in his views about the People's Commissariat for Justice:

> But where is the noise about *model trials* of the scoundrels abusing the New Economic Policy? There is no such noise, because there are no such trials.

> The P.C.J. has 'forgotten' that that is its business, that it is its duty to pull up, shake up and rouse the people's courts and teach them to be *ruthless and swift* in chastising—*with every means, including the firing squad*—for abuse of the New Economic Policy. *It* is responsible for this. There is no evidence of any vibrant activity in this sphere on the part of the P.C.J., because there is no such activity. (Lenin 1924)

Note the proposal is in effective show trials complete with the death penalty.

In 1922 the GPU (State Political Administration) was allowed to investigate party misconduct. Towards the end of his life Lenin arranged for the definition of treason in the penal code to include conduct that would objectively assist the enemies of the Soviet Union, and, of course, treason carried the death penalty. This provision is particularly alarming—criticizing the government, making jokes about the leadership, slacking at work could all be seen as objectively assisting the enemies of the Soviet Union.

Other political parties had already been banned because they had been involved in coups or conspiracies against the Bolsheviks—thanks to the behaviour of the czars, Russia had not developed a tradition of loyal opposition.

This is hardly an atmosphere conducive to the sort of socialist democracy advocated by Geras or Rosa Luxemburg. Trotsky himself, when out of power around 1930 called for the election of party officials by the secret ballot and the convening of a genuine party conference (Thatcher 2003, p. 172). There is a major problem about this, which was to haunt the Soviet Union right down to the days of Gorbachev. Imagine, for a very implausible minute, a successful Communist revolution in Britain and the installation of a single party state. If people were allowed to form groups or factions within the ruling party it would not be long before conservative, social democratic, Scottish Nationalist, groupings for example, emerged, and something resembling multiparty democracy started to reform. If there is an insistence on ideological homogeneity, on the other hand, things point towards the emergence of a small ruling group at the centre. In the Soviet Union this dilemma was eventually resolved by the complete breakdown of the system. There is a further problem inherent in the Soviet version of a planned economy, that it might well be possible to set overall economic priorities within a democratic framework—to some extent this occurs in democratic elections within capitalist societies. However, the sort of detailed economic planning required to decide exactly what should be done in particular factories and so forth is hardly amenable to thorough discussion by an elected assembly (there is a brief discussion of the problems of democratic planning in Thatcher 2003, pp. 174–175).

The above evidence on Lenin's restriction of democracy and willingness to use terror was available back in the 1970s when Geras was writing the material under discussion. It is reinforced by evidence from the recent biography by Robert Service, which benefits from the opening of archives following the demise of the USSR. Service details a series of issues and episodes that suggested Lenin's potential for ruthlessness. There was the admiration for Tkachëv, who glorified mass terror in order to inaugurate a post-revolutionary state in *What is to be Done?* (Service 2008, location 2882). Among the slogans Lenin put forward at the Third Party Congress in 1905 was 'mass terror' in defence of the revolution (Service 2008, location 3478). As early as 27 October 1917, in the immediate aftermath of the revolution, Lenin signed a decree allowing for the closure of newspapers that published anti-government material or significantly distorted facts (Service 2008, location 6288). In December 1917 the secret police (Cheka) was created and given a very free hand. In January 1918 a decree on food procurement allowed the shooting of speculators on the spot, and the government set about eliminating Soviets who had been unwise enough to elect Mensheviks (Service 2008, location 6878).

As part of the Red Army's advance into Poland with a view to spreading the revolution westwards, Lenin put forward the following plan to Trotsky's deputy:

> A beautiful plan. Finish it off together with Dzierżyński. Disguised as 'Greens' (we'll heap the blame on them afterwards) we'll advance 10–20 versts and hang the kulaks, priests, landed gentry. 100,000 rubles prize for each one of them that is hanged. (Service 2008, location 8022)

As Service points out, hanging priests was hardly likely to be popular with the Poles. We have seen earlier that Lenin placed considerable emphasis on the need to preserve unity in the Bolshevik party at the time of the introduction of the NEP in 1921. At the same time he emphasized that it was necessary to maintain firm government. Reacting to a proposal from Kamenev that the justice system should become more open, he responded:

> 'Bandits' should be shot on the spot. 'The speed and force of the repressions' should be intensified. Any constitutional or legislative reforms should

> be formulated in such a fashion as to sanction the possibility of the death penalty being applied in cases involving 'all aspects of activity by Mensheviks, S[ocialist]-R[evolutionaries], etc.' [Service continues] He gave a warning that the regime should not be 'caught napping by a second Kronstadt'. The Civil Code, he suggested, should enshrine 'the essence and justification of terror'. The peasant rebels of Tambov and elsewhere were still being attacked and quelled by the Red Army. In Georgia, the remnants of national resistance to the communists continued to be forcibly eliminated. Arrests of known officers of the White armies were still being carried out. Repression was conducted in abundance in the lands of 'Soviet power'. But Lenin wanted the scope widened. In the first months of 1922 he advocated the final eradication of all remaining threats, real or potential, to his state. For Socialist-Revolutionaries and Mensheviks he demanded the staging of show trials followed by exemplary severe punishment. For the Russian Orthodox Church hierarchy, or for a substantial section of it, he demanded the same. (Service 2008, location 8618)

He was successful in getting a show trial of the Socialist Revolutionaries, but not of the Mensheviks, and a show trial of leaders of the Russian Orthodox Church at which the death penalty was imposed. In terms of terror, Lenin's legacy is the setting up of the fundamentals for something on the lines of a collective Stalinist terror.

The Geras view of Trotsky appears vindicated by the following quotation, written by Trotsky in the early 1930s:

> In order to better understand the character of the present Soviet Union ... let us assume first that the Soviet bureaucracy is overthrown by a revolutionary party having all the attributes of the old Bolshevism, enriched moreover by the world experience of the recent period. Such a party would begin with the restoration of democracy in the trade unions and the Soviets. It would be able to, and would have to, restore freedom of Soviet parties. Together with the masses, and at their head, it would carry out a ruthless purgation of the state apparatus ... It would give the youth free opportunity to think independently, learn, criticise and grow. (Trotsky 1967, p. 252)

Service points out that it is not clear how Trotsky would have actually implemented these aims in the very unlikely event of his recall to lead the Soviet Union. This is particularly unclear in the light of previous support for terror and restrictions of democracy, as will be seen from the examples that follow.

Trotsky's ruthlessness, in dealing with the Kronstadt revolt, where the sailors stood for values very similar to those in the previous quotation, has already been discussed, including the way in which Trotsky, writing in 1938, defended his conduct in putting down the Kronstadt rebellion.

Almost certainly, this is not a matter of Trotsky's creative genius alone, but he was an early proponent of the use of concentration camps:

> As early as 4 June 1918, Trotsky called for a group of unruly Czech war prisoners to be pacified, disarmed, and placed in a kontslager: a concentration camp. Twelve days later, in a memorandum addressed to the Soviet government, Trotsky again spoke of concentration camps, outdoor prisons in which 'the city and village bourgeoisie … shall be mobilized and organized into rear-service battalions to do menial work (cleaning barracks, camps, streets, digging trenches, etc)'. (Appelbaum 2012, location 766)

As Commissar of War during the civil war, Trotsky's way of dealing with the problem of encouraging soldiers to fight was by ordering the shooting of every tenth man of units refusing to fight (Thatcher 2003, p. 102). In another famous incident during the Civil War he was felt to have crossed a line by ordering the execution of a Bolshevik commissar. The incident concerned a:

> certain Panteleev who was commissar of the 2nd Numerny Petrograd Regiment. When the battle around Sviyazhsk appeared to be going against the Reds, Panteleev and his men commandeered a steam-ship trying to escape upriver to Nizhni Novgorod. The vessel was boarded by other Red units and the fugitives were arrested. Trotsky ordered their summary execution. (Service 2010, location 4753)

Summarizing Bolshevik ruthlessness during the civil war, Service comments:

> They had shot innocent hostages. They had stripped large social groups of their civil rights. They had glorified terrorist ideas and gloried in their application. The Bolshevik party had treated even workers and peasants savagely whenever they had engaged in active opposition. (Service 2010, location 5656)

There are other examples of ruthlessness, however. Addressing the Kronstadt sailors in 1917 he said:

> I tell you heads must roll, blood must flow ... The strength of the French Revolution was in the machine that made the enemies of the people shorter by a head. This is a fine device. We must have it in every city. (Service 2010, location 3741)

Following the assassination attempt n Lenin fully approved the use of red terror involving the imprisonment of several thousand members of the middle and upper classes, some of whom were immediately shot and others were held as hostages (Service 2010, location 4767). Trotsky went along with Lenin's call for a show trial of the Socialist Revolutionaries in 1922 with a bloodthirsty speech (Service 2010, location 6213).

Trotsky's ruthlessness must have stemmed in part from an unrealistically utopian belief in the socialist future:

> Man will become incomparably stronger, more intelligent, more subtle. His body will be more harmonious, his movements more rhythmical, his voice more musical; the forms of daily existence will acquire a dynamic theatricality. The average human type will rise to the level of Aristotle, Goethe, Marx. It is above this ridge that new summits will rise. (Service 2010, location 6593)

It also stems from a view of morality that contrasts with views taken later by Geras:

> Civilisation can only be saved by the socialist revolution. To accomplish the overturn, the proletariat needs all its strength, all its resolution, all its audacity, passion and ruthlessness. Above all it must be completely free from the fictions of religion, 'democracy' and transcendental morality—the spiritual chains forged by the enemy to tame it and enslave it. Only that which prepares the complete and final overthrow of imperialist bestiality is moral, and nothing else. The welfare of the revolution—that is the supreme law! (Trotsky 1938)

If Trotsky seriously meant exactly what he says in the above passage, then absolutely anything is acceptable, provided the outcome is the success of the revolution.

Thus Alan Johnson's assessment of Geras's view of Trotsky, (see Cohen and Garrard 2017, p. 11), namely that he had badly lost his way between 1919 and 1921 when Trotsky asserted that the Communist Party had a right to impose its views on the working class when its temporary moods had gone astray, is simply inadequate.

There is thus a very big gap between Geras's desire for inner-party democracy and socialist pluralism, and much of the conduct of Trotsky when in power and his subsequent attitudes. Some of Lenin's conduct, also, was uncomfortably close to a mild version of Stalin.

The Rise of Fascism

Geras is not alone in praising Trotsky for his perspicuity in raising the alarm about the rise of fascism at a time when the Comintern policy was that of 'class against class', meaning that the social democrats and the fascists were just as bad as each other. In contrast to this, as is well known, Trotsky favoured a united front of communists and social democrats. He makes it clear, though, that this is to facilitate revolution:

> Capitalist society, particularly in Germany, has been on the eve of collapse several times in the last decade and a half; but each time it emerged from the catastrophe. (Trotsky 1975, p. 69)

There had been a revolutionary situation in Germany in 1923, but Stalin and his followers had urged restraint (Trotsky 1975, p. 75) (It will be recalled that this episode is discussed briefly in Chap. 2). Writing on Germany and the international situation in 1931 Trotsky described the situation in both Spain and Britain as pre-revolutionary (Trotsky 1975, p. 79). Revolution in Germany would lead readily to revolution in France (Trotsky 1975, p. 81). A revolutionary conflagration was likely in the USA and Japan (Trotsky 1975, p. 83). Turning to Germany:

> For us, the Communist Party is the subjective factor: the Social Democracy is an objective obstacle that must be swept away. Fascism would actually fall to pieces if the Communist Party were able to unite the working class (Trotsky 1975, p. 86). Cf. The moment that the masses are separated from the reformist leadership, any agreement with the latter loses all meaning. To perpetuate the left front would be to misunderstand the dialectical revolutionary struggle … from the united front in the name of defence to the conquest of power under the banner of Communism. (Trotsky 1975, p. 234)

Would a Social Democrat find this prognosis of the outcome of a united front particularly attractive? His party is scheduled to be swept away as part of a wildly optimistic forecast of revolution all over the place. And, following successful revolution, he is promised a fate similar to that of the

Socialist Revolutionaries and Mensheviks in Russia (Trotsky 1975, p. 108). Perhaps he would escape this fate because, like the majority of Social Democratic workers he will turn to revolution (Trotsky 1975, p. 122). Another theme in Trotsky, and certainly in subsequent Trotskyism, such as that of the Socialist Workers Party, is that the leadership of parties and trade unions is conservative, while the rank and file is willing to begin the struggle (see for example Trotsky 1975, p. 361). There may well be some truth in this on occasion, but in organizations that are internally democratic the leadership may very well simply reflect the will of the membership.

Certainly, some of Trotsky's assessment of Germany looks prophetic—he forecasts that the coming to power of the National Socialists would involve 'the extermination of the flower of the German proletariat … the hellish work of Italian fascism would probably appear as a pale and almost humane experiment in comparison with the work of the German National Socialists'. He also thought that a fascist Germany would attack the USSR (Trotsky 1975, pp. 89–91).

Once Hitler was properly installed, the Comintern dropped the disastrous class-against-class policy and instead promoted a united front comprising anybody opposed to fascism. Of all the policies adopted this is arguably the one with the best prospect of success, although, manifestly, it was adopted far too late. Neither Trotsky nor Stalin seem to have realized the extent of support in Germany for Hitler, which included large numbers of workers as well as the petty bourgeoisie and the monopoly capitalists they rightly saw as important. Given that, it is debatable whether Trotsky's policy or either of those coming from Stalin would have stopped the rise of Hitler. Italy provides a further comment about the disastrous Stalinist policy of regarding the fascists and social democrats as twins, and being foolishly unconcerned about the triumph of fascism. Fascism in Italy was certainly disastrous for the Italian left, but the depths of the disaster were not nearly as serious and dramatic as those in Nazi Germany. More generally, fascist regimes apart from Nazi Germany have been extremely bad for the left, but not as drastic as Nazi Germany.

Stalin emerged as a dictator from around 1928 onwards. He undertook a variety of sometimes startling changes of policy. Some of these made it difficult for Trotsky to keep up with him. The policy of incorporating the peasants into collective farms had been advocated by Trotsky, but he severely underestimated the depths of peasant resistance, and it is an interesting question as to what Trotsky himself would have done faced with the crisis of the late 1920s. The brutal way in which resistance was crushed was a major source of the expansion of the Gulag. Trotsky's theory was that Stalin was a representative of the Soviet bureaucracy. However, for a representative of the bureaucracy he sent surprisingly many bureaucrats to prisons and labour camps. Rather than representing bureaucratic stability, with the development of the Five-Year Plans starting in the early 1930s, he became involved in the dramatic and bloody collectivization of the peasantry, and in the development of industry at what was arguably excessive speed. Trotsky was, of course, assassinated by a Stalinist agent well before the end of the Second World War, and therefore was not in a position to discuss the extension of communism to Eastern Europe. It is, of course, arguable as to whether the planned societies that emerged had any resemblance to socialism or communism as envisaged by Marx and Engels, but the idea that the Soviet leadership had lost all interest in the development of communism elsewhere was plainly false.

Conclusion on Trotsky

Given Trotsky's very extensive writings, there is obviously a great deal more which could be said in this chapter. To reiterate the main points: the theory of permanent revolution is based mainly on a series of conceptual experiments, and a variety of other possibilities are not considered. Trotsky's general conceptions of politics were poor. His democratic credentials are very much open to question. He does not seem to have recognized the strength of bourgeois democracy, respect for law, political pluralism et cetera—this is arguably a general weakness in Marxism historically, but it is perhaps particularly acute in Trotsky's case. Although aspects of his analysis of fascism are acute, his major alternative was revolution, but the idea that there was a pre-revolutionary situation in Germany in the early 1930s is very debatable. Geras should have taken more cognizance of these matters back in the 1970s.

I end with a final comment on Trotskyism more generally. As mentioned earlier, basically Stalinist regimes were installed in a variety of countries in the years from the end of the Second World War through to the 1970s, it is very debatable as to whether there has ever been a Trotskyist revolution anywhere. Assuming that Geras was a committed and practical Marxist, this particular point might have made more impact on his thinking.

References

Applebaum, A. (2012). *Gulag: A History of the Soviet Camps* (Kindle ed.). Harmondsworth: Penguin Books Ltd.

Berkman, A. (1922). *The Kronstadt Rebellion*. Retrieved from https://www.marxists.org/reference/archive/berkman/1922/kronstadt-rebellion/ch2.htm.

Cohen, B., & Garrard, E. (Eds.). (2017). *The Norman Geras Reader 'What's There is There'*. Manchester: Manchester University Press.

Deutscher, I. (2003). *The Prophet Armed*. London: Verso. (This is a Reprint of the Earlier Penguin Edition Which Geras Would Have Used).

Geras, N. (1986). *Literature of Revolution: Essays on Marxism*. London: Verso.

Lenin, V. I. (1899). *The Development of Capitalism in, Russia*. Retrieved from https://www.marxists.org/archive/lenin/works/1899/devel/index.htm.

Lenin, V. I. (1920). *The Trade Unions, the Present Situation and Trotsky's Mistakes*. Retrieved from https://www.marxists.org/archive/lenin/works/1920/dec/30.htm.

Lenin, V. I. (1921). *The Tax in Kind* (Vol. 32). Moscow: Collected Works.

Lenin, V. I. (1922). *Speech at the Opening of the 12th Party Congress* (Vol. 33). Moscow: Collected Works, Progress Publishers, 1965.

Lenin, V. I. (1924). *On the Tasks of the People's Commissariat for Justice Under the New Economic Policy* (Vol. 36). Moscow: Collected Works, 1971.

Thatcher, I. (2003). *Trotsky*. London: Routledge.

Trotsky, L. (1906). *Results and Prospects*. Retrieved from https://www.marxists.org/archive/trotsky/works/pdf/prrp.pdf.

Trotsky, L. (1921). *On the Events at Kronstadt*. Retrieved from https://www.marxists.org/archive/trotsky/1921/military/ch61.htm.

Trotsky, L. (1931). *The Permanent Revolution*. Retrieved from https://www.marxists.org/archive/trotsky/1931/tpr/prre.htm.

Trotsky, L. (1938). *Their Morals and Ours*. Retrieved from https://www.marxists.org/archive/trotsky/1938/morals/morals.htm.

Trotsky, L. (1967). *The Revolution Betrayed*. London: Park Publications.

Trotsky, L. (1973). *1905*. Harmondsworth: Pelican.

Trotsky, L. (1975). *The Struggle Against Fascism in Germany*. Harmondsworth: Penguin.

Service, R. (2008). *Lenin* (Kindle ed.). Houndmills: Macmillan Publishers.

Service, R. (2010). *Trotsky: A Biography* (Kindle ed.). Houndmills: Macmillan Publishers.

CHAPTER 4

Marx and Human Nature

In this chapter my basic argument is that Geras's book: *Marx and Human Nature: Refutation of a Legend* (London: Verso, 1983) establishes that Marx had a theory of human nature, and establishes that there are some themes that persist throughout Marx's life, but that it does not establish that the youthful theory of alienation persists into the older Marx. Geras does not, in fact make this claim, beyond the point already made about the persistence of some themes, but the book has been taken by several commentators to establish that the Marx's youthful theory of alienation persists into his later writings. After summarizing the main claims made in *Marx and Human Nature: Refutation of a Legend*, I shall briefly make the case that there is a definite division between the younger and the older Marx. I shall argue that although Geras certainly does establish that Marx had a concept of human nature, and that to a considerable extent this is common to the younger and older Marx, this common human nature is relatively thin. Much of it would be subscribed to by people of any and every political persuasion. It does not form a good basis for arguing that the youthful theories of alienation persist into the older Marx. Geras makes the valid point that people who argue that the older Marx did not have a theory of human nature tend to rest their case on the *Sixth Thesis on Feuerbach*, and not a great deal else. I shall attempt to explain why theorists who argue that there is a division in Marx's work assert that the older Marx has no theory of human nature. I shall then go on to briefly summarize the evidence that there is a division, and will discuss some of

M. Cowling, *Norman Geras's Political Thought from Marxism to Human Rights*, https://doi.org/10.1007/978-3-319-74048-5_4

the apparent reappearances of the theory of alienation in the older Marx, arguing that these amount to considerably less than is frequently asserted.

The Basic Arguments of Marx and Human Nature: Refutation of a Legend

I shall now review the basic claims that Geras makes in the book. He lays down his approach as follows:

> You will not go very far in discussion either within or about Marxism before encountering the view that one of the things bequeathed to this intellectual tradition by its founder was a denial of the idea of a universal human nature. (Geras 1983, p. 11)

He continues by saying that not very much in Marx's work confirms this claim—there is only a single passage: 'The one item of any plausibility is some lines from the Theses on Feuerbach'—apart from that, and these lines themselves were unpublished, there are only 'a few other odds and ends which … amount to nothing at all' (Geras 1983, p. 12).

He continues:

> when the various possible meanings of this passage [from the Theses on Feuerbach] are placed within the only possible context for its proper assessment, the interpretation of Marx that has been so reliant on it is shown not to be a viable one at all. It is left without even the slenderest title to philological respectability. (Geras 1983, p. 13)

He emphasizes that he is taking the claim that Marx does not have a theory of human nature literally, meaning that Marx opposed 'not just this or that view about human nature but the very idea of one' (Geras 1983, p. 13). He makes it clear that, of course, 'Marx—like everyone else—did reject certain ideas of human nature' (Geras 1983, pp. 14–15).

Geras distinguishes between human nature, which he sees as a constant entity, a set of relatively permanent characteristics, and the nature of man meaning the character of human beings in a given context (Geras 1983, p. 24).

He says that the assertion by some Marxists, notably those influenced by Althusser, that there is no such thing as human nature must be intended to challenge the existence of a constant human character (Geras 1983, p. 24).

The next part of the book is, naturally, devoted to an extended analysis of the sixth *Thesis on Feuerbach*. This is well known, but the crucial to sentences seem to me to be:

> Feuerbach resolves the essence of religion into the essence of man. But the essence of man is no abstraction inherent in each single individual. In its reality it is the ensemble of human relations. (Marx and Engels 1975, Volume 5, p. 4)

He says there is a perfectly plausible account of what is going on here: Feuerbach is mistaken not because he views man as a species, but because he sees man exclusively in these terms (Geras 1983, p. 31). He also comments that it is perfectly appropriate to say that not too much should be derived from a very few unpublished sentences, but reasonably continues by pointing out that it is people who adopt a broadly Althusserian approach are putting a very heavy emphasis on these few sentences (Geras 1983, p. 37).

He then says that the Sixth Thesis could mean that:

> In its reality (i) human nature or (ii) the nature of man (a) depends upon, or (b) is disclosed by the ensemble of social relations. (Geras 1983, p. 38)

(i) (a) Geras dismisses as unattractive—the idea that a constant human nature could depend upon variable social relations just seems totally unlikely (Geras 1983, p. 39).

(ii) (a) the idea that the nature of man depends upon social relations Geras considers intelligible and compatible with the rest of the text (Geras 1983, p. 39). The more plausible version of this is that the nature of man may vary considerably because of changes in social relations, but that there are also more constant factors, some of which may constitute a human nature (Geras 1983, p. 40). A more drastic version asserts that the nature of man is completely and exclusively dependent on the ensemble of social relations (Geras 1983, p. 41). In this case there is effectively no human nature (Geras 1983, p. 42).

> (ii) (a) human nature is disclosed by the ensemble of social relations. The idea here would be that an invariant human nature would disclose itself in varying ways in different social totalities. A more drastic version of this option would say that human nature can be entirely reduced to the ensemble of social relations. (Geras 1983, p. 44)

> (i) (b) the nature of man is disclosed by the ensemble of social relations. If the nature of man is disclosed by the ensemble of social relations then plainly this is compatible with the idea of a human nature. (Geras 1983, p. 45)

It will be noticed that internally some of these alternatives come to be pretty much equivalent to particular interpretations of other alternatives, so that effectively three possibilities emerge:

> 1. The nature of man is conditioned by the ensemble of social relations.
> 2. Human nature or the nature of man is manifested in the ensemble of social relations.
> 3. In its reality the nature of man is determined by, or human nature is dissolved in, the ensemble of social relations. (Geras 1983, p. 46—slightly abridged)

The first proposition of the three above would seem to be an early formulation of the basic idea of historical materialism, and is perfectly compatible with the idea of a human nature because the dependence is not complete, and the obvious remaining part would be a nature of man due to stable, natural causes (Geras 1983, p. 47).

The second proposition, seeing the nature of man as manifested in social relations, would appear to be a way of emphasizing the social nature of man: a biological capacity to support language, for example, would only be manifested in society (Geras 1983, p. 48).

The third proposition, to the effect that human nature is dissolved in the ensemble of social relations does involve the denial of a human nature. Geras then finds a series of quotations from Bottomore, Cumming, Kamenka, Althusser, Suchting, Hook, Soper and Venable, all of which involve a denial of the idea of an essential human nature (Geras 1983 pp. 50–51). He continues by quoting Robert Tucker to the effect that in the Marxism that emerges after 1845 there is a 'mental world from which "man" seems to be absent', and, switches to another author who takes the same approach, where individuals are the 'bearers' of social relations (Suchting). The basic idea is that the fundamental concepts of historical materialism—the social formation, productive forces, relations of production, superstructure and ideologies supplant the concept of human nature (Geras 1983, p. 52).

Geras then sets about rebutting this approach, arguing that one needs to set the Sixth Thesis in a wider context (Geras 1983, p. 57). The obvious place to look is the exposition of historical materialism in *The German Ideology*. He quotes a series of places from this book in which Marx makes use of a concept of human nature. The one of these that I find the most persuasive and striking is the description of the proletarian as one 'who is not in a position to satisfy even the needs he has in common with all human beings'; one whose 'position does not even allow him to satisfy the needs arising directly from his human nature' (Geras 1983, p. 63). *The German Ideology* was not published in Marx's lifetime, but Engels tried to get it published for two years, and it can therefore be regarded as an accurate statement of their views at this point (Geras 1983, p. 63). Another very persuasive quotation reads in part 'of course, we cannot here go either into the actual physical nature of man, or into the natural conditions in which man finds himself' (Geras 1983, p. 66). The logic of these quotations is that if variations in the character of human beings are largely down to the relations of production, this production itself is to be explained by some general and constant characteristics (Geras 1983, p. 67). Summarizing what Marx has to say about these general characteristics in *The German Ideology*, Geras lists needs for 'other human beings, for sexual relations, for food, water, clothing, shelter, rest and, more generally, for circumstances that are conducive to physical health' (Geras 1983, p. 72). To this may be added a need of people for personal development.

A little later Geras points out that the idea of an underlying human nature is also to be found in the younger Marx, which makes the idea that similar quotations found later amount to a renunciation of the idea of an underlying human nature distinctly odd (Geras 1983, p. 77).

Summarizing his position on the question of one Marx or two, Geras says 'the real picture is of a theoretical development marked in places by genuine novelty and change, but marked equally by some stability of conception, by definite continuities and strong ones' (Geras 1983, pp. 78–79).

The above quotation does not place Geras firmly in either the group of authors who claim that there is only one continuous Marx, or the authors who think in terms of a radical division in about 1845.Geras then goes on to find examples of the use of the idea of an underlying human nature elsewhere in the later Marx. One striking quotation talks of Marx saying that there are 'immutable natural conditions' and 'absolute determinations of *human* labour as such' (Geras 1983, p. 82). Summarizing a variety of sources in the older Marx Geras produces a longer schedule of needs:

> Food, clothing, shelter, fuel, rest and sleep; hygiene, 'healthy maintenance of the body', fresh air and sunlight; intellectual requirements, social intercourse, sexual needs insofar as they are presupposed by 'relations between the sexes'; the needs of support specific to infancy, old-age and incapacity, and the need for a safe and healthy working environment. (Geras 1983, p. 83)

The deprivation of these by the capitalist system leads to what looks very like a moral condemnation of capitalism (Geras 1983, p. 84).

In the last part of the book Geras proceeds to look at the idea of human nature more generally. He suggests that Marx's idea from *The German Ideology* onwards that one can have a materialist conception of the idea of human nature, subject to scientific correction and research, somehow gets confused with the idea that Marx is disputing the very notion of a human nature (Geras 1983, p. 93).

Much is made by those of an Althusserian persuasion of the idea in *Capital* of individuals as the 'bearers' of economic categories. However, Geras points out that Marx also distinguishes people from their role as bearers (Geras 1983, pp. 92–93).

Geras finally asserts that Marx was right not to reject the idea of human nature. He accepts that there are reactionary uses of the concept, but asserts that it is surely not reactionary to protest against torture or hunger on the grounds that these are not compatible with human nature (Geras 1983, p. 96). He extends the longer of Marx's lists to include the capacity to make and enjoy music, and universal human emotions, which he says are linked to facial expressions, which are biological in origin (Geras 1983, p. 99).

He asserts that it is perfectly possible to have an ethical position resting on a conception of human nature. Indeed, the idea of socialism as a desirable outcome would seem to be readily expressed in terms of an idea of human nature (Geras 1983, pp. 102–103).

A little later he points out that there is massive and unmet human need on a global scale—children dying before they are five, people becoming disabled through poverty and malnutrition and so forth (Geras 1983, p. 105). The point of this is one can debate whether certain things are exactly in line with human nature or not, but hunger and torture are definitely not compatible with human nature. (This is obviously in a moral sense—our nature is such that we can go hungry or be tortured.)

Marxists and Socialists are committed to the idea of a radically different social order, and such social order requires people of a certain type—the exact list of qualities could be debated (Geras 1983, p. 109). Again, a theory of human nature would seem to be involved.

Even the Althusserian idea of a structure determining its elements must be false because the elements of the structure explain something of its character—the point here again being one of the elements of the structure is people, so that the structure partially contains some version of human nature, and this human nature affects the scope and limits of the structure (Geras 1983, p. 111).

Socialization obviously has biological limits—not just anything can be food, and some things are poisonous (Geras 1983, p. 113). '[B]leeding, sleeping, walking, running, grasping a tool in the hand' … and the 'feeling of acute physical pain' are examples of things which are not culturally specific (Geras 1983, p. 114).

Geras concludes: 'Marx did not reject the idea of a human nature. He was right not to do so' (Geras 1983, p. 116).

How Fixed Is Human Nature?

Before I go on to consider the issue of whether there is a division in Marx's work, which is the main subject of this chapter, I would like to make a brief observation about Geras's view that there is a relatively fixed human nature. Our biological nature is perhaps rather less fixed than one would imagine—one example would be that today in the advanced countries life expectancy is considerably longer than it was back in the Middle Ages. A whole variety of infections that were serious problems in previous times have now been eliminated or made much less serious. The changes in what we consider to be 'human nature' are particularly dramatic if one considers the variety of expectations placed upon women. In traditional peasant societies they were expected to carry out heavy physical labour. Indeed, prehistoric women developed stronger arms than those of modern day rowers because of the daily tasks they carried out (*Guardian*, 2 December 2017). In contrast, the sort of middle-class women depicted by Rubens, who would be deemed borderline obese by modern standards, would also be deemed incapable of engaging in serious physical exertion. In contrast again, women today are regarded as capable of considerable physical exertion, for example being able to run marathons, play rugby and football, complete triathlons, engage in boxing. They are also much less constrained than previous generations by biology, in particular, there are reliable contraception and disposable sanitary products, generally no expectation of virginity on marriage, and producing one or more illegitimate children is not seen as anything unusual, at least in much of Europe. So, while there may well be an underlying biological continuity, and all of these women need or would have needed food, shelter and so forth there is a very considerable variety of ways in which human nature is displayed, or alternatively perhaps the sensible way to understand it is as a family of ideas within which there is considerable variation. This question obviously needs considerable further discussion, but the argument of this paragraph points towards a thinner conception of constant and common human nature.

Geras and Continuity in Marx

The next step is to debate the extent to which Geras's conclusions in *Marx and Human Nature* impact the issue of continuity in Marx. Assuming for the minute that there might be a break in Marx's work, the obvious place to locate it is somewhere between 1845 and the writing of the first part of *The German Ideology* in 1846–1847. I think the claim that the concept of human nature disappears in the older Marx is actually an exaggerated way of saying that the concept of human nature and of man's alienation from his human nature is central to the Marx of 1843–1845, whereas in the older Marx the central concepts are historical materialism, the means, forces and relations of production, class, class struggle and so forth. The assertion is that the idea of alienation essentially disappears in the older Marx.

The majority of commentators on Marx writing in English take the view that the concept of alienation continues to be important in the older Marx. Many of these naturally date from the 1970s when there was a controversy stemming from the writings of Louis Althusser. Examples would be Avineri (1972), Cornu (1957), Garaudy (1967), Howard (1972), Hyppolite (1969), Kamenka (1972) (Geras, above, lists Kamenka as an author who asserts that there is discontinuity in Marx, but the general run of his book definitely points in the opposite direction); Korsch (1938, 1970), McLellan (1971, 1980, 1973, pp. 290–310), Maguire (1972), Mandel (1971, pp. 154–186), Mészáros (1970), Plamenatz (1975), Ollman (1971), Tucker (1967), Lewis (1972), Cornforth (1973), Kolakowski (1971), Thomas (1976). However, more recent commentators also take a similar view: Wilde (1998, 2004), Holloway (1997, 2002), Dyer-Witheford (2004). A curious point about this orthodoxy is that before the publication of Marx's *Economic and Philosophical Manuscripts*, what is now seen as an Althusserian approach was pretty much the standard one—writers such as Lukács (1971) and Korsch (1938, 1970) who picked out the humanist themes from what was then known of Marx's earlier writings were very much the exception. Writers linked to the Second and Third Internationals concentrated in varying ways on 'scientific' theories of society derived from Marx's writings about economics and the state.

A major reason why links with the theory of alienation were not made earlier is that those of Marx's youthful writings that were published were in fairly inaccessible places. Significantly, the most obvious traces of the theory of alienation to be found in Marx's writings after 1845 are in unpublished writings, most notably, of course, the *Grundrisse*. I can recall a conversation with Bertell Ollman in which he asserted that Marx's unpublished writings give a much better clue to what he was really thinking than do his published writings. Now this might well be true of a Machiavellian politician keen to deceive his adversaries, but it seems a very strange assertion about Marx—I can see no particular reason for him to hide his views about alienation. He was willing to adjust his views somewhat when involved with a committee or an organization, or in order to get round censorship, but neither of these apply in any obvious way to the theory of alienation. Indeed, given how very much he did publish during his lifetime, it seems very strange that he did not choose to publish a clear version of the *Economic and Philosophical Manuscripts*, updated to include aspects of the theories he developed in *Capital* and other texts. The summaries of the theories of *Capital* that he did produce, *Wages, Price and Profit* and *Value, Price and Profit*, are not generally claimed as places in which the alienation theories reoccur. The most obvious reason, I would argue, is that he realized that the theory of alienation did not fit very well with the basic ideas of historical materialism—if society, including major aspects of human nature and conduct are determined by the mode of production, this does not seem to leave an obvious space for stating that there is a communal, loving, powerful and creative human essence that is alienated in the economy, the state, religion, for example. To be clear, there is an obvious continuity in Marx's work at a general level in the sense that by 1844 if not slightly earlier he regarded himself as an atheist, a communist, someone who believed in the importance of the community, someone who thought that the economy is very important and who believed in revolution. However, this is a rather general belief that distinguishes Marx from Conservatives, Liberals, Christians and others but is very unspecific.

Human Nature and Human Need

Before we get any further with this exposition it is worth reiterating Geras's account of what Marx considers to be human nature:

> Food, clothing, shelter, fuel, rest and sleep; hygiene, 'healthy maintenance of the body', fresh air and sunlight; intellectual requirements, social intercourse, sexual needs insofar as they are presupposed by 'relations between the sexes'; the needs of support specific to infancy, old-age and incapacity, and the need for a safe and healthy working environment. (Geras 1983, p. 83)

It may be that everyone today has been influenced to some extent by Marx's heritage, but even a Conservative politician such as Theresa May might well agree with a list of this sort, even though her policies are making it more difficult for British citizens to ensure all of these. People of other persuasions might well broadly agree with this list but wish to add aspects or place a rather different emphasis. Thus trade union leaders would put special emphasis on higher wages as a way of attaining much of the above, and also consider a safe and healthy working environment to be particularly important. Remembering the report *Faith in the City* produced by the Church of England when Mrs Thatcher was in power, clerics might well agree with the list but obviously add spiritual needs. Feminists would wish to place particular emphasis on support for infancy, incapacity and old age, and, obviously, support for working women. Gay Lesbian and transgender activists, sadomasochists and so forth would doubtless describe Marx's statement of sexual needs as unimaginative, but might well be happy with the rest of the list.

It is also fairly obvious that from any of the standpoints, gross deprivation of most of the list would be seen as morally undesirable. I think this would be true whatever one's approach to ethics. In various places Geras points out that in large parts of the world there are people who are massively deprived of features of the list. He says that one can argue about exactly what of the obligations of people who are in a position to help, but that the level of need is so gross compared to the degree of help offered that there is an obvious and massive unmet need that should surely concern us. This is obviously very important, but does not particularly require a theory of alienation. To be quite clear, Geras's list is perfectly compatible with the idea that the theory of alienation persists in, or underlies the writings of the older Marx, but, as we have seen, it does not require this theory.

Alienation in the Older Marx

The general argument being pursued in this chapter is that there is a change of framework between the works of Marx before 1845 and after this date. However, it may be seen as facile to simply state this. It is necessary to bite the bullet, and carefully discuss and analyse the uses of the alienation vocabulary in the older Marx. This is a very considerable undertaking. I attempted it in an earlier article (Cowling 2006) in which I went carefully through the apparent uses of the alienation theory in the older Marx, and argued that these are very much exaggerated by people who wish to argue that there is one Marx.

I wish to start by assuming that readers are familiar with the basic outlines of the theory of alienation. I give a fuller account of this and of what I consider to be the differences between the younger and the older Marx in Cowling (1989). Very briefly, between 1843 and 1845 Marx asserted that man is alienated from the object of his labour, his means of labour, his fellow labourers and his species being. He is also alienated from the state, religion and philosophy. Linked to this there are several theories that are different from those of the older Marx. For example, the citizens are seen as an alienated from the state, rather than the state being described as a committee for organizing the common affairs of the bourgeoisie. Marx has at this stage a very stark theory of absolute poverty based on the idea of the alienation of the worker going to extremes, whereas later he was happy to note that the conditions of the working class had generally improved, but that they still suffered from relative poverty. There is no theory of the distinction between labour and labour power; instead Marx talks of the capitalist and the worker cheating each other. His economic theory generally takes its point of departure from Adam Smith, whereas in his mature writing the point of departure is generally the work of David Ricardo.

The points in the last paragraph are not generally as well recognized as they should be; this is probably because people who have studied sufficient philosophy to be reasonably familiar with the work of Hegel generally have not studied sufficient political economy to be familiar with Smith, Ricardo, and subsequent literature discussing them and comparing them with Marx and subsequent economists. Another matter that is not as generally realized as it should be is that what seems to be the central concept of the theory of alienation, the idea of being alienated from one's species being, is taken from Feuerbach, who saw human nature as intrinsically and naturally loving, powerful, knowledgeable and communal. A rival interpretation places greater emphasis on Marx's Hegelian heritage, but it is noteworthy that almost all of Marx's praise and condemnation of Hegel in the *Manuscripts* follows the same line as Feuerbach's praise and condemnation of Hegel. This tends to be recognized when dealing with Marx's *Critique of Hegel's Philosophy of Right*, but is less recognized when dealing with the *Manuscripts*. In order to make this point Althusser went so far as to translate some of Feuerbach's writings into French (on this issue, see Cowling 1995).

This paradox can be seen at work in Chris Arthur's very thorough work, *Dialectics of Labour* (Arthur 1986), which generally argues that what is at work in the *Manuscripts* is a set of ideas derived from Hegel, but Chap. 9 of which points to considerable links between Marx and Feuerbach: 'much of what Marx sees about the objective character of the man and his world is drawn from Feuerbach. It is possible to overlook this and to take as great discoveries of Marx things he copied wholesale from Feuerbach' (Arthur 1986, p. 118). Indeed, it can be argued that Chap. 9 undermines the rest of the book.

A further point about the *Economic and Philosophical Manuscripts* is that they are actually considerably more fragmentary in their original form than one would think from the version available in English. This version has been considerably reconstructed by the editors (see Marx and Engels 1982, 1.02, Rojahn 1983).

I shall now move onto a quick consideration of the appearances of the alienation vocabulary in the later Marx. The first thing to point out is that the major source for this vocabulary is the *Grundrisse*. The *Grundrisse* is a first draft of *Capital*, in which the alienation vocabulary is much less visible. The obvious conclusion would seem to be that Marx recognized that the logic of the approach he takes in *Capital* does not sit very readily with the alienation vocabulary.

The bulk of the uses of alienation terminology in the older Marx refer to the legal use of the concept of alienation in which it simply means that passing of the ownership of a thing from one person to another, normally by selling it. Thus we have Marx paraphrasing Sir James Steuart and talking of 'profit upon alienation' referring to the theory that profit is made by buying cheap and selling dear. It seems perverse to link this to the idea that the capitalist who is selling the goods is becoming alienated from his species being—he is simply supposed to be making money by buying cheap and selling dear. It would be possible to give many further examples of Marx using the alienation vocabulary in his mature economic texts to simply refer to either the legal concept of alienation or a somewhat extended version thereof.

It is worth reproducing here a passage from *Capital* that is cited by Geras in an article from 1973 as proof that the concept of alienation appears in *Capital*:

> On the other hand, the worker always leaves the process in the same state as he entered it—a personal source of wealth, but deprived of any means of making that wealth a reality for himself. Since, before he enters the process, his own labour has already been alienated from him (*selbst entfremdet*), appropriated by the capitalist, and incorporated into capital, it now, in the course of the process, constantly objectifies itself so that it becomes a product alien to him (*fremdem Produkt*). Since the process of production is also the process of consumption of labour-power by the capitalist, the worker's product is not only constantly converted into commodities, but also into capital, i.e. into value that sucks up the worker's value-creating power, means of subsistence that actually purchase human beings, and means of production that employ the people who are doing the producing. Therefore the worker himself constantly produces objective wealth, in the form of capital, an alien (*fremde*) power that dominates and exploits him; and the capitalist just as constantly produces labour-power, in the form of a subjective source of wealth which is abstract, exists merely in the physical body of the worker, and is separated from its own means of objectification and realization; in short, the capitalist produces the worker as a wage-labourer. (Marx and Engels 1975, Vol. 23, pp. 595–596, Marx 1965, pp. 716)

Whilst this certainly contains language and themes that can be tied in with the alienation theory of the younger Marx, the general point being made is that the reproduction of capitalism involves the reproduction of its elements, notably in this case the labourer. The passage does not *require* reference to the youthful theory of alienation.

Another fertile area for claiming that the theory of alienation appears in *Capital* is the theory of the fetishism of commodities. This theory is seen by some authors as a reappearance of the Feuerbachian theory that the gods are man's alienated essence. However, a straightforward reading of this theory is that the way in which the appearances of capitalist society are deceptive when compared with reality is revealed by the labour theory of value. Relations between products and producers of commodities appear to be natural relations between the commodities themselves; capital seems to produce profit; land seems to produce rent; and labour seems to produce wages. In fact, of course, surplus labour produces surplus value, and surplus value is distributed between profit, rent and interest; labour does indeed produce wages, but it produces a great deal more besides. Whilst it is possible to read the alienation theory into this, a straightforward reading might invite comparisons with Copernican astronomy—we know that sunrise is actually earth spin, but we still talk about sunrise and sunset. Likewise, when working for a capitalist employer a worker might accept Marx's theory of value, and therefore that his or her wages do not represent the full extent of the labour that has been expended, but is likely on a day-to-day basis to think in terms of 'fair' remuneration from one employer and exploitative terms of employment at another, meaning that the second employer is paying under the market rate for labour, whereas in fact according to the labour theory of value both employers are engaging in exploitation. Interestingly the discussion of fetishism includes many uses of the term 'bearers', which, although by no means decisive, is strange in a discussion that is supposed to link back to the theory of alienation.

Fetishism as Domination

In an early article Geras looks at fetishism as domination rather than as mystification (Geras 1973, pp. 288–289). He talks of the domination of the 'totality of economic relations' over 'all the agents of capitalist society', and says that this is 'a historical concept of alienation'. I think one could put forward an argument to the effect that the overriding theme in the concept of fetishism is mystification rather than domination, but the point that I would want to stress is that this concept belongs to a different theoretical framework from the youthful concept of alienation. In the young Marx alienation, ultimately alienation from man's species being, produces all the phenomena of bourgeois society. In contrast, Marx in his Marginal Notes on Wagner (the economist, not the composer) says 'Man? If this means the category "man" then in general he has "no" needs' (Marx 1975, p. 189). Marx's 'analytic method … does not start out from *man* but from the economically-given social period' (Marx 1975, p. 201). This really does not sound like the Marx of 1843–1845. He would appear here to be thinking in terms of a planned, socialist economy as the basic solution to the problems of capitalist society, rather than a reappropriation of the human essence.

The Domination of Living Labour by Dead Labour

Somewhat similar to this are passages where Marx talks of the domination of labour by capital—this contrasts with Geras's claims about fetishism, in which, according to him, everyone is dominated by capital. These passages include comments such as that the powers of labour appear as (what they have really become) the powers of capital. Science and the forces of nature seem to be powers of capital; the labourer is subsumed under the powers he has created (Marx 1965, pp. 195, 218, 233, 310, 361, 419, 423, 645, 1966, pp. 85–86, 264, 1969, 390–391, 1972, pp. 245, 259, 271–272, 1973, pp. 307–308, 450–456, 458, 462–463, 469–470, 485–487, 504f., 702, 831–833; Marx and Engels 1975, Vol. 5, 63–64, 78, 86–87.) These passages certainly look similar to the young Marx, but they are not properly integrated into a discussion of alienation in the older Marx, and are best seen as an emotive way of making an economic point. Here is one example:

> Some crippling of body and mind is inseparable even from the division of labour in society as a whole ... however, manufacture ... attacks the individual at the very roots of his life... (Marx 1965, p. 363)

The footnotes to the relevant chapter make it clear that views of this sort were expressed by factory inspectors and early social investigators who would have been unaware of the theory of alienation, but who would certainly have shared Marx's view that the crippling of body and mind is undesirable. There are many more quotations roughly similar to this one. There is nothing to stop these being interpreted as examples of alienation from one's species being, but all that is required in the context is the idea that under capitalism workers are forced to develop the forces of production, and that these appear as a natural property of capitalist relations. However, says Marx, this lays the foundations of a socialist society.

It is interesting to observe that passages in the *Grundrisse* that correspond with similar passages in *Capital* Volume 1 get to look less like the juvenile alienation theory in transition—faced with a choice Marx plainly decided to adopt terms of moral outrage that are more generally shared rather than give an explanation of the alienation theory, although, given the length of *Capital* Volume 1, let alone subsequent volumes, he would have had plenty of room to do so. If the theory of alienation is a really important foundation of *Capital* it seems very odd to suppress it rather than explain it.

The Many-Sided Man

The passages in the older Marx that most resemble the young Marx are those that discuss the many-sided man. Marx says that the capitalist mode of production makes people into one-sided men and women, and that the introduction of machinery exacerbates this (Marx 1965, pp. 360–361, 484, 645, 1973, p. 539). This looks very like the young Marx, however, some of the other things that Marx says on this question in *Capital* are rather different. He points out that to the extent that the needs of workers are met under capitalism they become increasingly many sided as consumers because their needs are met from diverse sources in the world market; and also there is something of a rise in the general standard of subsistence. This is rather a far cry from claims in the *Manuscripts* that of four children of the labourer two must die because of extreme poverty. However, in the most interesting passages Marx says that as capitalism develops it starts to require many-sided men who are adaptable and can change occupation is necessary (Marx 1965, p. 488, 1973, p. 539). I would not regard Marx as particularly prophetic, but the flexibility he is describing is increasingly required by capitalism today, and interestingly women may be particularly well suited to this type of change, at least given current practices concerning child rearing.

More to the point, it is very difficult to imagine the Marx of 1843–1845 seeing the many-sided man as required by capitalism. The older Marx is more dispassionate, and more capable of recognizing limited gains for working people under capitalism.

The logic of Marx's position in much of his writings on the many-sided man is that it does not matter whether or not people like being one sided or many sided, they are simply required to be like this by particular stages of capitalism.

However, there are definitely places where Marx argues that many-sided activity comprises the full realization of man's species powers. Most of these come from *The German Ideology*, and none of them were sent to the printers by Marx himself (Marx 1966, p. 820, 1972, pp. 487–488, 610–613; Marx and Engels 1975, Volume 5, pp. 44, 88). Two of these passages are from the *Grundrisse*, and the second of them may simply be Marx criticizing Adam Smith by talking about a logical possibility.

Conclusion

Geras's rigorous approach to the question of Marx and human nature is widely taken to have established that Marx has a theory of human nature, and that it persists throughout his writings. One argument of this chapter is that Geras's claim is valid, but that what he establishes is the continuity of a rather thin version of human nature that would be agreed by many who are by no means Marxists. However, this valid claim tends to be confused with a different claim, namely that Marx's theory of alienation, as found in his writings of 1843–1845, remains at the core of the theories of the older Marx. Except in an extremely limited way in an early article (Geras 1973), Geras does not make this claim. My argument in the second part of the chapter is that the claim that the alienation theory persists throughout Marx's writings is not valid. It is definitely not established by Geras.

References

Arthur, C. J. (1986). *Dialectics of Labour*. Oxford: Blackwell.

Avineri, S. (1972). *The Social and Political Thought of Karl Marx*. Cambridge: Cambridge University Press.

Cornforth, M. (1973, May). Some Comments on Louis Althusser's Reply to John Lewis. *Marxism Today*, 139–147.

Cornu, A. (1957). *The Origins of Marxian Thought*. Springfield, IL: C.C. Thomas.

Cowling, M. (1989). The Case for Two Marxes, Restated. In C. M. Cowling & L. Wilde (Eds.), *Approaches to Marx* (pp. 14–32). Milton Keynes: Open University Press.

Cowling, M. (1995). Marx's Conceptual Framework from 1843–5: Hegelian Dialectic and Historical Necessity Versus Feuerbachian Humanistic Materialism? *Studies in Marxism, 2*, 41–52.

Cowling, M. (2006). Alienation in the Older Marx. *Contemporary Political Theory, 5*, 319–339.

Dyer-Witheford, N. (2004). 1844/2004/2044: The Return of Species-Being. *Historical Materialism, 12*(Part 4), 3–25.

Garaudy, R. (1967). *Karl Marx, The Evolution of His Thought*. London: Lawrence and Wishart.

Geras, N. (1973). Marx and the Critique of Political Economy. In R. Blackburn (Ed.), *Ideology and Social Science* (pp. 284–305). London: Fontana.

Geras, N. (1983). *Marx and Human Nature: Refutation of a Legend*. London: Verso.

Holloway, J. (1997). A Note on Alienation. *Historical Materialism, 1*(1), 146–149.

Holloway, J. (2002). *Change the World Without Taking Power*. London: Pluto.

Howard, D. (1972). *The Development of the Marxian Dialectic*. Carbondale, IL: Southern Illinois University Press.
Hyppolite, J. (1969). *Studies on Marx and Hegel*. London: Heinemann.
Kamenka, E. (1972). *The Ethical Foundations of Marxism*. London: Routledge.
Kolakowski, L. (1971). Althusser's Marx. In R. Miliband & J. Saville (Eds.), *Socialist Register*. London: Merlin Press.
Korsch, K. (1938). *Karl Marx*. London: Chapman and Hall.
Korsch, K. (1970). *Marxism and Philosophy*. London: New Left Books.
Lewis, J. (1972, January, February). The Althusser Case. *Marxism Today*, 23–28, 43–48.
Lukács, G. (1971). *History and Class Consciousness*. London: Merlin.
Maguire, J. (1972). *Marx's Paris Writings*. Dublin: Macmillan.
Mandel, E. (1971). *The Formation of Marx's Economic Thought* (pp. 154–186). London: New Left Books.
Marx, K. (1965). *Capital* (Vol. 1). Moscow: Progress Publishers.
Marx, K. (1966). *Capital* (Vol. 3). Moscow: Progress Publishers.
Marx, K. (1969a). *Theories of Surplus Value, Part 1*. London: Lawrence and Wishart.
Marx, K. (1969b). *Theories of Surplus Value, Part 2*. London: Lawrence and Wishart.
Marx, K. (1972). *Theories of Surplus Value, Part 3*. London: Lawrence and Wishart.
Marx, K. (1973). *Grundrisse*. Harmondsworth: Penguin.
Marx, K. (1975). *Texts on Method* (T. Carver, Trans. & Ed.). Oxford: Blackwell.
Marx, K., & Engels, F. (1975). *Collected Works*. London: Lawrence and Wishart.
Marx, K., & Engels, F. (1982). *Marx-Engels Gesamtausgabe (MEGA)*. Berlin: Dietz.
McLellan, D. (1971). *Marx's Grundrisse*. London: Macmillan.
McLellan, D. (1973). *Karl Marx, His Life and Thought*. London: Macmillan.
McLellan, D. (1980). *Marx Before Marxism* (2nd ed.). London: Macmillan.
Mészáros, I. (1970). *Marx's Theory of Alienation*. London: Merlin.
Ollman, B. (1971). *Alienation, Marx's Critique of Man in Capitalist Society*. Cambridge: Cambridge University Press.
Plamenatz, J. (1975). *Karl Marx's Philosophy of Man*. Oxford: Clarendon.
Rojahn, J. (1983). Marxismus Marx Geschichtswissenschaft der Fall der so genannte „ökonomisch-philosophischen Manuskripte' Aus dem Jahre 1844". *International Review of Social History, 28*(1), 2–49.
Thomas, P. (1976). Marx and Science. *Political Studies, 24*(1), 1–23.
Tucker, R. (1967). *Philosophy and Myth in Karl Marx*. Cambridge: Cambridge University Press.
Wilde, L. (1998). *Ethical Marxism and its Radical Critics*. Basingstoke: Macmillan.
Wilde, L. (2004). *Erich Fromm and the Quest for Solidarity*. New York: Palgrave.

CHAPTER 5

Geras and Althusser

The purpose of this short chapter is to review two articles that Geras wrote about Althusser. In writing about Marx and human nature as discussed in Chap. 4, Geras plainly had as his target a view of Marx inspired particularly by Althusser. In Chap. 4 it was argued that Geras indeed manages to establish, contra Althusser, that the older Marx has a theory of human nature. However, it was also argued that this theory of human nature is a relatively thin one, and that it would be unwise to assume that it demonstrates a high degree of continuity in Marx's theories throughout his life. On the contrary, the younger Marx places a theory of alienation at the centre of his theories. In contrast from *The German Ideology* onwards the theory of historical materialism takes centre stage. Although a core of needs, abilities and so forth are common to all social formations, other aspects of human nature change with changes in the dominant mode of production and with the location of the subject within it.

For example, a man might migrate from being a poor peasant to becoming an industrial worker. He would find that his way of life in a town would be very different. Instead of supplying most of his needs from smallholding, almost all his items of consumption have to be supplied by the market. He discovers new needs. He learns to read and now needs newspapers. He requires a taste for curry, so he and his wife need curry ingredients, or a local takeaway.

His work involves the sort of detail labour described by Marx, and he finds it boring. However, perhaps his daughter or granddaughter finds

M. Cowling, *Norman Geras's Political Thought from Marxism to Human Rights*, https://doi.org/10.1007/978-3-319-74048-5_5

that the requirements of the capitalist mode of production have changed. She needs to be flexible, because her job involves a variety of requirements, and she actually needs to change career twice. And, who knows, perhaps her daughter finds herself living in a post-revolutionary socialist society with yet different requirements and opportunities. Marx, or we, or Geras, doubtless have attitudes to these various ways of life, and would, for example, find a life of detail labour unappealing. Obviously in one sense this is very important as it gives us an incentive for supporting a movement to socialism, on the assumption that it would bring a wider range of people greater benefits and opportunities. In another sense it does not matter at all. The differing developments of the mode of production bring with them their own requirements for their bearers, and whether or not the bearers find what is required of them to be deeply fulfilling or mind numbingly tedious does not matter—they are still required, and it is up to the individual how to come to terms with them.

With this as a background we come to Geras's account of Althusser. In a brief article from 1982, Geras outlines some major themes from Althusser, notably the idea that the problematic or theoretical framework of the texts of the young Marx is fundamentally different from those of the older Marx; there is an epistemological break (Geras 1986, p. 85). The ideas of a symptomatic reading that discovers a problematic, and of an epistemological break between two problematics, are seen by Althusser as part of a new philosophy founded by Marx (Geras 1986, p. 86). He goes on to outline the Althusserian idea of the movement in thought between Generalities I, II and III, meaning that what happens in thought is analogous to production in industry. Generalities I are the raw material of thought on which Generalities II, the intellectual means of production, work to produce Generalities III, knowledge (Geras 1986, p. 86).

Althusser was also distinctive in insisting that reality itself is irreducibly complex, subject to over-determination, and thus distinct from a Hegelian spiritual totality, which is permeated by a single essence. What this means particularly is that the social formation is not reducible to a single essence. The economy may be causally primary, but the other structures have their own effectivity, and can sometimes be dominant (Geras 1986, p. 87).

As one might expect, Geras is not sympathetic to the idea that Marx rejected all concepts of human nature, which he says to be textually insupportable, for reasons that should be plain from the previous chapter. He also rejects the Althusserian idea that a communist society will have its own ideology, its own 'imaginary representation of the real'. He asserts that both the young Marx and the older Marx saw communist society as a society transparent to its members. He dubs what Althusser is doing here as a form of obscurantism (Geras 1986, p. 88). There is definitely no contest that Geras is right here on textual grounds. However, whilst realizing that this is a very short piece, it might be worth thinking about ways in which the Soviet Union was represented: as a genuine socialist state, as a form of state capitalism, as a degenerated workers state, as a state that suffered from some form of revisionism from Nikita Khrushchev onwards—and this is just some of the ways in which Marxists have depicted the Soviet Union, let alone depictions from anti-Soviet critics. Whilst it is unlikely that many people now would describe the former Soviet Union as a genuine workers' paradise, and we are therefore looking at a society that was not communist in Marx's sense, the multiplicity of descriptions from people who are intellectually quite sophisticated suggests that Althusser may be looking at a genuine problem.

In a final section of the article Geras summarizes some of the changes that Althusser made to his set of theories, and suggests that they are a form of idealism, because it is not apparent how theory is supposed to relate to material reality—there appears to be a correspondence, but how the correspondence is established other than an onward development in theory is not clear.

He concludes that the theories were 'remarkably barren' in Althusser's own hands—for example, he admitted that he had nothing useful to say about Stalinism (Geras 1986, p. 89). Geras manages to pack a great deal into a very short piece, and much of what he says is well judged, although all the issues involved could do with a much more elaborate discussion—the theoretical gyrations of figures such as Cutler, Hindess, Hirst and Hussein illustrate one way of working through a complex set of questions.

Geras never discussed at any length the relationship between Marx or Marxism and Hegel. In the second article on Althusser he briefly approves of Althusser's criticism of Hegelian interpretations of Marx. Although he never branded himself an analytical Marxist, his approach to Marx was definitely analytical, and definitely made no use of Hegelian concepts and themes.

The other article, which Geras places after the one just discussed in *Literature of Revolution*, is entitled 'Althusser's Marxism: An Account and Assessment', and dates from 1971. The article comprises an assessment of Althusser's ideas in *For Marx* (Althusser 2005) *Reading Capital* (Althusser and Balibar 2007) and his subsequent partial change of theory in *Lenin and Philosophy* (Althusser 2001).

Geras starts with an exposition of Althusser's ideas that is careful, judicious and accurate. The central feature of what Althusser claims Marx to have achieved is a double innovation: a theory of history—historical materialism—and a new philosophy—dialectical materialism. Marxist philosophy is much less clearly articulated than is historical materialism, and it is Marxist philosophy that Althusser is aiming to elaborate (Geras 1986, p. 93). Marxist philosophy, for Althusser, is the 'theory of science and the history of science' (Geras 1986, p. 94).

The social formation comprises several different practices, which should not be collapsed into an undifferentiated notion of practice (Geras 1986, p. 95). The essential structure of a practice is a process of transformation similar to that described above in the production of knowledge (Geras 1986, p. 96). Dialectical materialism can alternatively be described as the theory of practice (Geras 1986, p. 98). Althusser distinguishes dialectical materialism from empiricism because he says that empiricism equates knowledge with one part of the real object that it deems to be essential. It thus confuses thought about the real with the real itself (Geras 1986, p. 100).

Geras then gives an account of the process of the production of knowledge, which is broadly similar to that in the previous, shorter, piece, but clarifies some points, notably that the raw material from which the process of the production of knowledge begins, Generalities I, is never reality as such, but an abstraction of one sort or another. Also, the end product, Generalities III, is always in the thought—it is the concrete-in-thought, and provides knowledge of the real-concrete, but itself remains abstract in the sense of still being within thought (Geras 1986, pp. 101–102).

Next, Geras considers the role of the problematic: it is unconscious, but is assigned the same role as that taken by the human subject in other epistemologies (Geras 1986, p. 104). The 'subject' plays the part assigned to it by the mechanism of the process, rather than playing the part that it thinks it is playing. Linked to the notion of the problematic, of course, is the epistemological break that separates Marxism from not just Hegel, Ricardo and other, but also from the ideological theories of his own youth (Geras 1986, p. 106). The sciences themselves provide their own forms of proof, which are internal to the theoretical practice of that science. The problem, according to Althusser, is to understand the mechanism through which a science produces knowledge (Geras 1986, p. 107).

Geras then turns to Althusser's account of history, reiterating the point that the social formation is irredeemably complex, comprising irreducibly distinct practices (Geras 1986, p. 109). What, then, is the interrelationship between the different practices, notably between those belonging to the superstructure and those belonging to the economic base? Some clue is given by the ideas of 'determination in the last instance by the (economic) mode of production' and the 'relative autonomy of the superstructure', but this obviously needs further elaboration. The social formation is a 'structure in dominance' but one element can replace another as the dominant one (Geras 1986, p. 111). Because the various levels of the structure are relatively autonomous they have relatively autonomous histories, and therefore are dislocated with respect to each other (Geras 1986, p. 112).

Althusser is, of course, critical of historicist interpreters of Marx who work with a Hegelian conception of the social totality complete with linear time. Along with this they tend to deprive theoretical practice/science of its autonomy and specificity. He emphasizes that except in his pre-1845 writings, Marx never included scientific knowledge as part of the superstructure. There is, therefore, no direct correlation between the science of Marxism and the ideology of the proletariat, and therefore Marxist theory needs to be imported into the working-class movement, as stressed by Kautsky and Lenin. Indeed, ideology is an essential part of every society, including communist society: it is the way in which people experience their world (Geras 1986, pp. 114–115).

In the final part of his exposition of Althusser, Geras deals with the concept of structural causality. Althusser distinguishes linear causality, the effect of one element on another—presumably this corresponds to one billiard ball striking another, and causing it to move on the one hand; and expressive causality, the determination of the parts by the whole in the manner of a Hegelian spiritual totality. He says that these two forms of causality are characteristic of pre-Marxist philosophy. Marx identified a new form of causality, structural causality, which exists in the totality of its elements, but is not completely present in any one of them. The 'subjects' of history are the relations of production and the political, ideological and social relations (Geras 1986, pp. 116–117).

We then move on to Geras's assessment of Althusser. He says that he thinks that Althusser seriously misreads both Marx and Lenin, but his assessment will not rest on this, because he could be accused of dogmatism. It is plain that Geras is examining Althusser's ideas on their own merits. In particular, he considers that Althusser's account of science is idealist, and that his account of the relationship between theory and politics is incorrect and harmful (Geras 1986, p. 118).

Nonetheless, Geras considers that Althusser has some positive features. In particular, the questions he asks are eminently appropriate: 'the problem of the specificity of the different practices/instances and of their complex inter-relationship' (Geras 1986, p. 120). Moreover, his criticism of Hegelian and humanist Marxism is well judged. Humanism and alienation, the themes emphasized by many contemporary interpreters, are not '*by themselves*' adequate to think through the question immediately above, which is a crucial one for determining political practice. The concept of the problematic is also helpful as a way of criticizing teleological approaches to Marx, which discover early versions of his theories in *Capital* in his schoolboy essays, and assume that alienation must be exactly the same concept in the early Marx as in *Capital* (Geras 1986, p. 121).

Geras moves on to consider 'the contradictions of Althusser's science' (Geras 1986, p. 121). Althusser is right to assert that the content of science is universal; it is not dependent for its validity on particular social groups or a particular historical epoch. However, things go wrong from this point. He cannot be clear about what is the 'mechanism' of the knowledge effect, which is a crucial point for identifying science. More seriously, the autonomy of science appears to become absolute for Althusser, yet it talks about its relative autonomy, and plainly recognizes that it is related to other social practices, but the nature of this relationship remains a mystery (Geras 1986, p. 123).

For Geras there are a series of problems in Althusser's conception of science that point towards it being idealist. To start with, science is outside the superstructure, and therefore outside the social formation. And the history of science is absolutely autonomous, outside the history of social formations. Althusser says ideology is dominated by interests and social functions beyond the necessity of knowledge. This, in turn, implies the absolute autonomy of science. In addition, Althusser fails to offer any account of what distinguishes Marxism from other sciences. We thus have a picture of an autonomous science introduced to the working class from outside: 'When knowledge celebrates its autonomy, the philosophers celebrate their dominance' (Geras 1986, pp. 124–127).

Geras emphasizes that Marxist theory may have been produced by bourgeois intellectuals, but the bourgeois intellectuals were those who had 'linked their fate with that of the working class', and become involved in the struggle for socialism. Geras suggests a series of things that Marxists have learned from the working class—Marx learned the necessity of smashing the bourgeois state from the experience of the Paris Commune; Lenin learned the significance of Soviets and of dual power; Rosa Luxemburg learned the importance of the mass strike; and Trotsky learned the importance of permanent revolution from the experience of 1905. Marxist theoretical work has political conditions, and is unlike other sciences because it is so bitterly contested (Geras 1986, pp. 127–129).

Geras considers that Althusser is perilously close to a position in which Marxist science could be considered as neutral and value free. It is plain, says Geras, that *Capital* is value laden. Moreover, Althusser emphasizes that the realm of ideology is one of mystification, illusion and so forth. The masses appear to be lumbered with ideology, although hopefully an ideology produced by the intellectuals. This, says Geras, violates 'the first principle of revolutionary politics—to tell it as it is' (Geras 1986, p. 130).

Finally, Geras indicates that after 1965 Althusser revised his theories, and seemed to be particularly troubled by the areas that Geras found unsatisfactory. However, the new theories that he produced seemed also to be fundamentally incoherent (Geras 1986, p. 131).

It would be possible to say a very great deal more about Geras's criticisms of Althusser—one could, as was indicated above, follow through the theoretical trajectory of Cutler, Hindess, Hirst and Hussein (for example, Hindess and Hirst 1975, 1977, Cutler et al. 1977, 1978. For my own view of their work at the time, see Cowling 1980). This would be exceedingly lengthy. A few comments will have to suffice. Geras's claim that Althusser's theory of science is idealist makes a lot of sense—as Geras says, the background in which science is produced is left unclear, as is the relationship between what Althusser called the concrete-in-thought, meaning the elaborated final product of science, and the concrete-real, the real material world. This issue of the relationship between theory and the real will be returned to in the discussion of two variants of postmodernism criticized by Geras, to be found in Chaps. 8 and 9.

A limited defence of Althusser could be mounted on a couple of points. The things that the various Marxists are alleged to have learned from the working class are all to do, in one way or another, with political practice. It would be worth asking whether there is anything in particular that made them learn these particular lessons rather than, for example, the entrenched character of political democracy in much of Western Europe, and the ways in which parliamentary democracy might be respected and extended for socialist purposes. Second, the bulk of Marx's theoretical work was in the area of political economy. Whilst one can certainly gain a degree of perspective on the economy on the picket line, the main work in this area involved critical theorizing about the work of the political economists using data from real economies. This would appear to be a matter of intellectuals sitting in libraries rather than something learned in interaction with workers, though such interactions might well provide the motive for the work in economic theory, and perhaps it is primarily this work that is introduced to the working class from outside. Whilst by no means vindicating Althusser, this perhaps is some of the explanation—or certainly would be a good explanation—of his insistence on the merits of the idea that theory is introduced to the working-class movement by bourgeois intellectuals.

References

Althusser, L. (2001). *Lenin and Philosophy.* New York: Monthly Review Press.

Althusser, L. (2005). *For Marx.* London: Verso.

Althusser, L., & Balibar, E. (2007). *Reading Capital.* London: Verso.

Cowling, M. (1980). Resolving the Contradictions of Althusser's Philosophy: Popperian Falsificationism as an Alternative to Hindess and Hirst's Anti-Philosophy. *Scottish Journal of Sociology, 4*(2), 169–192.

Cutler, T., Hindess, B., Hirst, P. Q., & Hussein, A. (1977 and 1978 respectively). *Marx's Capital and Capitalism Today* (Vol. 1 and 2). London: Routledge.

Geras, N. (1986). *Literature of Revolution: Essays on Marxism.* London: Verso.

Hindess, B., & Hirst, P. Q. (1975). *Pre-Capitalist Modes of Production.* London: Routledge.

Hindess, B., & Hirst, P. Q. (1977). *Mode of Production and Social Formation: An Auto-Critique of Pre-Capitalist Modes of Production.* London: Routledge.

CHAPTER 6

Marx and Justice

Geras's discussion of Marx and justice emerges particularly in two articles: 'The Controversy about Marx and Justice' (Geras 1986, pp. 3–58) and 'Bringing Marx to Justice' (Geras 1992).

I will summarize the content of these two papers, and then offer some critical reflections. It needs to be said immediately that the papers offer an excellent introduction both to the relevant parts of Marx's work, and to the writings of a wide range of authors on this issue up to the date of the papers. Whilst there has obviously been much subsequent writing on this issue, the general lines of the debate are very much those sketched out in Geras's articles. As Paul Raekstad says: 'The contribution these have made to Marxist thought is beyond dispute: jointly, they are both the definitive summary of the arguments on either side of the debate and the best summary presentation of the arguments for the position Geras defends' (Raekstad 2014, p. 1).

Why Marx Did Not Have a Theory of Justice

Geras starts by considering a set of reasons for thinking that Marx did not have a theory of justice. The first argument is that the wages paid to the labourer in exchange for his or her labour power are a fair exchange. This is 'a piece of good luck for the buyer, but by no means an injury towards the seller' (Geras 1986, pp. 6–7; Marx 1965, p. 301). A second argument

M. Cowling, *Norman Geras's Political Thought from Marxism to Human Rights*, https://doi.org/10.1007/978-3-319-74048-5_6

is that the present day distribution is fair, indeed it is the only 'fair' pattern of distribution on the basis of the current mode of production (Geras 1986, p. 7). A third argument reinforces this. Geras quotes from Critique of the Gotha Programme 'right can never be higher than the economic structure of society and its cultural development conditioned thereby' (Marx in Marx and Engels 1975, Vol. 24, p. 87). Standards of justice are internal to specific historical modes of production (Geras 1986, p. 8). A further argument is that this is a reformist way of looking at things because it focuses on distribution within the capitalist system rather than its abolition. Geras makes this point by quoting from *Wages, Price and Profit*: 'Instead of the *conservative* motto "A *fair day's wage for a fair day's work*!" They ought to inscribe on their banner the revolutionary watchword "*Abolition of the wages system!*"' (Geras 1986, p. 10; Marx in Marx and Engels 1975, Vol. 20, p. 149). A sixth argument points out that a focus on distributive justice directs attention away from 'concrete revolutionary goals'. The focus instead should be on tendencies, social forces and movements that are capable of producing a revolution (Geras 1986, pp. 10–11). A seventh argument is that principles of justice are juridical principles, and therefore part of the state apparatus, which is destined to wither away in a communist society (Geras 1986, p. 11). An eighth argument considers Marx's account of communism, a society of material plenty where principles of justice are not needed—this is the implication of the famous slogan 'From each according to his abilities, to each according to his needs!'. If there is no scarcity, principles of distribution are not necessary (Geras 1986, p. 13). What about the point that Marx obviously condemned capitalist society? He condemned it because he valued 'freedom, self-realisation, well-being and community', in other words because of values other than that of distributive justice (Geras 1986, p. 14).

Why Marx Had a Theory of Justice

Geras then presents a series of arguments that point in the opposite direction. The first of these is that although Marx does start by saying that the exchange of wages for labour power is fair according to capitalist principles of distribution, he then goes on to show that the wages relationship is not an exchange of equivalents at all because work involves the extraction of surplus value (Geras 1986, pp. 14–16). A second argument is that exploitation, the extraction of surplus value, is theft, robbery, embezzlement. This point is reinforced by Marx's discussion of primitive accumulation.

Capitalism, he says, comes into being through 'conquest, enslavement, robbery, murder' (Geras 1986, pp. 16–18; Marx 1965, p. 874). A second argument is that Marx plainly thinks that 'from each according to his abilities, to each according to his work' is a higher principle than that of capitalist exploitation, but a lower principle than 'from each according to his abilities, to each according to his needs'. In turn this must imply some kind of trans-historical principle of justice (Geras 1986, pp. 18–19). A fourth argument develops the above by asserting that Marx is offering a realist principle of justice, meaning that it is anchored in particular societies with their economic structures, but that there is nothing to stop such a principle making judgements about societies other than its own (Geras 1986, p. 19). A fifth argument takes up the claim made at the end of the set of arguments which claimed that Marx did not have a theory of justice, and points out that Marx was certainly concerned about such things as freedom, fulfilling activity and general welfare, that this is a form of discussion of distribution, and (sixth) the moral censure of capitalism involved in making this judgement can contribute to advancing revolutionary change (Geras 1986, pp. 20–21). Seventh, principles of justice are not bound exclusively to the capitalist legal system, but can be discussed more widely (Geras 1986, p. 21). A further argument is that the principle 'to each according to his needs' involves a commitment to an equality of self-realization, and that this, in itself, is a principle of justice (Geras 1986, pp. 22–23). A final argument is that if the previous point is accepted then it seems inappropriate to deny the existence of principles of justice in Marx which extend beyond the capitalist system (Geras 1986, p. 24).

Geras's Conclusion: Marx Had a Theory of Justice, But Did Not Think That He Had One

Geras starts his own assessment by giving two reasons why no conclusive resolution of the issue under consideration can be achieved. First, Marx was not a moral philosopher, and therefore there is no reason to expect him to be entirely consistent in this area. The second is that there is what Geras describes as 'dialectical play' in this area, notably the question of the wage relationship. The exchange of wages for labour power is an exchange of equivalents. However, labour power has the peculiar property that when it is utilized by a capitalist it produces more value than the value of labour power. This extraction of surplus value tends to attract terms such as 'robbery' (Geras 1986, pp. 24–25). There is a dialectical inversion in which the exchange with equivalents becomes theft (Geras 1986, p. 27).

Geras then moves on to consider some explanations given by interpreters who consider that Marx did not have a theory of justice for terms such as 'robbery'. There are several of these. In some cases Marx is considering the theft of health or time rather than surplus value. Marx's discussion of capitalist accumulation attracts many comments on the lines of 'robbery', but perhaps Marx intended to refer to the standards prevailing at the time rather than to make his own accusation of justice. A similar strategy could be used in discussing the extraction of surplus value. In particular, the regular extraction of surplus value corresponds to the given mode of production, which is just on Marx's account. The term 'theft' refers to coercion, not to injustice. Or perhaps it is simply rhetoric. Marx's views on ideology prevent him from having a criterion of justice. Geras says that this last explanation is what underlies the others, and that they are basically feeble (Geras 1986, pp. 29–30). He then responds briefly to some of these arguments. The first argument, the one about health, is one of the strong ones in the sense that sometimes when Marx is talking about 'robbery' he does indeed refer to the theft of health. However, his plain meaning in the majority of the relevant quotations is that the extraction of surplus value is robbery (Geras 1986, p. 30). The plain meaning of Marx's denunciation of primitive accumulation is that he is condemning its horrors himself, on his own behalf. Again, the most obvious interpretation of places where Marx talks of the extraction of surplus value is, likewise, that he is condemning it on his own behalf (Geras 1986, p. 31). Geras concludes what there are looking at here are 'ad hoc and speculative attempts to explain away material that versus the interpretation of Marx these writers favour' (Geras 1986, p. 32). The reason that these writers engage in this sort of ad hoc explanation is that they are attempting to make Marx's work consistent when it simply is not.

He concludes that Marx had a theory of justice, but, paradoxically, that he did not believe that he had a theory of justice: 'Marx did think capitalism was unjust but he did not think he thought so' (Geras 1986, p. 36). Geras then moves on to try to reconstruct the conception of justice, which he considers to be implicit in Marx's work, a broader conception of justice than the one that Marx clearly formulates (Geras 1986, p. 37). There is certainly, he says, a judgement in Marx that the distribution of burdens, free time, and opportunities for free development is 'morally illegitimate'. Marx is therefore committed to some more acceptable pattern of distribution (Geras 1986, p. 40), and it is the role of capitalism to develop the forces of production to make this better pattern of distribution possible (Geras 1986, p. 41).

What about the argument that actions are only historically effective if they are in pursuit of class interests? This is not compatible with the idea that the pursuit of justice is a major theme in Marx (Geras 1986, p. 42). However, there is nothing in this argument that prevents the view that when the proletariat struggles for its own interests it is struggling for a just and universal aim 'the free development of all' (Geras 1986, p. 43). A fundamental feature of Marx's theory of justice, says Geras, is that there is no moral right to private ownership (Geras 1986, p. 45). Putting this together with his comments about usurpation and robbery the obvious conclusion is that Marx condemns the current distribution of the means of production as unjust (Geras 1986, p. 46). Seen in this light the principle 'from each according to their ability, to each according to their needs!', is an integral feature of Marx's notion of a just society (Geras 1986, p. 47). He points out that there is a passage in *The German Ideology* that can legitimately be regarded as an early formulation of this idea, which in any case is not, as such, original to Marx and Engels (Geras 1986, p. 48).

Geras then moves on to consider the argument that principles of justice will be redundant under communism because it is a society of such abundance that it will have no need for principles of justice. Marx does not make it clear what he means by abundance. It is pretty clear that Marx does not simply mean satisfying a very minimum standard of need: self-realization plainly requires something more than this. On the other hand, the idea that everyone could satisfy limitless needs is pretty obviously an absurdity: as Geras puts it: if I need Australia 'undisturbed by the presence of other people' this would obviously not be all right. The conclusion must be, therefore, that Marx should have been thinking in terms of a 'large and generous' standard of reasonable needs, but that the idea of abundance without limits is a fantasy (Geras 1986, pp. 52–53). In order to determine what counts as reasonable, and to deal with potentially conflicting needs Geras assumes that there will be 'authoritative social norms, including distributing funds, which people more or less voluntarily accept' (Geras 1986, p. 54). In turn this implies that although the coercive state will wither away there will be 'public institutions in which the community collectively deliberates and decides on its common affairs' (Geras 1986, p. 54). Geras plainly considers that there is some kind of harmony in Marx between the real onward movement of history and the realization of freedom and a just distribution of opportunities for self-realization. He concludes that it is time to produce 'a properly elaborated Marxist conception of justice' (Geras 1986, p. 56). This, in turn, points towards an engagement with political philosophy, which can be seen in Geras's later work.

In the second article Geras brings his work on Marx and justice up to date by considering work published between 1986 and 1992. Obviously, much more has been written on this theme since.

Critical Discussion of Geras and Justice

Geras undoubtedly provides a brilliant overview of the main arguments in both main directions of the debate about Marx and justice, and a powerful set of arguments for his conclusion that Marx has an unacknowledged theory of justice. Nonetheless, inevitably, there is room for debate. I shall start by summarizing some critical comments from McLellan, and then go on to provide some critical comments of my own.

McLellan comments that when Geras says that distributive justice is part of the communist enterprise, and that Marxists who deny this now need to learn about this 'in liberalism's more advanced school' (Geras 1992, p. 67) and presumably has in mind authors such as Rawls, he is sounding 'more like Bernstein than Luxemburg' (McLellan 2012, p. 38). Discussion of justice was obviously pushing Geras in the direction of liberalism.

McLellan rightly pursues this theme of a turn to liberalism, referring to Geras's discussion of the dilemmas of revolutionary violence (Geras 1990, p. 50), where Geras says that even if revolution involves violence and war and there are 'circumstances to make some moral crimes unavoidable, it is still necessary to have rules and constraints which define them as crimes and which serve as a barrier against unavoidable ones' (McLellan 2012, p. 39). This is discussed further in Chap. 7.

McLellan takes this further, pointing out that Geras also moves further away from straightforwardly Marxist socialism when he says that the homeless or people who are generally in need 'should be regarded as part of the core [of socialism] in their own right' (Geras 1992, p. 69). Geras is perhaps less explicit about what is going on here than he might be. Marxists tend not to like explicitly affiliating themselves with revisionists such as Eduard Bernstein. What Geras definitely did not do was take a rather waffly pathway from classical Marxism via Gramsci and postmodernism in the manner of authors such as Ernesto Laclau and Chantal Mouffe (see Chap. 8).

McLellan points out some further features of Geras's turn towards liberalism. In the late article on Rosa Luxemburg he comments that she has a deterministic approach in her discussion of barbarism in which the only thinkable positive outcome is socialism, and that this is a threat to democracy, as citizens do not get to freely choose the outcome (Geras 1994, p. 104; McLellan 2012, p. 40). McLellan says that it is not surprising that Geras now describes Marxism as 'a programme of research' and 'a tradition of enquiry' (McLellan 2012, p. 40). McLellan is also pointing out that the implicit theory of justice that Geras finds in Marx is—not surprisingly—fairly undeveloped, hence Geras's turn to liberalism to provide a more specific theory.

I have some reservations about Geras's conclusion that Marx had a theory of justice, based on my critical discussion in Chap. 3. There, in discussing Marx and human nature, I accept that Geras demonstrates that the older Marx had a theory of human nature, but argued that it is very thin. Seen from this perspective, there are reasons for thinking that the older Marx considers himself to be dealing with a scientific approach to society to which moral judgements would be extraneous. Marx's economic thought, particularly, suggests that the concept of exploitation is rather different from the day-to-day idea we might have about exploitation. For example, a worker who is part of a small team that sets in motion an enormous chemical plant is likely to be well paid, but will also very likely generate his or her wages in the first few minutes of the week, and is therefore very exploited. In contrast, a worker in a Third-World sweatshop who generates her wages over eight hours every day and surplus value over the last four, taking home a scandalously low wage is less exploited. The situation I am about to describe would obviously not persist indefinitely, but firms frequently experience periods where they are temporarily making a loss. If they are continuing to pay their workers in this situation, it may well be that, rather than surplus value being extracted, the workers are actually being paid more than their labour power is producing. In terms of exploitation it is they who are exploiting the capitalist. The experience of work, and the relationship of alienation, for those who assume that this concept continues into the older Marx, does not seem to correspond at all well with the relationship of exploitation. The workers in the loss-making firm, for example, might well still experience their work as drudgery.

The argument of the previous passage is reinforced if we consider a popular writer from the early-nineteenth century who summarized the work of the classical political economists in a simplified form. Mrs Marcet, in her book on political economy, commented: 'I have always thought it one of the most beneficent ordinances of Providence that the employment of the poor should be a necessary step to the increase in wealth of the rich' (Marcet 1821, p. 98). Ricardo makes it clear that profit originates in labour beyond that needed to pay wages.

That said, the direction in which Geras was led by his conclusions about this question of justice was entirely appropriate for socialists today, given that the 'scientific' aspects of the later Marx actually do not work in some crucial respects. Most notably, the declining rate of profit, which is supposed to result in a capitalist crisis seems to be based on a confusion between the mass of machinery that is used and its cost—one of the features of the last 30 years has been the very rapid cheapening of computing facilities. To take two very minor illustrations, I recently purchased in a supermarket for about £5 a calculator that is considerably more powerful than the one installed by NASA in the spacecraft that went to the moon.

I started word processing on my university's mainframe computer in the mid-1980s. It was enormous and boasted somewhere between 2.8 and 4 MB of RAM. My current desktop computer has 16 GB of RAM, and not surprisingly easily performs tasks that were not actually possible in the 1980s. Again, it was quite cheap, certainly compared with the cost of a mainframe computer in the 1980s. Because computers are used very widely in the economy generally the effect is to reduce the overall cost of all sorts of items in the production of which computers are involved, meaning that the cost of capital goods involved in production has tended to decrease relative to the cost of labour, and the rate of profit will accordingly have tended to rise over the past 35 years. Moore's law conflicts with the old Moor [Marx's nickname]. The 'mass' of machinery that Marx talks about when explaining why there is a falling rate of profit is not relevant as a matter of economics, the relevant question being the value of machinery.

Perhaps linked to this, and perhaps also as a consequence of the fall of the Soviet Union and the Chinese turn to capitalism, the idea of a militant working class moving inevitably towards a socialist future has become very much less plausible, and some form of moral advocacy of socialism has become highly appropriate, so that Geras's subsequent development of interest in moral philosophy was well chosen.

References

Geras, N. (1986). *Literature of Revolution: Essays on Marxism*. London: Verso.

Geras, N. (1990). *Discourses of Extremity: Radical Ethics and Post-Marxist Extravagances*. London: Verso.

Geras, N. (1992). Bringing Marx to Justice: An Addendum and Rejoinder. *New Left Review, 195*, 37–69.

Geras, N. (1994). Democracy and the Ends of Marxism. *New Left Review, 203*, 92–106.

Marcet, J. H. (1821). *Conversations on the Principles of Political Economy* (4th ed.). London: Longman, Hurst, Rees Orme and Brown.

Marx, K. (1965). *Capital* (Vol. 1). Moscow: Progress Publishers.

Marx, K., & Engels, F. (1975). *Collected Works*. London: Lawrence and Wishart.

McLellan, D. (2012). The Marxism of Norman Geras. In E. Garrard & S. de Wijze (Eds.), *Thinking Towards Humanity* (pp. 27–42). Manchester: Manchester University Press.

Raekstad, P. (2014). *Marx and Justice: A Re-Examination of the Arguments*. Political Studies Association Annual Conference, 2014, Marxism Panel.

CHAPTER 7

Marxism, Socialism and Morality

Accept for the sake of argument that Marx had a theory of justice. It is perfectly clear from the previous chapter that it was not at all well elaborated. Indeed, it takes extensive argument from Geras to reach his conclusion that Marx had a theory of justice, and much of the very extensive literature on this subject that Geras so ably summarizes and criticizes is generated because of Marx's numerous contradictory statements in this area. To the extent it is there, Marx's theory of justice condemns capitalist robbery, notably of surplus labour. A minimal theory of distribution is perhaps implicit in the thin account of human nature that Geras found in Marx and elaborated in Chap. 4. If humans have needs of food and shelter, for example, then they should have access to these if possible, even at the expense of property relations. The same applies to the rest of the short list of needs. Some kind of theory of distribution is also implied in the communist slogan found in the Critique of the Gotha Programme: 'from each according to his abilities, to each according to his needs', although exactly what this means is not spelled out.

Geras concluded that Marxism required a theory of justice, and further that aspects of this needed to be drawn from non-Marxist writers, notably from liberals. This is a theme of several essays.

M. Cowling, *Norman Geras's Political Thought from Marxism to Human Rights*, https://doi.org/10.1007/978-3-319-74048-5_7

Marxism and Moral Advocacy

The first issue tackled in this essay is that of human needs. The satisfaction of human needs, says Geras, uncontroversially, has always been a central Marxist principle, but precisely what it means is difficult to specify beyond bare needs for survival. Marx saw communism as a society of abundance, but the idea that this abundance would be so great that absolutely any needs could be met makes 'no sense' (Geras 1990, p. 5). Aside from ecological problems, there will always be some human goals too extravagant to meet from existing resources. Beyond this, the idea of 'to each according to their needs' is an egalitarian principle, but equality of what? Geras argues that it must mean equality of welfare rather than exact equality of resources, but would there not be limits to acceptable inequalities of resources that would arise? Presumably people would get rewards for doing 'tedious or unpleasant, but necessary' work (Geras 1990, p. 6). This, he says, points towards a *social definition*. This point becomes even more apparent if one considers activities that involve using other people as part of the resources—for example, making an epic film. It is pretty obvious that such a project would have to be agreed in some way between large numbers of people, and not everybody's epic film would get made. Politics in the sense of debate in the public sphere would have to continue under communism (Geras 1990, p. 7).

Geras then comes up with one of the comments that make his work so appealing. He says that we know enough about human needs to know what is required for a 'decent human existence' for everybody: adequate nourishment, protection against the elements, medical care, education, free time, against a background of civil and political liberty. 'Suppose everybody had "only" this. Now wouldn't that be something!'—it makes such a contrast with capitalist societies at present as to be revolutionary (Geras 1990, p. 8; Cohen and Garrard 2017, p. 55). At this point he should, perhaps, have said something about China since 1981, where some 500 million people have been lifted out of extreme poverty. This is not as good as the 'decent human existence' described above, and China's human rights record over those years leaves much to be desired, but it is still quite something. What would Geras think about this pattern? How would he rate this compared to India? These are very big topics, but would surely be the type of practical question someone from a Marxist background ought to be asking.

Moving on to another issue, writing in the piece from the Cohen and Garrard collection, he also says that we shouldn't lose sight of moments of maximum utopia, which we find in society already. For many people an example might be supreme moments of sporting excellence, but there is also 'deep or intense love, outstanding acts of friendship, compassion, courage' (Cohen and Garrard 2017, p. 52).

The obvious question is how to get there, and this leads him to praise Marx's disdain for empty moralizing by looking at claims made by Robert Nozick in *Anarchy, State and Utopia*, (1980) a book that places a great deal of emphasis on the legitimacy of unequal property holdings provided that they are justly acquired. However, when it comes to rectifying historical injustices that have contributed to contemporary inequalities, for example slavery, he has extremely little to say. He is not overly interested in a rounded appraisal of the world as it stands (Geras 1990, pp. 9–12).

Geras then moves on to consider a more respectable example of empty moralizing. This is the claim by Peter Singer that, given the extent of famine, disease and so on outside the advanced countries, people there ought to donate relief resources to a point where they and their dependents are beginning to experience serious suffering themselves. Brian Barry extends this into a claim that the amount of GNP given by affluent countries such as the USA to relieve distress should be massively increased. Geras regards these claims to conscience as well-intentioned but so grossly unrealistic that they are unlikely to have any purchase in the real world. What is needed is plainly a radical social transformation toward socialism, based primarily on the material interest of the working class—meaning all the exploited (Geras 1990, pp. 12–17). At this point he is accepting a broadly Marxist approach, although one modified in a social democratic direction. However, in the final part of this chapter it will be seen that, although the egalitarian thrust of the argument is retained, his approach could no longer be seen as Marxist.

The Ethics of Revolution

By 'revolution' Geras has in mind 'the overthrow or very radical transformation, within a relatively brief period, of the basic economic and social relations of a society; or of its governing political institutions; or both' (Geras 1990, p. 22). The ethical question he is concerned about is the justification of violence against persons in order to bring about revolution.

He asserts that there is a right of revolution against grave social injustice, including capitalist forms of it. The basic idea of a right to revolution against tyranny goes back to John Locke. The example that Geras chooses, in order to have an example most readers will recognize is that of revolution in South Africa against apartheid—it will be recalled that apartheid came to an end not long after Geras's book was published (Geras 1990, pp. 22–25).

What criteria might be used to identify justifiable forms of violence? First of all, they must stand a chance of success. Violence should be minimized, subject to first criterion. Significantly, he contrasts this with quotations from Trotsky and Lenin to the effect that there is no restriction on revolutionary violence by the proletariat (Geras 1990, pp. 25–27). After noting that he is not alone in wanting to place restrictions on the scope of revolutionary violence, mentioning statements by Herbert Marcuse (1966), Anthony Arblaster (1975) and Kate Soper, Geras considers some activities that occurred in the upsurge of black resistance in South Africa in 1985. These included the bombing of police stations and a shopping centre, the murder of black policemen and town councillors, the murder of informers and of people who violated an economic boycott. It also included particularly horrific forms of murder, notably necklacing (the placing of a burning tyre round the neck of a victim). What of this could be regarded as legitimate? The socialist literature is too unspecific to be helpful. Instead, Geras proposes turning to just war theory (Geras 1990, pp. 28–37).

Geras is not, of course, claiming that combatants always stick to the rules of war, simply that there is a much more elaborate literature in this area. One issue where just war theory is helpful is the question of targets. Crudely, enemy combatants are legitimate targets whereas enemy civilians are not. The ANC publicly stated, similarly, that its targets were police and military, not civilian. Thus the bombing of shopping centres and restaurants, the taking and killing of innocent hostages, making people targets because they are members of a particular class or ethnic group is morally wrong, a crime (Geras, pp. 40–41). This, he points out, is a specific criticism of Trotsky, who, in *Their Morals and Ours*, argued in favour of taking hostages based on their social class. Geras points out that this massively expands the numbers of people who are legitimate targets, and includes many who are not directly threatening. Obviously this criticism of Trotsky would also apply to liberal statesman such as Winston Churchill and Harry Truman (Geras 1990, pp. 41–42). Geras does not spell this out, but presumably has in mind the saturation bombing of German cities by Winston Churchill, notably that of Dresden, and the use of the atomic bomb by Harry Truman.

The second kind of rules in which Geras is interested concern legitimate ways of stopping enemy combatants. Weapons and methods should not aim to inflict torture or maim (Geras 1990, p. 43). This clearly rules out necklacing and a variety of other horrible ways of inflicting death—there is a need for restraint even if suffering under an oppressive regime is brutalizing. Individuals have rights against being killed or violated that may not be set aside unless the individuals are making war in defence of injustice (Geras 1990, p. 45).

Both of these kinds of rules depend upon an assertion of rights, which is characteristic of liberalism. Geras is not spelling the matter out, but he is plainly introducing at least some fundamental liberal tenets into a Marxist framework. Given that the obvious alternative would be to stick to the framework, spelled out by Lenin and Trotsky, where anything goes in class warfare, Geras obviously feels constrained to introduce liberal features into his original Marxist approach: he has changed into what he describes himself in his later years—a liberal Marxist. In turn, this would be thought to imply a repudiation of at least some aspects of his youthful Trotskyism, but, as will be seen in Chap. 11 and also in the conclusion, Chap. 13, this is less clear-cut than might be imagined.

Geras then moves on to the issue of popular consent. He argues that in established parliamentary democracies, which enshrine basic civil and political rights, there is a degree of popular political consent such that the sort of grave injustice that is the basis of a right of revolution is lacking. There is certainly a case for substantial changes in the economy with a view to getting rid of the massive inequalities characteristic of capitalism, but not for the violent extra-parliamentary revolution traditionally advocated by Marxists (Geras 1990, p. 51). However, Geras finds the idea of a purely parliamentary advance to socialism unthinkable. Active commitment and participation of very large numbers of people outside parliament would be required, and the committees, campaign bodies and so on that they had formed would need to continue in existence after the transition (Geras 1990, p. 53).

The Euston Manifesto

The Euston Manifesto is readily available online, but the references here are to the version in the Cohen and Garrard collection (2017, pp. 114 et seq.). Geras was the main author of this, which was intended as a focus of socialist and progressive thinkers online—it was obviously inspired by the success of normblog in reaching a wider audience using the relatively new medium of the Internet. For our purposes it is a good summary of the main ideas that Geras subscribed to in the last decade or so of his life.

It starts by emphasizing a commitment to the central values of liberal, pluralist democracy. It is unwilling to make excuses for regimes and movements that are reactionary and hostile to democracy. It places a central value on human rights, and condemns violations of them whoever is responsible. It espouses equality. It is hostile to simple reflex anti-Americanism. It favours a two-state solution to the Israeli–Palestinian conflict, thus respecting the right of both peoples to self-determination. It is against racism, including anti-Semitism in the guise of anti-Zionism. It is hostile to terrorism, even in a just cause, including Islamic terrorism. The Manifesto favours humanitarian intervention once a state goes beyond a threshold of inhumanity.

These values plainly set Geras and the other authors of the Manifesto at loggerheads with much liberal and socialist opinion, not just the Socialist Workers Party, but also the values expressed by many Guardian readers.

In an 'Elaboration', the Manifesto is forthright in regarding the overthrow of the Baathist regime in Iraq as a liberation of the Iraqi people. It will be recalled that in 2006 Iraq was in a state of near civil war, but the Manifesto simply condemns the various forms of opposition to the US forces in Iraq, and commends efforts to rebuild Iraq's infrastructure. This view will be extensively criticized in Chap. 11.

Justice and the Labour Theory of Value

Geras wrote virtually nothing on Marx's theory of political economy, but then in 2013 co-authored a lengthy online article critical of the labour theory of value (Harvey and Geras 2013). Given Geras's background, it seems a reasonable surmise that the economic theory aspects of the article largely come from Geras's co-author, Mark Harvey, and that the implications of this for a theory of justice are Geras's contribution.

The article is devoted to trying to help solve the paradox that there are urgent problems of the material basis of life, including such issues as climate change, land use, the availability of food, water resources and the price of oil, but yet Marxist movements are at their weakest ever (Harvey and Geras 2013, p. 1). Although, they say, Marx's mature economic writings contain many valuable hypotheses, the theory at their core, the labour theory of value, is simply indefensible. A major problem has been apparent for a very long time: the transformation problem, the transformation of values into prices. It is simply unsatisfactory to carry on blithely on the basis that there is no problem. There is, in fact, a recent claim that the transformation problem is soluble, although this is a formal claim, meaning that, if it is right, Marx is internally consistent, not that his theories that are linked to the successful solution of the transformation problem, such as the theory of the falling rate of profit, are valid when applied to the real world (Kliman 2007). However, this is a controversial area with an enormous scholarly literature, so it may simply be best to assume that Harvey and Geras are right. Moving on then from this assumption that it has long been established that the transformation problem is not soluble, Harvey and Geras point out that, nonetheless Terry Eagleton, Fredric Jameson and David Harvey, a diverse trio of authors, behave in this way in recent books (Harvey and Geras 2013, pp. 2–4).

Harvey and Geras then introduce the central line of their critique of the labour theory of value. It will be recalled that the labour theory of value asserts that the value of commodities is determined by the quantity of labour that they contain. Other inputs such as raw materials, tools, machines make no contribution to the value of commodities. Prices are ultimately determined by values. Harvey and Geras identify a crucial problem with this analysis. Marx accepts that the value of labour power includes an historical and cultural content. The only way in which this can be satisfactorily dealt with is by looking at the price of labour power. However, this then introduces an irremediably circular problem at the core of Marx's theory (Harvey and Geras 2013, p. 6). Moreover, they note that Marx acknowledges that, however much labour and object may contain, if there is no effective demand for it, then it has no value. Why, they say, should effective demand enter Marx's theory in this way, but otherwise be totally excluded (Harvey and Geras 2013, p. 7)?

As part of my critical discussion of Geras's account of Marx's theory of justice at the end of Chap. 5 I said that some of the crucial economic propositions of Marx's theories in *Capital* do not work, and that I therefore agree with Geras that a socialist theory of justice is needed today whether or not Geras is right about Marx himself subscribing to a theory of justice. For this reason I am happy to simply accept Harvey and Geras's criticisms of the determination of value by labour. If I were an economist I would want to ask some more questions. Harvey and Geras's criticisms are not particularly original, and it would therefore be worth looking at previous attempts to answer them. Over and above this, why do economists, be they classical economists in the tradition of Smith, Ricardo and Marx or neo-classical economists such as Marshall, Jevons, Pareto or Walras think it important to have a theory of value, whether a labour theory of value or a marginalist theory of value? Might there, as neo-Ricardians such as Sraffa and those influenced by him thought, be problems in the marginalist theory of value that do not arise in a properly stated version of the labour theory of value (see, for example, Sraffa 1960; Steedman 1977)? Harvey and Geras seem to have opted out of having a theory of value at all. Are there any problems about this? This topic plainly requires an extremely lengthy discussion that would not be appropriate here. Suffice it to say that their rapid dismissal of the labour theory of value cannot simply be the end of the story.

In the next part of their exposition, Harvey and Geras point out that the appropriation of surplus labour occurs in any society in which people who do not work receive the fruits of some of the labour of workers. Marx says that this only takes the form of exploitation, the appropriation of surplus value, in capitalist society. Thus the idea of exploitation is not needed in order to demonstrate the appropriation of surplus labour. Moreover, Marx is not consistent in making a moral claim that exploitation is unjustified. In a communist society where distribution is according to need, surplus labour is transferred to, for example, the sick, but this is not regarded as exploitation (Harvey and Geras 2013, p. 11).

Harvey and Geras now start to discuss the range of issues that they see as their contribution to the development of historical materialism. They point out that, for much of the time in *Capital*, Marx behaves as if there is a straightforward encounter in the market between the capitalist and the worker. However, they point out, in different capitalist societies there are different moral, legal and cultural constraints on the way in which labour may be used. Also, the worker is largely produced outside the market, by the family and in education. Marx has a picture of the worker becoming exhausted during labour and needing to be refreshed, but skills and education may actually be enhanced as part of the labour process. Thus at one end we have highly skilled workers encountering the capitalist against a favourable background, and on the other literal slavery, debt bondage and modern slavery, all of which can be made use of in a capitalist framework (Harvey and Geras 2013, pp. 12–14).

After some more criticism of writers who simply stick with the framework put forward by Marx in *Capital*, Harvey and Geras start to consider in more depth the reproduction of labour outside the market. They mention feminist criticisms of Marx for failure to analyse the role of the family in reproducing labour, pointing out that the situation of women and their role in relation to paid work varies greatly between different capitalist societies. They then move on to role of education, a great deal, at least, of which takes place outside market relationships. Thus a large and more or less continually increasing part of the labour force is withdrawn from the market. The household and the education system break the circuit of capital, as they do not sell their outputs. Access to education is selective and plays a role in reproducing inequalities (Harvey and Geras 2013, pp. 18–23).

Their next target is the assumption in *Capital* of an individual buyer confronting an individual seller in conditions of equality. This is evidently false. Where labour power is concerned, workers may or may not be unionized, for example, and firms will have different constitutions. Also, larger firms, for example supermarkets, may be in a position to impose unequal terms of exchange on small farmers. Equality before the law is assumed, but the fact was achieved over a substantial period of time, and cannot simply be assumed. Marx assumes that the worker must sell his labour power or die, but the degree of constraint varies. In particular, capitalists need the knowledge and skills of the worker to set the physical means of production going, so that the relationship between these areas and publicly available knowledge is to be considered. Legal and fiscal constraints also vary—compare the position of labour under the Poor Law of 1834 and the varying provisions available in the post-war welfare state. This is an area of variation and struggle across Europe.

Marx talks about the purchase of labour power, but the situation is more like hiring—the purchase is for a limited period of time and there are contractual constraints on what may be done with labour power, just as there are with hired equipment. Moreover, unlike other purchases, workers exercise constraints over what may be done with them, which may be reflected in the law. The purchase and use of knowledge and skills introduces another area of variation (Harvey and Geras 2013, pp. 24–32). After reiterating the circularity problem in determining the value of labour power because of its social and cultural elements, they point out that the purchase of labour power in contemporary Britain occurs in conditions very different from those prevailing in Lyons.

They return to the notion found in Marx of the use of labour power in the production process, and set a relatively affluent level of what is needed to restore the worker's ability to work, thus reinforcing the point about the cultural element in the wage. But they insisted again that knowledge acquired in the production process does not get used up in the same way, and argue that more attention needs to be paid to the manner in which it is used (Harvey and Geras 2013, pp. 33–36).

The labour theory of value measures the value of commodities in terms of the quantity of simple labour that they contain, so that skilled labour is a multiple of simple labour. They are sceptical both that, for example, carpentry and bricklaying can be satisfactorily equated, and that highly skilled labour is simply a multiple of unskilled labour. And the idea that, under capitalism, all labour is tending to turn into simple labour is just ridiculous. Instead they think that it is more fruitful to analyse the various forms of labour and their interrelation in the production process and relationship with the society generally.

The above scepticism about the labour theory of value is strongly reinforced by the consideration of slavery and its relationship to the development of capitalism. Capitalist development in the New World depended upon forms of forced labour, starting with attempts to use the labour of indigenous people, and then moving on to indentured labour, and most notably the enslavement of some 15 to 18 million Africans, and the widespread use of indentured labour from India, which accounted for perhaps another 3 million people. Slavery may well have been crucial to getting industrial capitalism going. Certainly, it was highly profitable, and much of the profit was recycled into other areas. Moreover the industrial economy was highly dependent on raw materials and food produced by slaves. Marx simply assumes that the basis of the capitalist economy is the wage labour of free labourers, but the major role of slavery places this in doubt. Indeed, modern slavery, child labour under oppressive conditions and various forms of debt bondage are integrated into capitalism today (Harvey and Geras 2013, pp. 37–47).

In summarizing their critique of Marx, Harvey and Geras again contrast their own profoundly historical and spatial analysis of capitalist production with the closed system found in *Capital* (Harvey and Geras 2013, pp. 48–53).

In the final part of the article they summarize some political conclusions from their analysis. They start by stressing that those on the left must be committed to genuine democracy, to democratic economic and political participation. There is no room for making excuses for supposedly anti-capitalist but totalitarian regimes (Harvey and Geras 2013, p. 56).

This is certainly in line with Geras's general commitments by this stage of his life, but does not automatically follow on from the above analysis. Their general argument, at any rate, is that their approach highlights a whole variety of areas where issues to do with equality need to be debated and struggled for, and this can only be done within a democratic framework—mature electorates will not accept anything less. What follows on directly from their overall analysis is that the uni-dimensional approach to bringing about equality by bringing exploitation to an end, which would appear to flow from *Capital*, is seriously inadequate. In addition to significant economic inequalities, it is necessary to address many other issues, for example:

> There are gendered inequalities, differences in access to educational opportunity, differences in access to available work, or to well-paid work, and to space and housing and health and insurance, and to a clean environment, and to water, and more. (Harvey and Geras 2013, p. 58)

These are the sorts of issues that are regularly discussed in the British Labour Party and its equivalents elsewhere. It is immediately apparent that it would be unrealistic to expect everyone to be equal in all of these dimensions—just compare, for example, someone living in the Highlands of Scotland and someone living in London. In the Highlands there is a beautiful environment and plenty of room, but it would be unrealistic to expect to have available the variety of work or the speed of ambulance response available in London.

A commitment to equality, in fact, leads on to some issues already considerably rehearsed in political philosophy. For example, given discrepancies of need, equality of resources is not appropriate. The issue of equality of opportunity is well known to be difficult because it is not possible to equalize, for example, family backgrounds and personal capacities. Issues of this sort need serious debate, rather than simply asserting that Marx had all the solutions (Harvey and Geras 2013, p. 60). In concluding, they reiterate the point that they made at the beginning of the article: that despite the ongoing ramifications of the crisis of 2008, there has been no serious revival of the left. In order to achieve this, the issues raised in the article need to be seriously addressed (Harvey and Geras 2013, p. 62).

There is a great deal to be commended in the Harvey and Geras article. Certainly drawing attention to the very wide range of conditions under which labour is performed, the wide variations in educational and skilled resources that workers bring to the marketplace, the role of the unions and of law and their suggestion for issues that should be considered in developing an egalitarian politics are all very important. There are at least two issues that they do not consider, but which definitely arise from their work. First, many of the issues they discuss are frequently also discussed in the Labour Party and the trade unions, so there is a question of the extent to which Harvey and Geras are bringing anything new to these forums. It would obviously require a very lengthy excursion from the general themes of this book to deal with this, but it is an important task for people impressed by their contribution. Second, an issue that will be discussed further in the conclusion (Chap. 13): their conclusions plainly stem from an analysis of Marx, but so much of what is often seen as the core of a Marxist position is rejected so that it might be better to think of what they produce as a set of liberal egalitarian ideas developed from a critique of Marx.

References

Arblaster, A. (1975). What Is Violence? In R. Miliband & J. Saville (Eds.), *The Socialist Register 1975*. London: The Merlin Press Ltd..

Cohen, B., & Garrard, E. (Eds.). (2017). *The Norman Geras Reader 'What's There is There'*. Manchester: Manchester University Press.

Geras, N. (1990). *Discourses of Extremity: Radical Ethics and Post-Marxist Extravagances*. London: Verso.

Harvey, M., & Geras, N. (2013). Marx's Economy and Beyond. Retrieved from http://normblog.typepad.com/files/meabpdf.pdf.

Kliman, A. (2007). *Reclaiming Marx's 'Capital': A Refutation of the Myth of Inconsistency*. Plymouth: Lexington Books.

Marcuse, H. (1966). Ethics and Revolution. In R. T. De George (Ed.), *Ethics and Society* (pp. 139–187). Garden City, New York: Anchor Books.

Nozick, R. (1980). *Anarchy, State and Utopia*. Oxford: Oxford University Press.

Sraffa, P. (1960). *Production of Commodities by Means of Commodities: Prelude to a Critique of Economic Theory*. Cambridge: Cambridge University Press.

Steedman, I. (1977). *Marx After Sraffa*. London: New Left Books.

CHAPTER 8

Geras and Postmodernism 1: Laclau and Mouffe

The subject of this chapter is a Geras's critique of Laclau and Mouffe's *Hegemony and Social Strategy* (Laclau and Mouffe 1985). However, their book is an important part of the development of a postmodernist approach that is still influential in the arts and social sciences, and similarly, Geras's critique (Geras 1990) is part of a defence of Marxism, science and Enlightenment values by a range of philosophers, Marxists and scientists.

Postmodernism: Major Features and Criticisms

A full discussion of postmodernism and its critics would be extremely lengthy, but it will help to locate the discussion in this and Chap. 9 if some of the main features of postmodernism and main lines of criticism are identified.

Among the many definitions of postmodernism the one by Terry Eagleton (Eagleton 1996, p. vii) is particularly succinct. Some major features of postmodernism are:

- We are now in the postmodern period.
- Enlightenment or modernist notions of progress, grand narratives—meaning large-scale explanations of society and history—truth and reason simply do not work.
- The world is diverse, unstable, indeterminate.

M. Cowling, *Norman Geras's Political Thought from Marxism to Human Rights*, https://doi.org/10.1007/978-3-319-74048-5_8

- Identities are fluid and multiple. Thus, rather than identifying somebody as a worker, she is a disabled Scottish black lesbian working in a service industry who is passionate opera lover. Different aspects of these identities will come to the fore in different circumstances. Thus identity politics replaces class politics.
- As the subject is disintegrated, the idea of liberation, so powerful in the Marxist tradition, recedes. Foucault, particularly, sees the subject as constituted by power (see, for example, Dews 1987, p. 190).
- Postmodernism is linked to the dominance of consumerism and service industries over traditional manufacturing.
- Postmodernism is linked to a form of art that is playful and eclectic, blurring the boundaries between art and everyday experience.
- Postmodernism has been particularly popular amongst literary critics because it tends to see all texts as being on a level. There is also an emphasis on the role of language, which is seen as determining everything because everything is described in language.
- There are no clear criteria for choosing between one way of seeing things and another, between one discourse and another. Overarching criteria such as comparison with the physical world are ruled out because we cannot access the physical world outside of discourse.
- Postmodernism can therefore lead to a version of idealism in which it is denied that there is an extra-discursive reality, or certainly, as we will see later in the case of Laclau and Mouffe, ambiguous formulations in this area.

Some major criticisms of postmodernism:

- The boundaries between modernism and postmodernism are very foggy. Callinicos (1989) devotes much of the early part of his book to this criticism.
- Postmodernism itself is a grand narrative, so that it is hypocritically regards all grand narratives as invalid except for postmodernism (Eagleton 1996, p. 34).
- Thinking particularly of Foucault, prisons, the body and so forth are seen as acceptable subjects of discourse whereas modes of production are not—the choice of legitimate totalities to discuss is arbitrary (e.g. Eagleton 1996).
- For postmodernists essentialism is a serious theoretical error. Eagleton points out that this displays ignorance of the history of

philosophy and differences between, for example, Bentham and Locke (1996, pp. 101–102). Taken to extremes, the critique of essentialism knocks away any foundations of social criticism or political action (Meiksins Wood 1998, location 72).

- Valuing plurality in itself is formalistic: would British social life be enriched if there were more fascist parties? (Eagleton 1996, p. 127).
- The postmodernist equation of science with, for example, astrology as alternative approaches to truth that are equally valid is simply ridiculous. For example, a leading postmodernist journal happily accepted a spoof article about physics that would have been immediately rejected by any reputable scientific journal (see Sokal and Bricmont 1999).
- Dealing with questions about whether or not scientific theory is better than, say, astrology, Boghossian (2007) provides a very thorough set of arguments, some of which will be rehearsed below in the discussion of Rorty in Chap. 9. Interestingly, he points out that, while literary theorists and sociologists have been very enthusiastic about postmodernism, on the whole philosophers regard it as obviously invalid.
- Boghossian also provides a lengthy and careful set of arguments concerning the validity or otherwise of idealism, which is implied by the idea that there is nothing outside discourse, again arguing for some form of realism.
- Callinicos (1989, p. 9), amongst others, points out that there is a connection between loss of faith in a socialist revolution and the growth of postmodernism.
- Given that one major feature of postmodernism is an assault on the values of the Enlightenment, critics of postmodernism tend to mount at least a limited defence of Enlightenment values, perhaps following Habermas in defending communicative rationality, meaning not the defence of a substantive set of values but of un-coerced discussion in the public sphere. Callinicos has some reservations—Habermas thinks that mass democracy, state intervention in the economy and the welfare state have rendered Marx's picture of capitalism outdated, whereas Callinicos thinks capitalism is very much alive and kicking, thus affecting unconstrained discussion. And, even if unconstrained discussion in the public sphere were possible, the resulting consensus might still not be true. He therefore looks to the idea of valuing truth on the lines advocated by Lakatos (see, for example, Callinicos 1989, pp. 94 et seq.; Dews 1987, pp. 237, 271 et seq.).

- Callinicos has doubts about the thesis of de-industrialization, the replacement of manufacturing by services (Callinicos 1989, pp. 122–123).
- Peter Dews (1987) provides an extremely detailed and erudite critique of postmodernist thought. A very few particularly telling points are mentioned here.
- Dews is excellent on the subject of Foucault and power—there is a contradiction in Foucault between notions of oppression that appear in some places and his stress on the ubiquity of power. Successful resistance would itself become another power, Dews says, which leads the late Foucault to abandon the concept of power (Dews 1987, pp. 207, 265).
- Foucault also runs into ambiguities when it comes to his well-known linkage of power and knowledge. At times he wants to argue that his own approach, that of genealogy, is on the side of resistance, but finds it difficult to do this coherently (Dews 1987, p. 233).
- These are just a few of a variety of points where Dews points out that poststructuralist and postmodernist thought is riven by contradictions. He concludes that a commitment to the coherence of thought is required if it is to have emancipatory power (Dews 1987, p. 297).

Hegemony and Social Strategy

Laclau and Mouffe's *Hegemony and Social Strategy* made a considerable impact when it was first published—it seemed to be an idea whose time had come. Before moving on to Geras's critique a short exposition of some main points is in order.

We can start, as Geras could not, with the Preface to the second edition of the book, written in 2000. Earlier on we find:

> The problems of a globalized and information-ruled society are unthinkable within the two ontological paradigms governing the field of Marxist discursivity: first the Hegelian, and later the naturalistic. (Laclau and Mouffe 1985, location 185)

Geras could start by disputing that Marxism is necessarily governed by either paradigm in a straightforward way—if it is Hegelian, some sort of inverted Hegelianism is involved. If it is naturalistic, then the scientific method used has to be modified because society, not simply natural phenomena, is the object of study. Either way, Marxist ideas about globalization are often regarded as one of Marxism's success stories. And a society ruled by information is a wonderful onward development of the Hegelian Idea. (The work of Manuel Castells is the most obvious source for a thorough and erudite discussion of the notion that contemporary society is characterized by the processing of information. For an article which attempts to link the idea of the information society with Marxism, and which includes references to the main books by Castells, see Cowling 2014).

Then in the same place Laclau and Mouffe go on to say that their approach is 'grounded' in 'privileging' the 'moment' of political articulation, particularly hegemony. 'Moment' is a typically Hegelian term. And why 'privilege' political articulation rather than anything else? Social antagonisms are inherent in politics, but they are not objective relations—they would appear to just crop up. Social division is inherent in the political (Laclau and Mouffe 1985, location 160). The convoluted and pretentious language of the original has been largely omitted, but it appears to be a way of saying that they now subscribe to the standard definition of politics as contestation in the public sphere. Thinking in terms of hegemony enables the Left to seek a credible alternative to the supposed inevitability of globalization, which is in fact part of the neo-liberal world order (Laclau and Mouffe 1985, location 216). A whole variety of people and groups had developed ideas about challenging neo-liberal globalization by the year 2000, so this is hardly earth shattering.

Moving on to a brief summary of the major features of the book itself, the starting point is that contemporary society presents so many different struggles that the traditional Marxist view of a revolution made by the working class in which all the antagonisms of capitalist society are eventually overcome under communism is no longer credible (Laclau and Mouffe 1985, location 292). This classical picture was very strongly there in Kautsky, who regarded the working class as already unified, and saw the development towards revolution as the inevitable outcome of onward economic development, but broke down considerably amongst neo-Kantian Marxists, and almost completely in Bernstein, who denied the inevitability of revolution and saw the working class as increasingly diverse (Laclau and Mouffe 1985, pp. 4–30). The concept of hegemony developed first in Russia where the concerns of workers had to be articulated with those of a variety of other classes. Thus a practice of hegemony was required, which could be democratic or autocratic. In the democratic practice of hegemony social interests lose any necessary connection with classes; instead we have social groups reconstituting themselves and the 'precarious' articulation of 'subject positions' (Laclau and Mouffe 1985, pp. 39–49).

The potential that Laclau and Mouffe see here is the development of democratic politics as understood by conventional theorists of democratic pluralism such as Robert Dahl, in which politics is seen as a contestation between a variety of interest and advocacy groups (see Dahl 2005, 1977). Dahl's work generated a massive literature, both applying his ideas and opposing them. No discussion of this whatsoever appears in Laclau and Mouffe, partly because it would reveal the position that they achieved nothing very extraordinary at all: 'we've just realised that the conventional study of politics is much better than the Marxist one!!', and partly because Dahl and his critics generally write in straightforward English without lots of abstruse terms. The only Marxist thinker who got close to the above position was Gramsci (Laclau and Mouffe 1985, pp. 55–60).

They then turn to attempts to link the economic interests of the working class to the political struggle for socialism, but argue that concept of 'economic interests' lacks any theoretical foundation whatsoever, and should therefore be abandoned (Laclau and Mouffe 1985, p. 74). A naive response to this might be that one minimal way of finding a unity of economic interests would be to ask whether people who rely on working for a living support the welfare state on the grounds that they need it or might need it. To a considerable extent the welfare state is delivered according to need, and can therefore be seen as a socialist element in a capitalist society. A great deal would need to be said about capitalist interests in a healthy and well-educated workforce, features of the welfare state being used to subordinate people who use it, its bureaucratic and undemocratic pattern of delivery and so forth, but still the basic idea could be maintained. However, Laclau and Mouffe focus on these negative aspects (e.g. 1985, pp. 141–146), and do not consider the naive response.

They pursue their version of the concept of hegemony by stressing that a radical alliance has to be put together from a wide variety of social positions that are themselves fluid, and their relation to the rejected radical alliance cannot be presumed but must be analysed in each case (Laclau and Mouffe 1985, p. 77).

Their view of discourse is very important in taking the analysis further. Every object is constituted as an object of discourse. They see discourse itself as material. The opposition between thought and reality is thus abandoned (Laclau and Mouffe, pp. 91–96). Wonderful things can be done with the idea of discourse. A major objection to Engels' *Dialectics of*

Nature is that his claim that logical contradictions can exist in the real world is spurious. However, Laclau and Mouffe point out that propositions are part of the real, contradictory propositions exist empirically, therefore logical contradictions are part of the real (Laclau and Mouffe 1985, p. 110). A more serious point, which is taken up by Geras, and which crops up again in the discussion of Rorty in Chap. 9 is whether Laclau and Mouffe are committed to some form of idealism, because they deny that objects can be constituted as objects outside discourse.

Because there is a multiplicity of political struggles there is also a multiplicity of political spaces (Laclau and Mouffe 1985, p. 123). Subordination to capital is a feature of numerous aspects of social life, and this helps to generate many varied struggles (Laclau and Mouffe 1985, pp. 144–148). Rather than trying to relate everything to class, the Left should support the democratic revolution against oppression (Laclau and Mouffe 1985, p. 160). Not surprisingly in the light of what has gone before, there is no possibility of a unified discourse of the Left (Laclau and Mouffe 1985, p. 174). This reader, at least, is left very unclear as to what Laclau and Mouffe would count as the Left. Here is one example. There has been a democratic struggle against oppression in recent years to achieve equal rights for gays and lesbians. Thus, from homosexuality being illegal before 1967, gay marriage is now widely supported and enjoys legal status. I consider it a cause for celebration that it is now possible to be an overtly homosexual Conservative MP. Even better, the popular and successful leader of the Scottish Conservatives, Ruth Davidson MSP, is well known as a lesbian and kickboxer, something which would have been inconceivable a few years ago. However, whether this has anything particular to do with the Left is open to question. Similar comments could be made about numerous other struggles. Laclau and Mouffe have so completely gutted the traditional concept of Left that I am left completely unclear as to what it comprises, or as to what criteria could be used to work out what should count.

Geras's Critique of *Hegemony and Social Strategy*

Geras's critique is rigorous and thorough. Having commented briefly on the possible role of post-Marxism in people's intellectual development (Geras 1990, pp. 61–64), he says that he will go on to show that the book is the result of 'an intellectual malady … theoretically profligate, dissolute … without regard for normal considerations of logic, of evidence or of due proportion' (Geras 1990, pp. 64–65). This is one of the best sets of insults I have come across in academic writing! Is it justified?

The book, he says, is organized around a single principle of construction, the distinction between simplicity and closure on one hand and complexity and openness on the other—for them, the mere idea of society having a centre has no meaning (Geras 1990, pp. 67–68). This derives originally from Althusser's distinction between an expressive totality as found in Hegel and many versions of Marxism, and what he identified as an over-determined totality, to be found in the later Marx. Geras comments that this had some justification in opening up research in historical materialism rather than just regarding Marx as another philosopher. However, in Laclau and Mouffe things are taken further, so that virtually any general explanation of society can be condemned because it closes off openness and indeterminacy, it is a form of essentialism (Geras 1990, p. 71). In particular, they define Marxism in the most rigidly economistic and deterministic terms, and thus condemn it for essentialism. The idea of relative autonomy is a dead end: entities are either explained by the basic determinations, in which case there is no autonomy; or there is real autonomy, which undermines the idea of, for example, economic determination. In opposition to this Geras offers an example in which he is chained by the ankle to a post. This allows him to do some things, makes other activities impossible, and requires him to do yet further things. But it would be arbitrary to say that the chained Geras is either autonomous or determined. If this is accepted, then why not accept that there are, for example, genuinely different types of capitalist state, that this might be linked to different political outcomes, but that capitalist relations of production are primary in explaining these states (Geras 1990, pp. 72–75)?

Geras moves on to briefly consider Laclau and Mouffe's critique of Rosa Luxemburg. Luxemburg considered that mass strikes would bring the relatively fragmented working class together. She is subjected to the economic necessity versus pure fragmentation critique that we have come to expect. Geras responds by arguing that a wide variety of workers are subjected to similar problems because of their situation within the capitalist economy, and that this provides a solid basis for unifying socialist politics. This is a critique on very much the same lines as the comments above in the exposition of Laclau and Mouffe about the welfare state. The same sort of approach, says Geras, is used on a wide variety of Marxists from Kautsky to Gramsci to Althusser (Geras 1990, p. 79).

Bifurcation is also applied to the development of the concept of hegemony as it developed in the Russian revolution. The concept had to be developed because the Russian bourgeoisie was too weak to make a bourgeois revolution; increasingly the Mensheviks, Lenin and above all Trotsky recognized the need for the working class to lead the other classes. They were thus acknowledging the idea of a decisively political bond, but it was one that left the underlying class identities intact. Gramsci took this concept further. His social agents were strictly speaking 'collective wills' rather than classes, who were united in a historical bloc. But ultimately the unifying principle of every hegemonic formation was a fundamental class, meaning that Gramsci was an essentialist after all. Any Marxist can be shown to be guilty of essentialism by showing that they use a central Marxist category. Laclau and Mouffe take up Althusser's idea that many forms of Marxism are guilty of essentialism, but they take it further and conclude that all forms of Marxism are guilty of essentialism, thus vitiating any other merits that they may have (Geras 1990, pp. 81–86).

Geras considers in more detail Rosa Luxemburg's theories about the mass strike. In mass strikes a series of processes are involved that tend to unify the working class. Laclau and Mouffe say that this shows that Luxemburg recognized the 'defining characteristic of the symbol: the overflowing of the signifier by the signified'. This bizarre interpretation helps Laclau and Mouffe to demonstrate that there is a dualism in Luxemburg between this and a rigid conception of economic determinism. They thus disregard seven or eight interesting ideas about the mass strike, but manage to find essentialism and dualism (Geras 1990, pp. 87–92).

Geras comments that this finding of essentialism and dualism everywhere is effectively a way of breaking with historical materialism, and of denying the validity of any form of systematic social explanation based on Marxism (Geras 1990, p. 96). This is a very apt comment. Indeed, any attempt at general social explanation relies on taking some aspects of society and using them to explain others, which is an essentialist way of proceeding.

The next part of Geras's critique concerns the concept of discourse. Geras takes issue with the claim in Laclau and Mouffe that objects could not constitute themselves as objects outside any discursive condition of emergence. He considers that this implies that nothing exists outside discourse. If that is the case, then the normal basis for communication across different viewpoints is removed (Geras 1990, pp. 97–100). Geras makes this point well and succinctly here. There is a further discussion in the final section of this chapter; Geras's main discussion of this issue was in his critique of Rorty, and is taken up more fully in Chap. 9.

The main issue, though, is to do with hegemonic articulation. This involves the incomplete and open character of the social, which comprises many floating elements. A hegemonic articulation divides these into two camps by combining and redefining the elements involved. However, says Geras, here lurks a problem. If the elements of the social structure are fully autonomous then they are fixed in themselves, so we have an essentialism. But we also have an essentialism if these elements are regarded as moments of a totality, as would be typical in Marxism. So Laclau and Mouffe opt for an intermediate region between the two, where there is neither absolute fixity nor absolute non-fixity. So society is neither totally possible nor totally impossible (Geras 1990, pp. 100–106).

Geras comments, very reasonably, that we are left with complete theoretical vacuity: for example, is there any reason to think that some hegemonic practices will succeed better than others? Would one discourse be more attractive than another and why? Laclau and Mouffe have cut away any criteria for making sense of such issues. He points out that occasionally such terms as 'advanced capitalism' or 'imperialist exploitation' are mentioned, but surely these belong to Marxism, which is discredited and essentialist? They also use the term 'progressive', but the obvious bases for saying something is progressive—objective interests, a conception of human nature, a trans-historical notion of justice—have all been discarded. They talk about 'subordination', which becomes 'oppression' when it leads to 'antagonism', but they have left themselves no clear basis on which to found these concepts. For example, capitalists forced to put up with trade unions could be described as oppressed—the idea of progressive politics has become arbitrary (Geras 1990, pp. 108–115).

Laclau and Mouffe see themselves as advocates of radical democracy, which is pluralist. They suggest that democracy has hitherto been foreign to socialism, and thus assimilate socialism to Stalinism. Geras insists that there has been a very strong commitment to democracy amongst a wide variety of thinkers in the Marxist tradition, and that this commitment has been particularly strong amongst Marxists over the past couple of decades. In contrast, Laclau and Mouffe have virtually nothing to say about what form their pluralist democracy might take. They are obviously trying to accommodate new social movements to do with gender, ecology, nuclear power, war and peace and so forth, but provide no helpful basis on which to do this. For example, if there is 'no logical connection whatsoever' between positions in production and the mentality of producers because 'political practice constructs the interests it represents', presumably the same logic applies to feminism, which has no particular connection to the position of women (Geras 1990, pp. 115–119). He concludes by suggesting that Laclau and Mouffe should be regarded more as anti-Marxist than as post-Marxist.

Ellen Meiksins Wood's Critique of Laclau and Mouffe

By the time that Geras's assault on Laclau and Mouffe appeared, there was already a book by Meiksins Wood (1998 in what follows, but the first edition was published in 1986), which was also a critique of *Hegemony and Social Strategy*. Geras was aware of the book. Why did he feel the need to publish his own critique? Meiksins Wood conceptualizes the work of Laclau and Mouffe and other similar figures as a new form of the True Socialism, which Marx and Engels criticized in *The German Ideology*: in both cases abstract concepts take the place of the class struggle (Meiksins Wood 1998, location 139). For the New True Socialists, socialism becomes the more attractive the more it is detached from material interests:

> This, then, is the new 'true' socialism. Needless to say, there is a great deal in it which is hardly new. To a large extent, it is just another repetition of banal and hoary right-wing social-democratic nostrums. (Meiksins Wood 1998, location 226)

This is rather sweeping and not very specific, a comment that could be applied to much of her book. She defends class politics against quite a variety of figures, making the interesting point that for some of those involved post-Marxism is a staging point on the route from Althusserian Maoism to Eurocommunism and beyond, which she illustrates at some length in a discussion of Poulantzas (Meiksins Wood 1998, locations 530–980).

The next stage of her assault on post-Marxism involves well-aimed criticism of Laclau and Mouffe's notion that material interests do not exist unless they are translated into political objectives (Meiksins Wood 1998, location 1222). What motive force is there to socialist politics, she asks, if not the interests of the working class (Meiksins Wood 1998, location

1816)? However, part of the Laclau and Mouffe attempt to justify this point is an insistence that the working class is fragmented, an issue that a variety of Marxists tried to deal with in different ways, but which Meiksins Wood regards as not a serious issue. Geras, in contrast, deals with this at some length and very effectively as we have already seen.

Two chapters follow in which Gareth Stedman Jones and Gavin Kitching are taken to task over the detachment of socialist politics from class. She then attacks a variety of figures including Laclau and Mouffe for regarding liberal democracy as a neutral form rather than as a source of mystification that promotes capitalist hegemony (Meiksins Wood 1998, location 2748). Geras leaves the impression that he would require a longer and more nuanced discussion of this issue. However, given his vigorous defence of the democratic aspects of socialism, he is happy to agree with Meiksins Wood's claim that aspects of liberalism such as civil liberties, the rule of law and protection of privacy would be required following a socialist revolution (Meiksins Wood 1998, location 3193). Towards the end of the book there is a trenchant defence of the idea that the working class is exploited, therefore it has an interest in socialism (for example Meiksins Wood 1998, location 3470). However, this has something of the air of the defence of an article of faith. There are, of course, various ways of making sense of the economic system of the Soviet Union. It is by no means obvious that Soviet workers were exploited in the same way as workers in West. On the other hand, the collapse of the Soviet system in 1989 was definitely caused, in part, by a realistic perception that exploitation in West left workers much better off than the absence of it in the East. To put the same point differently, the fence that divided East and West Germany was not erected by West German capitalists fearful of losing their workers. Plainly a great deal more argument would be needed to demonstrate the validity of this analysis. However, it does suggest that there are problems in assuming that capitalist exploitation automatically gives workers an interest in socialist revolution. Perhaps part of the explanation for Meiksins Wood's defence of a rather fundamentalist Marxist line is the background of the overt and vigorous defence of capitalist interests that was being undertaken by the Thatcher government at the time she was writing.

Thus, although Meiksins Wood's book contains a lot of well and vigorously argued contentions, it by no means contains the forensic dissection of Laclau and Mouffe found in Geras.

Laclau and Mouffe's Response to Geras

Geras's attack on Laclau and Mouffe was originally an article in *New Left Revue* (Geras 1987). Laclau and Mouffe responded with a shorter reply of their own (Laclau and Mouffe 1987). A summary of some main points in this reply follows, although I agree with Geras's view that they say virtually nothing to clarify the issues in dispute.

Their project in their book, they say, was based on the need to respond to profound changes in recent years, including the decline of the classical working class in the post-industrial countries and the penetration of capitalist relations into many areas of social life leading to new forms of protest (Laclau and Mouffe 1987, p. 80). In other words, one might think, a project based around changes in the essence of capitalism and its effects. They duly exchange insults with Geras, who they see as a fading epigone of Marxist orthodoxy, but are not concerned with his motives as they are not his psychiatrists (Laclau and Mouffe 1987, p. 81).

They start by explaining discourse, which they say is a combination of the linguistic and the non-linguistic, so that speech and writing are only a part of it. Nature and natural objects are the result of a lengthy historical construction, but this does not commit Laclau and Mouffe to a form of idealism. Apart from Geras's response, which will be seen later, these assertions also relate to the general discussion of postmodernism above and the discussion of Rorty on similar issues in Chap. 9.

They say that what distinguishes idealism from materialism is that idealism asserts the ultimately conceptual character of the real. Traditional materialism is actually to a great extent idealist (Laclau and Mouffe 1987, pp. 86–88).

Moving on to the issue of relative autonomy, Geras offers the example of having a chain round his ankle that is attached to a post as a possible example. However, the chain does not determine what Geras does, so the example is useless. A more traditional way to look at the idea of relative autonomy is to say that there is a series of complex mediations between the base and the superstructure, but this does not help because the totality ultimately determines its contents. If there is full autonomy there is a question of what links the elements of the social whole. What they are aiming for is a position somewhere between determination in the last instance and full autonomy (Laclau and Mouffe 1987, pp. 92–95).

They revisit their attack on the idea of objective interests, saying that only God and Geras know how to preserve this idea whilst avoiding essentialism (Laclau and Mouffe 1987, p. 96).

Geras was critical of their history of Marxism. What they were trying to do was to avoid a relatively static set of concepts and emphasize a development in the direction of an increasing use of the idea of hegemony, found particularly in the work of Gramsci (Laclau and Mouffe 1987, p. 99).

They emphasize the logic of the symbol in a series of Marxist texts. Geras fails to understand this (Laclau and Mouffe 1987, p. 100). They see the struggle for socialism as part of a struggle for democracy, which has been taking place over the past 200 years. Anti-capitalism is part of the democratic revolution (Laclau and Mouffe 1987, p. 103). There are numerous points of antagonism between various parts of the global population and capitalism. The straightforward antagonism between the working class and capitalism has not occurred, so that rather than there being intrinsically anti-capitalist relationships, there are relationships that could become anti-capitalist. 'Marx correctly observed that capitalism only expands through permanent transformation of the means of production and the dislocation and progressive dissolution of traditional social relations.' A variety of phenomena are connected with 'combined and uneven development', which give rise to struggles connected to the issue of identity (Laclau and Mouffe 1987, p. 104). This appears to be accepting a dubiously large dose of traditional Marxist essentialism. In its turn, it also raises acutely the issue raised above about lesbian kickboxing Scottish Conservatives. Ruth Davidson's popular and successful leadership of Scotland's Tories involves a triumph of democratization, but has nothing obvious to do with anti-capitalism.

Finally in this chapter we come to Geras's response to Laclau and Mouffe's counterblast to his criticisms. His first point of substance is that they mis-state his critique of what they have to say about rigid oppositions. He is *not* criticizing them for basing their own conclusions on rigid oppositions, but rather for allowing themselves imprecise and evasive intermediate solutions. His criticism rather is of Laclau and Mouffe reducing a variety of Marxist ideas to rigid oppositions. He gives as examples first their rejection of the idea of relative autonomy in Marxism by arguing that there is a polarity between complete autonomy and absolute subordination, whereas they allow intermediate positions, second their misunderstanding of Geras's example of being chained to a post, which they failed to recognize as a valid but limited example of powerful but less than total determination, and third of determination of the superstructure by the base, which they see as a relation of expression, whereas in Marx there are a variety of formulations. He again offers examples of intermediate positions between economic reductionism and sheer plurality within the Marxist tradition

(Geras 1990, pp. 128–137). One particularly spectacular example of the distortion of Marxist writing by Laclau and Mouffe is where Geras lists 13 aspects of Rosa Luxemburg's discussion of the mass strike, which Laclau and Mouffe reduced to a central linguistic mechanism of the 'overflowing of the signifier by the signified' (Geras 1990, pp. 147–148).

For about one-sixth of his critique, Geras criticized the way in which, for their own purposes, Laclau and Mouffe are very free and easy with concepts such as fixity and interiority, and points out that their response is to say nothing (Geras 1990, p. 149).

We now come to the issue of in what sense Laclau and Mouffe's politics may be said to be progressive? Part of their answer is the value of humanism, the humanist conception of 'man'. Obviously, however, there are various conceptions of 'man'. One way to choose between them is to ask which corresponds best to human nature, but they have ruled out any conception of human nature. There is a similar problem in giving any substance to their support for the ongoing democratic revolution. It is that any reason for supporting it would be bound to be some form of essentialism (Laclau and Mouffe 1987, pp. 150–152).

After insisting that he and other Marxists in recent years have been very much concerned with democracy, Geras moves on to diversions in which Laclau and Mouffe devote considerable energy to matters that were a very minor part of his criticisms. The first of these is to do with ontology and epistemology: Laclau and Mouffe accept that objects exist outside thought in formal terms, but in a way that denies this acceptance of any theoretical weight. Geras's response here is a good one (Geras 1990, p. 157), but to save duplication a thorough discussion of this issue is postponed until Chap. 9. The second diversion is their complaint that Geras is using intemperate language. He says that because there is virtually no real reply to his criticisms in their counterblast he thinks that they just thrash about for anything that gives the appearance of a reply (Geras 1990, p. 161). I have to say that I very much concur with this judgement—Laclau and Mouffe's response looks to be very hastily thrown together, and amounts to asserting things which are deemed to be obvious from their lofty perspective.

References

Boghossian, P. (2007). *Fear of Knowledge: Against Relativism and Constructivism*. New York: Oxford University Press.

Callinicos, A. (1989). *Against Postmodernism: A Marxist Critique*. Cambridge: Polity.

Cowling, M. (2014, January). Manuel Castells and Historical Materialism. *Open Journal of Political Science (online), 4*(1). Retrieved from http://www.scirp.org/Journal/PaperInformation.aspx?PaperID=41399.

Dahl, R. (2005). *Who Governs?: Democracy and Power in an American City, Second Edition (Yale Studies in Political Science): Democracy and Power in the American City*. New Haven, CT: Yale University Press.

Dahl, R. (1977). *Polyarchy: Participation and Opposition*. New Haven, CT: Yale University Press.

Dews, P. (1987). *Logics of Disintegration: Post-Structuralist Thought and the Claims of Critical Theory*. London: Verso.

Eagleton, T. (1996). *The Illusions of Postmodernism*. Oxford: Blackwell Publishing.

Geras, N. (1987, May, June). Post-Marxism. *New Left Review*, 163.

Geras, N. (1990). *Discourses of Extremity: Radical Ethics and Post-Marxist Extravagances*. London: Verso.

Laclau, E., & Mouffe, C. (1985). *Hegemony and Social Strategy: Towards a Radical Democratic Politics*. London: Verso. (1985 is the Date of Original Publication; References Will be Made to the Kindle Second Edition, 2014).

Laclau, E., & Mouffe, C. (1987, November, December). Post-Marxism Without Apologies. *New Left Review*, 166.

Meiksins Wood, E. (1998). *The Retreat from Class: A New True Socialism* (2nd ed.). London: Verso.

Sokal, A., & Bricmont, J. (1999). *Intellectual Impostures*. London: Profile Books.

CHAPTER 9

Geras and Postmodernism 2: Richard Rorty

Geras's second confrontation with postmodernist philosophy and political theory is to be found in his book *Solidarity in the Conversation of Humankind: The Ungroundable of Liberalism of Richard Rorty* (Geras 1995).

Geras identifies, as one central theme, the issue of a universal human nature. Rorty denies that there is a universal human nature, but continues to make moral judgements without one. Geras describes his own book as a sequel to his *Marx and Human Nature: Refutation of a Legend*. It will be recalled from Chap. 3 that the major theme of this book is Geras's claim that the older Marx retains a concept of human nature. My claim was that the concept of human nature, which Geras finds in the older Marx, is a thin concept, and that it is not a basis for a widespread impression that Geras proves the retention of a theory of alienation in the older Marx. If the reader accepts my account of the older Marx instead of that given by Geras, the upshot is that our image of the older Marx is closer to the one fostered by Engels and largely accepted at the time of the Second and Third Internationals of Marx as the founder of scientific socialism.

However, at some points in the book he also argues for the validity of a concept of human nature. Whilst it is possible to make judgements about ethical issues based on intuitions and without a conception of human nature, I very much agree with Geras that worthwhile accounts of ethics (for example, Moore 1903; Stevenson 1944), and still more of social

M. Cowling, *Norman Geras's Political Thought from Marxism to Human Rights*, https://doi.org/10.1007/978-3-319-74048-5_9

justice, require a conception of human nature. Such a conception is likely to have things to say about our need for happiness, or things which are likely to promote happiness, such as at least a minimum of food and shelter, healthcare, education, a degree of freedom and so forth (for a lengthy and well-researched account of human nature and human need, see Doyle and Gough 1991).

Geras organizes his discussion of Rorty around four chapters:

First, a critique of Rorty's account of solidarity. Second, an argument that Rorty's various usages to do with human nature and that their inconsistencies lie behind his flawed analysis of solidarity. Third, a defence of universalist moral thought, together with an argument that liberalism without foundations is 'neither persuasive nor conducive to democracy' (Geras 1995, p. 5). In the final chapter Geras engages with Rorty's anti-realism, arguing that this is implausible and links to his denial of a universal human nature. Most of this chapter comprises of an exposition of the book, but the discussion of the final chapter argues that in a longer book it would have been better, ideally, for Geras to spend more time discussing the implications of Rorty's anti-foundationalism.

Although Geras discusses other parts of Rorty's voluminous writings, his main target is Rorty's book *Contingency, Irony and Solidarity.* An important claim Rorty makes in the book is that the reason people help each other is not because of an abstract respect for humanity, but because of some sort of prior connection.

> Consider, first, those Danes and those Italians. Did they say, about their Jewish neighbors, that they deserved to be saved because they were fellow human beings? Perhaps sometimes they did, but surely they would usually, if queried, have used more parochial terms to explain why they were taking risks to protect a given Jew—for example, that this particular Jew was a fellow Milanese, or a fellow Jutlander, or a fellow member of the same union or profession, or a fellow bocce player, or a fellow parent of small children. (Rorty 1989, pp. 190–191)

Rorty says more on similar lines. He does this on the basis of pure speculation. It fits with his anti-foundationalism, his general dismissal of universal human rights and philosophical principles. Perhaps it simply seems obvious to him? After all, it isn't silly to say that we would be more likely to help a member of our own family than a stranger. What Rorty fails to do is to engage in any empirical research about why people help each other.

Geras's later work is particularly strong in this respect. He gives very thorough empirical evidence as the basis of philosophical positions that he takes. He does not engage in primary research, but reads extensively in a good range of secondary sources. What he finds is overwhelming evidence that rescuers did not select those they rescued on the basis of prior association of the sort Rorty imagines. The evidence points to rescuing on the basis of human need.

Rescuers did not belong to a particular category. Men and women, workers, peasants, middle-class people, believers, non-believers all risked their lives (Geras 1995, pp. 17–18). A high proportion of rescuers helped strangers. This is particularly marked in large-scale as opposed to impressionistic studies (Geras 1995, p. 20). A virtually unanimous finding was that rescuers' motivations were universalist: helping people in need, helping victims. This includes recollections afterwards, diary entries at the time and people who were involved in helping friends. People who referred to their own communities did so in universalist terms (Geras 1995, pp. 21–23). Briefly, then, he gives a very thorough demonstration that Rorty is talking through his hat when it comes to this particular speculative assumption. (For a splendid satirical version of the points Geras is making see Eagleton 1996, pp. 114–115.)

He then moves on to question of human nature. Rorty claims that there is nothing to people except what has been socialized into them.

'All we share with other humans is the same thing we share with all other animals—the ability to feel pain' (Rorty 1989, p. 177).

He says that human beings who have been socialized in any language culture can all be humiliated by the deliberate tearing down of their structure of language and belief—this result, humiliation, is the worst aspect of torture.

Rorty says that there is no in-built human solidarity to use as a reference point. Perhaps Rorty creates a human nature straw man, thinking that human nature is an inner structure that leads 'all members of the species … To recognise the same theories, virtues and works of art as worthy of honour, whilst refusing individual diversity' (Geras 1995, pp. 60–61).

Geras starts his critique of Rorty in this area by commenting: Isn't a 'common desire to avoid pain and humiliation something which sounds like a—minimal—human nature'? (Geras 1995, p. 63, cf. p. 89).

Although Rorty gives a couple of references to justify his statement that humiliation is the worst aspect of torture, he does not go into detail, and Geras could perhaps have taken this up. If one considers the series of tortures arranged for Damiens the regicide, who tried to stab Louis XV, including having his flesh torn with red hot pincers and boiling oil and molten lead poured into the wounds, followed eventually by being torn apart by four horses, one for each limb, perhaps just being humiliated might be preferable. Tartaglia (2007, pp. 79 et seq.) in an excellent guide to Rorty's *Philosophy and the Mirror of Nature* is also happy to talk about torture without any empirical evidence, although perhaps with more excuse. He considers somebody who is attached to a torture machine and told he is to be tortured, but then finds that pain is not inflicted, as if this would be the end of the matter. However, a classic method of torture is the fake execution. Just because the firing squad bullets are blanks, or the helicopter is just above the ground when the victim is thrown out, it does not mean that the experience is trivial. Geras could certainly have gone to town on such discussions.

However, on the substantive point that Rorty is actually implicitly making use of a concept of human nature, Geras is quite right. He reinforces his criticisms by following up Rorty's comments about Jean-Paul Sartre. Rorty agrees with Sartre that there is no human nature because 'there is nothing else but that which he makes of himself… man is as free to choose new descriptions … for … himself'.

Geras then quotes a series of writers who identify free activity as a central part human nature (Geras 1995, pp. 68–69). Thus, we now have a desire to avoid pain and humiliation and free activity as features of human nature. Freedom to remake yourself is certainly not a feature of trees or lumps of iron. Perhaps at this point Geras could also have made reference to his Marxist background, and said something about limits to individual freedom based partly on our nature as animals, and our level of technology. For example, in our society women can decide not to give birth to children, which was much more difficult before the development of reliable means of contraception and safe methods of abortion. However, with current technology men cannot decide to personally give birth. Obviously also the freedom that Sartre espouses in his *Being and Nothingness* (Sartre 2003) is individual freedom, and other people are mainly seen as restrictions on individual freedom. But other people can also enhance our freedom, making it possible to choose to get married, fly from Britain to South America and so on. And the individual freedom of plutocrats is much greater than that of the average cleaner or factory worker, so that space tourism might well be available to the plutocrat but is highly unlikely to be an option for ordinary people.

What about the problem of extending sympathy beyond our culture?

Rorty talks about manipulating our feelings, as happened to white Americans who read *Uncle Tom's Cabin* and other works of literature that extend our sympathies to and make us think about groups of people we might not have previously thought much about, or novels that make us realize that we might, as individuals, be doing things which upset other people (Rorty 1989, pp. 63, 88–89, 147).

In trying to extend people's sympathies it is common to appeal to human goods or lack of them 'to pain, hunger, illness or disease, to mockery and insult, to assault upon the integrity, of the body, or the mind, or the beliefs', and this is generally found more persuasive than referring to certain poets or saying 'we just do' (Geras 1995, p. 95; cf. Rorty 1989, location 149). This is an appeal to human nature.

A clinching argument is the issue Rorty himself raises of dehumanizing people as part of the process of legitimizing their subjection to inhuman treatment—saying, for example, that Muslims are not real human beings. If you have to dehumanize somebody in order to mistreat them, this is acknowledging that humanity is a powerful moral argument (Geras 1995, p. 97; Rorty 1994, p. 111).

Rorty acknowledges that a human-rights culture is a welcome fact of our world and is morally superior to other cultures. This appears to be a change of heart, but in his Amnesty lecture he chose the one that we have been cataloguing thus far (Geras 1995, p. 100; cf. Rorty 1999, p. 87).

Rorty certainly opens himself to the kind of criticism Geras makes elsewhere when he discusses the issues of the suffering of oppressed people, that is, that he presumes are things that need to be studied. Amongst other things, he says:

> As I said earlier, pain is nonlinguistic: It is what we human beings have that ties us to the nonlanguage-using beasts. So victims of cruelty, people who are suffering, do not have much in the way of a language. That is why there is no such things as the 'voice of the oppressed' or the 'language of the victims.' The language the victims once used is not working anymore, and they are suffering too much to put new words together. So the job of putting their situation into language is going to have to be done for them by somebody else. (Rorty 1989, p. 94)

He is making the point here that the people who put the situation of oppressed people into language tend in our society to be novelists and poets. However, his claim that people who are oppressed are unable to speak for themselves is open to debate. Rorty seems to be almost wilfully referring to Paolo Freire's *The Pedagogy of the Oppressed* (Freire 1996). In the book Freire is opposing a banking conception of knowledge in which an outsider tells oppressed people what they should be thinking and doing. Instead, he advocates that the outsider should take the language and thoughts of oppressed people and re-present it to them in a more coherent or theorized form. So, what Freire, who worked with oppressed people, is saying is that they are able to give an account of their situation, but one that is capable of improvement. Or consider the claim made by Lenin and Kautsky that working people on their own could only attain trade union consciousness, meaning that they would demand a fair day's work for a fair day's pay, whereas Marxist science demonstrates the necessity of ending the wages system. Whatever one might think about this claim, Lenin and Kautsky would certainly share with their critics the idea that working people on their own can attain trade union consciousness. As I am writing this, a major topic of public debate in Britain is the horrific fire that spread rapidly through the Grenfell Tower block in London on 15 June 2017, killing some 80 people. The survivors and the relatives of those who died have been able to give a very good account of a whole series of failings by the local council ultimately responsible for the building. They have certainly received all sorts of support from a variety of other people, but do not particularly seem to need poets and novelists. Finally, to offer a much more extreme example, some six weeks after Abraham Lincoln's declaration of the ending slavery on 1 January 1863, slaves in Brazil were singing about how Abraham Lincoln was coming to set them free (which, unfortunately, he wasn't). Just on the face of it one would expect female slaves to be particularly oppressed, and hence particularly silenced, but actually women slaves in Cuba and Brazil, two societies where slavery ended late, were able to articulate legal claims that their owners had abused them in various ways and that they should therefore be freed (see Cowling 2013).

The point of the previous paragraph is not to deny that there is a role for novelists who write about oppressed people; it is that oppressed people are perfectly capable of articulating their situation whatever Rorty may say on the basis of—in this instance—limited reading and thought, thus reinforcing Geras's claim that Rorty is prone to make generalizations either on the basis of his own intuitions or the basis of limited reading.

We now come to the fourth and final chapter of Geras's book, which is arguably the most potent part. It concerns his assertion that if truth is 'internalised to particular discourses or language games or social practices, there is no injustice'.

This is the most fundamental challenge to Rorty's philosophical enterprise. Rorty describes himself as a pragmatist, and an anti-foundationalist. By this he means, briefly, that he rejects the traditional philosophical enterprise of epistemology or the philosophy of science in which philosophy investigates the foundations of knowledge. This involves a conception of nature that is out there, and which we gradually get to know better. Rorty wants to replace this with the notion of a conversation between discourses that is driven more by what is useful than by a conception of truth. As Terry Eagleton tartly points out, this approach to truth as a question of usefulness rather than correspondence to reality would be particularly useful to Stalinists. In this context he pretty clearly means the tendency in the Soviet Union under Stalin for the truth to be crudely bent in whatever way suited the regime (Eagleton 1996, p. 13).

Geras suggests that non-linguistic awareness comes before linguistic awareness and remains after the development of language. He thinks that his instant recognition of his cat and his cat's instant recognition of him do not involve language.

Geras makes a claim, which I would endorse, that language reaches beyond itself—conversations are typically about other people or other things (Geras 1995, p. 117, cf. Eagleton,). Geras also points out that other forms of awareness such as sexual pleasure, pain, performative knowledge such as how to ride a bicycle or knowing that a voice is a voice—all these things can be put into language, but are initially experienced directly (Geras 1995, p. 115).

There is a problem about Rorty and relativism. He frequently insisted that he was not a relativist, and certainly held that some beliefs were better than others. However, he also insists that competing language games or opposed intellectual worlds are incompatible (Geras 1995, p. 121).

For Rorty the way to argue for one belief rather than another is to make the other belief look bad. Another form of argument, which he emphasizes, is that one belief helps us cope better than another, but what counts as coping is not at all self-evident (Geras 1995, pp. 122–123).

Rorty adheres to a coherence theory of truth, but this basically seems to be regarded as self-evident within his work. He regards logical arguments as devices to get people to change their practices without admitting that they have done so (Geras 1995, pp. 125–126).

Geras was a political philosopher of some stature, but did not display very much interest in epistemology. Because of this, his critique of Rorty in this area is weaker than it might be. To reinforce Geras's arguments above, and to explore the basic weaknesses of Rorty's pragmatism, we need to consider his book, *Philosophy and the Mirror of Nature* (Rorty 1980), which was popular amongst sociologists because it eroded the distinction between the hard natural sciences and soft and unreliable social sciences, much in the manner of Thomas Kuhn's *The Structure of Scientific Revolutions* (Kuhn 1962).

Some of the sort of criticisms to which Rorty is open in this area can be found in the book by James Tartaglia (2007), which is an extended philosophical critique of *Philosophy and the Mirror of Nature*. Much of Tartaglia's book summarizes work by a range of other philosophers. Thus, although his book was published after Geras's critique of Rorty, many of the criticisms it includes or refers to were available to Geras. Here are some of the main points made by Tartaglia.

Rorty has a series of philosophical heroes, including Heidegger, Wittgenstein and Dewey. Tartaglia comments that there are literally scores of articles by specialists who write on these philosophers but who would dispute Rorty's interpretations. Rorty makes use of work by Quine and, as we have seen, Kuhn, but both of these disowned the use he made of them (Tartaglia 2007, p. 22).

As we saw above, fundamentally in *Philosophy and the Mirror of Nature*, Rorty is challenging the conception of knowledge as reflecting nature, and proposing the idea of looking at a variety of ways of understanding. One of the ways in which he challenges this traditional view is to question the role of vision in epistemological theorizing. Vision has been the dominant way of getting to know about things since the time of Plato. We could just as well make rubbing up against something, crushing it underfoot or having sexual intercourse with it as the dominant way of knowing (Rorty 1980, p. 39; Tartaglia 2007, p. 58). Tartaglia points out that there are a series of ways in which Rorty can be challenged on this. Psychologists accept vision as the dominant sense. It is a good guide to a variety of features of a thing, such as colour, texture, size, position, and offers useful clues to whether it is slippery, climbable, hot and so on. Our sense of smell is much more limited. A variety of practical difficulties suggest themselves when it comes to thinking about sexual intercourse as a way of getting to know things! Vision links naturally to geometry, which was seen by the Greeks as the dominant way of getting reliable knowledge, and it is typical of Western philosophy to link the study of epistemology to what is regarded as the best science of the day. For Plato geometry was an important route to knowledge of the forms, which were unchanging. However, we can certainly watch as things change. Rorty thus rushes to judgement on this issue in an arbitrary way, motivated by his desire to undermine the idea of the mirror of nature (Tartaglia 2007, pp. 58–59).

Tartaglia follows Rorty through a long and complicated discussion of the philosophy of mind, and in particular of eliminative materialism, an approach that attempts to reduce the mind to brain states, and which was particularly associated with Australian philosophers such as Armstrong (see: https://en.wikipedia.org/wiki/David_Malet_Armstrong). However, a large number of objections to eliminative materialism are possible, as indeed they are to any other position on the relationship between mind and brain (see, for example, https://en.wikipedia.org/wiki/Eliminative_materialism). Thus, although there is a great deal of lengthy philosophical discussion in Rorty's book about hypothetical Antipodeans who use terms about the stimulation of particular neural fibres instead of about a sensation such as pain, it is open to doubt how seriously it should all taken. Is he just trying to establish his credentials as a widely read philosopher who can discuss analytical philosophy with the best of his colleagues, when really what he is interested in doing is questioning the validity of the philosophical enterprise as a whole? Indeed, just at the point where Rorty appears to be about to acknowledge that he is an eliminative materialist, he actually says that he holds no particular position on the mind–body problem. The best view of it is boredom (see Rorty 1980, p. 127; Tartaglia 2007, pp. 72–73, 97).

Despite this, Rorty seems to be committed to physicalism, the thesis that everything in the world is ultimately physical. Physicalism is the successor to materialism, which is best understood as a form of philosophical monism, which holds that matter is the fundamental substance in nature, and that all things, including mental things and consciousness, are results of material interactions. Physicalism is the successor to materialism in a world populated by increasing numbers of subatomic particles. Physicists are currently worried about their belief that they can't find 96% of the universe, one-quarter of which is dark matter and the remainder of the missing part comprises dark energy. Materialism where we have good evidence for only 4% of matter is rather embarrassing, so a commitment to the best current scientific evidence about matter seems the wisest course.

Although Rorty says that he is a physicalist, as Tartaglia points out, Rorty's physicalism is of a very limited and unenthusiastic sort. Its basis is pragmatism, which takes usefulness as the criterion of truth and falsity: 'Archangels are on a par with tables for Rorty, simply because they are both things we talk about'—the key question is what we like to talk about (Tartaglia 2007, p. 92).

Thus, for Rorty, physics is a persistent story that we tell rather than the paradigmatic science. Rorty is committed to the view that philosophy as we understand it was invented in the seventeenth century, notably by Descartes, but was then developed by others, in particular by Kant. Tartaglia is very sceptical about the claim that the ancient Greeks would not have understood the sort of issues raised by Descartes. Unlike non-Western traditions, much ancient Greek culture and thought was central to the culture of seventeenth-century Europe (Tartaglia 2007, pp. 98–99, 102).

Tartaglia's conclusion to Rorty's discussion of the mind–body problem is that it is a dismal failure:

> Moreover, even with the complete carte blanche of science-fiction, it does seem that Rorty has proved unable to imagine people who are just like us except for their lack of a mind–body problem. Maybe this just goes to show that you cannot 'escape from history'; maybe it just shows that Rorty is wrong about the mind. (Tartaglia 2007, p. 99)

The area that has been under discussion so far in this summary of some criticisms of Rorty (1980) is of interest to philosophers specializing in the philosophy of mind. A good recent book on this is Kim (2010). Although it goes back to the philosophical origins of the issues raised by the philosophy of mind, the real strength of the book is a very wide-ranging account of the issues in the area and of the contributions made to it by numerous contemporary philosophers. The impact that Rorty made in this area, despite the above-mentioned popularity of Rorty (1980) amongst sociologists, is that there is no discussion whatsoever of Rorty anywhere in the book, although there is extensive discussion of both the issues and the authors he concerns himself with.

Reverting to the summary of Tartaglia's critique of Rorty, he next guides the reader through Rorty's discussion of Sellars and Quine. In dealing with both philosophers Rorty is attempting to undermine the tradition established at least since the Enlightenment of making a sharp distinction between analytic statements such as those of logic and mathematics, or definitions such as 'a bachelor is an unmarried man' and synthetic statements that need to be based upon observation, be they about grass being green or the qualities of subatomic particles. Quine's argument is that it might be possible for the meaning of 'bachelor' to shift in such a way that the above definition becomes eroded. If we accept this, then rather than have a sharp distinction between analytic and synthetic statements we would have a distinction between statements central to our knowledge and those that are more peripheral, meaning that we are more willing to give up the peripheral statements. Rorty wants to take this much further than Quine, and simply to distinguish between views that are more or less useful. Thus for Rorty modern science is not a more accurate representation of the world than mediaeval science, it is simply more useful for us (Tartaglia 2007, p. 160). If I tell somebody to turn right at the end of my road to get to the nearest hospital, I am simply misdirecting them. When they get to the end of my road they will see a sign telling them to turn left for the hospital, which is indeed the way to get there. In common parlance my instruction to turn right is just plain wrong. I am pretty sure that somebody telling NASA that they should be using Ptolemaic astronomy to guide their next interplanetary probe would be told exactly the same, and for the same reasons. In virtually any everyday context, Rorty's theories in this area would be seen as just plain wrong.

We now come to the use that Rorty makes of Kuhn (1962). Stated very baldly, the argument of Kuhn's book is that scientific theories are not replaced by others because the first theory is falsified, as Popper (see, as a starting point, Popper 2002) would argue. The sort of evidence that Popper would regard as decisive is seen by Kuhn as merely a small part of a process involving such things as older scientists retiring or dying, fashion and so forth. As mentioned above, whatever may be said about the natural sciences, the process that Kuhn is describing appears to fit the bill rather well when thinking about sociology.

The above mention of astronomy leads the discussion on to Tartaglia's summary of an assault on Rorty and others like him by Paul Boghossian, *Fear of Knowledge: Against Relativism and Constructivism* (Boghossian 2007). The first point of contention concerns a debate that took place when Galileo was summoned to the Vatican to defend his views. Ranged against him was Cardinal Bellarmine, a sophisticated defender of Ptolemaic astronomy. Bellarmine's contention was that Ptolemaic astronomy is consistent with the Bible, whereas Galileo's was not. Galileo relied upon telescopic observation, for example he observed the four moons of Jupiter, and contended that visual evidence is good evidence, and that therefore the interpretation of Scripture should be less literal. Of this Rorty says that they were simply working within different frameworks, one based on scripture and one on observation. Boghossian's argument is:

> Rorty's view is 'incoherent': he wants us to reject all claims of absolute justification, and yet in order to think of our beliefs as even relatively justified requires us to accept the claims to absolute justification constitutive of our epistemic system. (Tartaglia 2007, pp. 191–192)

Tartaglia considers that Rorty can avoid this argument by emphasizing his pragmatism: it is a question of what is useful, and usefulness is charged within a particular framework. Nonetheless, the arguments offered above about finding the hospital or the work of NASA do suggest that Rorty would be leading a very difficult life if he confined himself to a mediaeval set of beliefs. And if Rorty happened to be transported back to the Middle Ages, wouldn't he still find that a simple misdirection, as in the hospital example, would be seen as just plain wrong in the same way as today?

Another argument of Boghossian's, which I find persuasive, is that 'we have a stock of ordinary and fundamental epistemic principles, rooted in observation, induction, and deduction, to which it is very difficult to imagine any genuine alternative' (Tartaglia 2007, p. 193). The point about this is that somebody who is committed to an account of astronomy based on the Bible still reads the Bible using his eyes rather than just using his intuition; assumes that his copy of the Bible will not change every few minutes, thus accepting the uniformity of nature, and deduces the validity of Ptolemaic astronomy from the Bible (Boghossian 2007, p. 193). This is a powerful criticism of the view that people such as Bellarmine and Galileo have such radically incompatible outlooks that there is no way of choosing between them. In fact there is a degree of overlap, and this is surely part of the reason why people manage to persuade others that one point of view is better than another. Tartaglia regards Boghossian's criticism as valid, adding the comment that another paradox that Rorty fails to deal with satisfactorily is that he is wanting to both take a stand against philosophy and also to argue against an objective account of truth, which, of course, is a philosophical position (Tartaglia 2007, p. 195).

This brief summary of some main points from Tartaglia is itself, of course, a summary of much more extensive work from a variety of sources. At this point I want to add some comments of my own based on the latter part of Rorty (1980).

In identifying knowledge and human ends, and in the latter part of *Philosophy and the Mirror of Nature* a search for knowledge with personal development, based on some affinities between Rorty's position and the ideas of Gadaemer Rorty seems to me to underplay the role of intellectual curiosity.

I can't think of any use whatsoever for knowing the origins of the universe, or whether there are parallel universes, but these seem to be very interesting questions that have probably been going in one form or another since people developed.

Curiosity about beliefs also tends to arise as something additional to more practical concerns. Here are three examples:

Suicide bombers get 72 virgins on arriving in Paradise, unless there is a problem of interpretation and they actually get 72 grapes. But doesn't this story immediately make you want to know more? What happens if there is a rush of suicide bombers? Do the virgins ever temporarily run out? Might some suicide bombers be happier with respectable widows of men who had become apostates, and who had had some practice? Why do women suicide bombers only get to be in charge of the virgins?

If you are a mediaeval Christian and believe in angels, what size is an angel? How many of them could dance on the head of a pin?

What about a therapist who deals with paedophiles? She knows some techniques that appear to reduce offending, and practices them. But she is surely likely to wonder why some adults become attracted to children sexually whilst others don't.

The Notes and Queries section of *The Guardian* is full of such questions, and very many of them have no potential use whatsoever.

There are thus plenty of reasons for believing there are significant problems with the more strictly philosophical positions that are in the background of *Contingency, Irony and Solidarity*.

Having indicated that Rorty's pragmatism is open to a wide range of objections, we can move back to the part of Geras's critique that deals with the effect of Rorty's denial of an objective sense of truth when it comes to questions of oppression.

People who were in concentration camps want justice, and even if they know they are going to die they want somebody else to be able to tell what happened. They therefore need a statement of what happened to be believed as truth. Obviously a camp guard, for example, might have a different version of the truth. If there is 'no way things really are' how are we to choose between the two accounts (Geras 1995, pp. 127–133)?

In some places Rorty is happy to talk about 'facts about economic oppression or class struggle', and indeed cites a lot of 'obvious' facts of the sort that a social democratic American would be concerned about. Are these, asks Geras, merely 'facts' within a given vocabulary or language game (Geras 1995, pp. 134–135)?

The other possibility, Geras suggests, is that Rorty actually takes his anti-realist ideas back. He is certainly keen to emphasize that he is not an idealist—but how does he know the world is out there?

Perhaps he would be unable to cope with the overwhelming paradox and absurdity that would follow upon losing the world behind one's beliefs. He is perilously close to saying that because we must talk in words, we can only talk about words (Geras 1995, pp. 137–139).

Overall, then, Geras's critique of Rorty is well thought through and well argued. For obvious reasons he fails to go into the issues linked to Rorty (1980) to the extent that would ideally be desirable, but if this is done Geras's position is merely reinforced.

References

Boghossian, P. (2007). *Fear of Knowledge: Against Relativism and Constructivism.* New York: Oxford University Press.

Cowling, C. (2013). *Conceiving Freedom: Women of Color, Gender, and the Abolition of Slavery in Havana and Rio de Janeiro.* Chapel Hill, NC: University of North Carolina Press.

Doyle, L., & Gough, I. (1991). *A Theory of Human Need.* Houndmills: Palgrave Macmillan.

Eagleton, T. (1996). *The Illusions of Postmodernism.* Oxford: Blackwell Publishing.

Freire, P. (1996). *The Pedagogy of the Oppressed* (2nd ed.). Harmondsworth: Penguin.

Geras, N. (1995). *Solidarity in the Conversation of Humankind: The Ungroundable of Liberalism of Richard Rorty.* London: Verso.

Kim, J. (2010). *The Philosophy of Mind* (3rd ed.). Boulder, CO: Westview Press.

Kuhn, T. (1962). *The Structure of Scientific Revolutions.* Chicago: University of Chicago Press.

Moore, G. E. (1903). *Principia Ethica.* Retrieved from http://fair-use.org/g-e-moore/principia-ethica/.

Popper, K. (2002). *The Structure of Scientific Revolutions* (2nd ed.). London: Routledge.

Rorty, R. (1980). *Philosophy and the Mirror of Nature.* Oxford: Blackwell.

Rorty, R. (1989). *Contingency, Irony and Solidarity.* New York: Cambridge University Press.

Rorty, R. (1994). Human Rights, Rationality and Sentimentality. In S. Shute & S. Hurley (Eds.), *On Human Rights: The Oxford Amnesty Lectures 1993* (pp. 111–134). New York: Basic Books.

Rorty, R. (1999). *Philosophy and Social Hope.* London: Penguin.

Sartre, J. P. (2003). *Being and Nothingness* (2nd ed.). London: Routledge.

Stevenson, C. L. (1944). *Ethics and Language.* New Haven, CT: Yale University Press.

Tartaglia, J. (2007). *Routledge Philosophy Guidebook to Rorty and the Mirror of Nature.* London: Routledge.

CHAPTER 10

The Enlightenment and Modernity

The Enlightenment and Modernity is the title of an edited collection based on a series of seminars at Manchester University (Geras and Wokler 2000). In the nature of such a collection most of the contributions are by other people. However, given that Geras was one of the editors of the collection, and that it is a brilliant book, some further details are appropriate.

The book as a whole is an excellent corrective against the over-simplified view of the Enlightenment that has become popular thanks to the influence of Foucault and postmodernism. The particular context in which I have encountered this argument is as a lecturer in criminology. Criminology students are required to study a certain amount of criminological theory as part of their degrees. Criminological theory is mainly devoted to explaining why people commit crime. In order to do this it looks at a range of theories taken from other disciplines, and asks how they contribute to the explanation of crime. Obviously most criminologists do not wish to devote the bulk of their time to the analysis of theories—they wish to move on to studying crime in one way or another. They have generally not undertaken an extensive study of either political philosophy or the Enlightenment.

They therefore tend to read Foucault's *Discipline and Punish*, (Foucault 1991), and accept an account on the following lines. Punishment under the Ancien Regime involved the state demonstrating its power on the body of the subject. Foucault takes the example of Damiens the regicide, who attempted to assassinate Louis XV in 1757. His horrific execution,

M. Cowling, *Norman Geras's Political Thought from Marxism to Human Rights*, https://doi.org/10.1007/978-3-319-74048-5_10

described in Chap. 9, was much discussed across Europe, and was one of the influences on the penal reformer Cesare Beccaria, whose book, *On Crimes and Punishments* (Beccaria 1764), was widely influential across Europe. He cites the execution as part of his case against the use of torture and the death penalty. He was very much an Enlightenment figure.

In the nineteenth century, in contrast, there was what at first sight was a more humane and civilized way of dealing with criminals. Foucault gives a description of the very detailed schedule for the day of prisoners that was being prescribed. He identifies this with a shift in the regime of truth and way in which the subject is disciplined. He sees the very detailed day laid down for the prisoners as part of the development of the panopticon, originally the design of prison proposed by Jeremy Bentham in which a guard in a central tower can watch all the prisoners, and each prisoner never knows whether or not he is being watched.

The panopticon is, for Foucault, a metaphor for a wider society. The members of the society are disciplined and observed in schools, military institutions, factories and other places. The disciplines of medicine, criminology and psychology contribute to the process of disciplining and surveillance. These disciplines are part of a different regime of truth.

Thus, rather than seeing the development of a more humane prison regime as one beneficial outcome of the spread of Enlightenment ideas, Foucault sees it as part of a different regime of power, backed up by a different regime of truth.

Linked to this, the ideas of the Enlightenment tend to be condemned. They are seen as Eurocentric, failing to take into account non-European ways of living and of understanding the world. They are condemned because they led on to the mass slaughter of the world wars and the Holocaust, which are seen as the outcome of science. They are falsely universalizing, whereas forms of truth are more localized, and there is no grand narrative of truth. Enlightenment ideas were seen as compatible with subordination of women and with slavery.

This gloomy picture of the Enlightenment, which combines Foucault and postmodernism, is a very popular picture with criminologists, and I suspect with social scientists generally. The edited volume from Geras and Wokler serves as a magnificent corrective to this. Geras's own contribution is either identical, or virtually identical, to his discussion of Miliband, which is dealt with in the third section of Chap. 11. Given that the other chapters of this edited collection are written by an assortment of people who are not responding particularly to Geras, it is not appropriate to discuss their contributions in any detail. Some indication of themes is perhaps helpful.

Ursula Vogel demonstrates that thinkers during the Enlightenment were, contrary to a frequent criticism, aware of, and able to think about human diversity.

Geraint Parry discusses the Enlightenment's excitement at the idea of the possibilities afforded by education, and contests Foucault's idea that for the Enlightenment education was basically a form of discipline.

Andrea Baumeister demonstrates that Alastair MacIntyre has a simplistic view of Kant's approach to morality as just concerned with obedience to rules. Ian Carter continues the critique of MacIntyre. His claim is that the conception of the good in MacIntyre and the Enlightenment notion of human perfectibility, which includes ideas about liberty and equality, are closer together than MacIntyre would have us believe. Ian Holliday looks at the relationship between the English Conservative tradition stemming from Burke and Enlightenment rationalism. He argues that most of the features of society that held life together in Burke's day now no longer function. The justifications used by English Conservatives today are rationalistic ones.

Maurizio Passerin d'Entrèves takes as his starting point a late essay by Foucault in which he takes a more positive view of the Enlightenment than the one for which he is best known, in which it inaugurates a new regime based on detailed surveillance and discipline. He takes a more positive view of Kant's justification of the French revolution. d'Entrèves reminds us that Foucault had a Nietzschean dimension, which made him more willing to celebrate dramatic change than would be thought from US interpreters, for whom he is basically a conservative figure.

In the final chapter Vittorio Bufacchi emphasizes the diversity of Enlightenment thought by considering the differing approaches of Hobbes and Kant to the idea of a social contract, demonstrating that this has echoes down to our own day, with David Gauthier continuing on Hobbesian lines in contrast to Rawls, whose use of the social contract is closer to Kant.

Overall this very well thought out and scholarly collection demonstrates the diversity and continuing interest of Enlightenment thought, and is an excellent corrective to contemporary over-simplification based on postmodernism and an uncritical assimilation of Foucault.

References

Beccaria, C. (1764). *An Essay on Crimes and Punishments*. Available in Numerous Editions and Several Internet Locations, Including https://en.wikisource.org/wiki/An_Essay_on_Crimes_and_Punishments.

Foucault, M. (1991). *Discipline and Punish*. Harmondsworth: Penguin.

Geras, N., & Wokler, R. (2000). *The Enlightenment and Modernity*. Houndmills: Macmillan.

CHAPTER 11

The Contract of Mutual Indifference

The Contract

Geras was at his very best when combining detailed analysis of an issue with Marxist analysis in his earlier writing, or political philosophy in his later writing. His work on the Holocaust is a striking and, particularly in *The Contract of Mutual Indifference* (Geras 1998), frequently terribly poignant and thought-provoking example of this. Chapter 9 includes his demolition of Rorty on the question of the motivation of people who rescued Jews. Geras, it will be recalled, pointed out, using a great deal of detailed evidence, that rescuers were virtually invariably motivated by common humanity or decency rather than prior acquaintance all because of belonging to, for example, the same trade union. Here, however we have a much longer and more detailed analysis of the horrors of the Holocaust and, particularly, the question of the duties of bystanders.

The book's main theme is best introduced by a wonderfully Gerasian quotation that was used for the cover blurb:

> The idea which I shall present here came to me more or less out of the blue. I was on a train some five years ago, on my way to spend a day at Headingley, and I was reading a book about the death camp Sobibor. Headingley, for those who may not know this, is a cricket ground in Leeds. At Sobibor between May 1942 and October 1943, the Germans killed a quarter of a million people. The particular, not very appropriate, conjunction involved

M. Cowling, *Norman Geras's Political Thought from Marxism to Human Rights*, https://doi.org/10.1007/978-3-319-74048-5_11

> for me in this train journey ... had the effect of fixing my thoughts on one of the more dreadful features of human coexistence, when in the shape of a simple five-word phrase the idea occurred to me. (Geras 1998, p. 1)

The basic idea of the contract of mutual indifference, which will be elaborated, is that human beings manage to be unconcerned about the terrible suffering of other people. The best way to make sense of this is to say that there is a tacit contract between human beings to the effect that they will ignore each other's suffering.

The initial part of the book concerns the indifference of bystanders to the Holocaust. Geras talks of a woman watching the first great deportation of Jews from the Warsaw ghetto who carries on watering flowers. Elsewhere just outside the ghetto wall, children were laughing and playing on a roundabout, and passers-by smiled at them, though shooting could be heard on the other side of the wall. The Jews throughout the Third Reich felt abandoned. Their neighbours and friends no longer talked to them; many people were indifferent, or yelled insults, or spat or mocked. Many of the inhabitants of Warsaw went up to their rooftops to watch the entertainment when the Germans bombarded and burnt the ghetto (Geras 1998, pp. 3–8).

Geras continues to consider this theme of the Jews feeling abandoned, and quotes Ian Kershaw: 'the road to Auschwitz was built by hate, but paved with indifference', noting the same thesis in Zygmunt Bauman's book, *Modernity and the Holocaust*, but with the addition of the idea that modern industrialized society increases the distance between people to the extent that moral responsibility and moral inhibitions are attenuated (Geras 1998, p. 18).

This introduction to Geras's book certainly shakes the reader up. Might we behave like that? Geras was obviously in some sense including himself: he was going off to watch cricket for the day in a world where other people are suffering torture, human-rights abuses generally and the gross deprivation of the necessities of human life such as food, clothing, shelter, medical care, education.

Thinking of myself as an ordinary German during the 1930s and 1940s, I might have joined street demonstrations organized by the SPD or KPD. It would not have bothered me that the leaderships of both organizations included Jews. I like to think that, following the rise of Hitler I would have continued to shop in Jewish shops, talk to Jewish neighbours and give up my tram seat to elderly Jews. Even public kindness to Jews continued to occur in the early war years (Finkelstein and Birn 2014, location 562). Before Hitler's accession to power Germans carried on this way in spite of Nazi discouragement (Finkelstein and Birn 2014, location 389). Once the Nazi regime was properly installed, and particularly with the Nuremberg laws of 1935, which made association with Jews a reason for prosecution, and made people who were friendly to Jews liable to be arrested by the Gestapo, such contacts generally ended (sees Finkelstein and Birn 2014, location 456). At that stage, my natural cowardice and fears for my family would probably have led me to fall in line. The extent to which Germans resisted the regime in one way or another, and also the degree of fear inspired by the Gestapo, can be seen from the statistic that, between 1933 and 1945 some 3 million Germans ended up at one point or another in prison or concentration camps on political grounds (Gill 2014, location 351). In 1935 some 715 pastors of the Confessing Church were arrested in Prussia alone on the eve of a planned denunciation of Nazi ideology (Gill 2014, location 888). In November 1935 there were mass trials of Social Democrats and Communists (Gill 2014, location 1179). Nevertheless, on the eve of the Holocaust, Germans were less inclined to support incitement to racist violence than people living at that time in the Southern USA (Finkelstein and Birn 2014, location 543). Very near the end of the war there were horrific death marches to move Jews from one concentration camp to another. During these, ordinary Germans tended to offer food to the Jews, but the guards frequently forbade this (Finkelstein and Birn 2014, location 923).

In the previous paragraph there is a mixture of statements about the conduct of ordinary Germans and about how I think I might have behaved myself. The overall picture is a less pessimistic one than is found in the opening pages of Geras's book: ordinary people behave fairly decently unless intimidated by a totalitarian state. The degree of intimidation was very considerable indeed. The question then would be how do totalitarian states come to be set up, or alternatively, how do particular totalitarian states come to be set up? This leads on to the thought that Geras is taking a particularly pessimistic view of human nature in order to set up a puzzle in political philosophy. Perhaps spending several years studying the Holocaust, as opposed, for example, to studying how London has become an increasingly multicultural and generally tolerant place to live over recent years, pushes one direction of a pessimistic view as implied by the contract of mutual indifference. On the other hand, there was every reason for Jews in general to feel abandoned both in Germany and in most of the territory conquered by the Nazis.

Geras moves on to something that is certainly a legitimate question. He quotes not only Ian Kershaw but also Edmund Burke and Martin Niemoller to the effect that the precondition of evil is indifference and inaction (Geras 1998, pp. 18–21). He then quotes some appeal leaflets from Amnesty International describing with illustrations dreadful events during ethnic cleansing in Bosnia, followed up with sickening descriptions of torture (Geras 1998, pp. 21–22). He obviously finds it difficult to actually read this material. My wife had a similar reaction, saying that she was very happy to donate money to Amnesty International provided they did not send her any leaflets! Significantly, Amnesty then go on to point out that Western firms supply all sorts of torture equipment, making millions in profit. Geras then comments that Amnesty in Britain has a membership of about 100,000, and worldwide a membership of about a million, while there are at least 60 and perhaps as many as 100 of the world's governments that employ torture. Given that members of Amnesty International do not have to do anything more than donating money and helping to put pressure on oppressive governments, without risk to themselves, this is not very impressive. He then mentions a series of genocides—East Timor, Cambodia, Bosnia, Rwanda—noting that each time everyone says 'Never again'. And finally the fact that one-fifth of the world's population lives in extreme poverty. Overall this places almost all of us in the position of the indifferent bystanders to the Holocaust (Geras 1998, pp. 23–24).

Geras then proceeds to give a more exact exposition of the contract of mutual indifference. He says that it does not rely on a supposed state of nature, or an 'original position' as found in Rawls (Rawls 1999). The core idea is this:

> If you do not come to the aid of others who are under grave assault, in acute change or crying need, you cannot reasonably expect others to come to your aid in similar emergency; you cannot consider them to be obligated to you. Other people, equally, unmoved by the emergencies of others, cannot reasonably expect to be helped in deep trouble themselves, or consider others obligated to help them. (Geras 1998, p. 28)

He indicates that this is a reluctant proposal. He knows that the contract is an exaggerated model of our world. However, it is too close to the way that extremely large numbers of people behave to be disregarded. Of course, there can be no expectation that anyone can solve a huge problem of the sort involved, but people can certainly do something, which will encourage others. People cannot be expected to devote their lives to those in crying need, but how about 10% of their free time and disposable income (Geras 1998, pp. 28–33)?

He next considers some reasons why his model might be considered an illegitimate over-simplification. Families and communities take care of each other. However, Jews and Bosnian Muslims took care of each other, but this was not enough to protect them from genocidal assault, so the protection from the community can be completely overwhelmed. A second response is that states and governments often provide aid and care. Geras responds, very appropriately, that they are often the source of the problem. Some very extensive examples, involving Iraq, the USA and Britain in a context where I am criticizing Geras on other grounds, will be found in the Chap. 12. A third issue is that of ignorance, but this really does not stand up in a world of global 24-hour news. When it comes to the extent to which Germans knew about the Holocaust, Geras quotes David Bankier's comment that they knew enough 'to know that it was better not to know more'. This is from a footnote. In the text Geras says 'prefer not to know any more'. Geras's version is certainly appropriate for the television viewer who switches from news about genocide in South Sudan to Graham Norton, but Germans had the Gestapo to worry about—was it actually dangerous to know too much (Geras 1998, p. 35, including f. 64)? It was certainly dangerous to try to do anything to resist it. The fourth criticism is that people can conceive concern and mutual aid only on a small scale, to which Geras basically responds that they could easily try a bit harder (Geras 1998, pp. 33–36).

Is there any escape from this gloomy situation? Could we say that people have a right to expect aid in dire emergency, and a corresponding duty to provide it? He goes on to say that this right and duty could be derived from an elaborated moral theory or from religious faith, but Geras is more interested in the point that one could hardly assert that it would not be consistent to invoke a right to assistance in dire emergency without accepting a duty to help people suffering such an emergency (Geras 1998, pp. 37–39).

There are also some criticisms of over-simplification that Geras regards as legitimate. There are certainly people who devote anything down from total to at least substantial efforts on behalf of others in distress, including the heroic people who saved Jews from the Nazis (see Chap. 9). Also, the idea of an obligation to assist others in distress is abstract. There are obviously people so close to being in distress themselves that it would be unreasonable to expect to do anything much for others. (I cannot recall the exact details, but a few years ago there was a scheme in which communities in Canada were providing help to extremely poor people in part of Africa. After some time, Canada was affected by heavy rains and experienced some flooding, and a modest bundle of blankets arrived from Africa.) The question obviously arises as to how well off a person needs to be in order to encourage substantial obligation to assist others. Are psychological and ideological influences to be taken into account? (In that case, the New Right theories that have been so influential since the 1980s would leave wealthy people with hardly any obligations to assist). Indeed, Geras probably did not want to get tangled up in a whole set of claims about New Right theories, but they come perilously close to the contract of mutual indifference—recall Mrs Thatcher's famous 'there is no such thing as society, only individuals and their families' (Geras 1998, pp. 41–43, Thatcher 1987).

Escaping the Contract of Mutual Indifference: The Duty to Bring Aid

Assuming that Geras has made a good case for a duty to bring aid, what would be involved? He starts by considering the question of guilt. Geras quotes Primo Levi talking first of a feeling of shame that came from witnessing appalling horrors, for example being made to watch a hanging at Auschwitz. Germans under Hitler, says Levi, deluded themselves that not seeing was a way of not knowing, and not knowing relieved them of guilt. There is a question here as to how much Levi knew about the knowledge the average German had of the Holocaust. This obviously raises a significant problem of historical research. My impression is that the disappearance of Jews from German towns would have been evident, but that exactly what had happened to them was less clear. There were not, for example, triumphant radio and newspaper announcements of that month's achievements in the death camps. Assuming that you did know about what was going on, at least to the limited extent of watching Jews being taken way, there is then the question of what you could do about it. Essentially the choice was to try to save individual Jews by sheltering them, or to engage in underground resistance to Hitler. Either of these carried grave personal risk, essentially of death.

The point Geras is largely driving at is the one mentioned above about a feeling of shame, which he also finds in the writings of Karl Jaspers. He notes a corresponding feeling of great satisfaction in people who helped to keep Jews safe (Geras 1998, pp. 50–57). Both of these are, in different ways, evidence of a sense of responsibility for other people:

> Only by way of such a moral culture, one that would be at least *very much* informed by the sense of a generalised obligation for the security and well-being of others, can we escape the darkness of the conclusion of the contract of mutual indifference. (Geras 1998, p. 57)

What could underpin such a moral culture? Geras argues that the values of liberalism underpin the contract of mutual indifference. The basic liberal approach in this area is of an obligation not to harm others, but actively helping them is up to individuals. Moreover, liberalism basically links to capitalism, in which the wealth of some is achieved through the hardship of others (Geras 1998, pp. 58–59). Socialism is certainly one possible way of placing care for others at the centre of society's values. A less fleshed out conception that would underpin caring for others can be found in Kant (Geras 1998, pp. 60–62).

Geras next wonders, in trying to be more specific about a duty to bring aid, quite how demanding it is. He spends some time considering the extreme situation of people in concentration camps. Prisoners had to prioritize themselves and, if they were there, their families. But beyond that there was a widely recognized obligation not to steal from other prisoners in ways that would seriously harm them; and also to save them if at all possible. So even in that extreme situation, it can be argued that there was a limited duty to bring aid. But what of the obligations of people with a reasonable amount of leisure and resources? Geras argues that, in the current situation, where much more help is needed than is available, their obligations are very substantial. However, in a society where the duty was much more widely recognized, the demands on individuals would be less (Geras 1998, pp. 64–73).

How do we get to such a society? Geras comments that the problem of the agents of change is hardly new, but the sort of society required would have to be one with 'robust democratic political institutions and the egalitarian economic and social relations that would be apt to those more caring dispositions' (Geras 1998, pp. 74–75). He continues by stating that it is unlikely that the interests of those involved would solve matters on their own, thus, obviously, rejecting the idea that the victory of the proletariat would solve everything. But he also insists that a political dimension is essential (Geras 1998, pp. 76–77). Geras is thus leaving all but these bare outlines of how to get from a relatively abstract duty to bring aid and the notion that a democratic socialist society would be a better framework in which to implement it as effectively his conclusion. In other words, he is obviously interested in the question of moving from a capitalist to a socialist society, but is leaving any details for consideration elsewhere.

The issues that Geras is considering in his discussion of the contract of mutual indifference and the duty to bring aid are some of the most fundamental moral issues for someone living in our society that I can imagine, alongside any issues where there is a serious danger of the destruction of humanity, such as an immediate risk of nuclear warfare, or global warming beyond a certain level. Obviously, other issues will be paramount for particular people in particular situations—consider a woman thinking about whether to have an abortion, or a police detective wondering about falsifying evidence to convict someone he is convinced is guilty of a serious offence—'noble cause corruption'. But for most people in our society most of time the duty to bring aid is fundamental. So Geras has plainly identified something really important.

That said, quite a variety of issues warrant further discussion. I have raised them in a series of bullet points:

- Is it worth making a distinction between 'acts of God' and iniquities perpetrated by people? Thus, every so often, many people in Bangladesh need help because there has been a storm and they have lost what little they have in a flood. In the long term, issues to do with climate change need to be considered, which raise all kinds of questions to do with the impact of human activity on the environment. However, just at this minute, the people in question have obvious immediate needs for rescue, shelter, clean water, food, replacement for lost possessions and so on. It would be callous in the extreme to explain to Bangladeshi flood victims that we are doing everything we can to alleviate global warming, which completes our responsibilities to them. Just for now we have to behave as if the Bangladeshi floods were acts of God. At the other extreme, Jews in Germany and Poland had no major problems apart from those suffered by other citizens before the coming of the Nazis. All they needed was to be left to get on with their lives.

- In the exposition of the contract of mutual indifference found above, I ask whether it is abstract because ordinary people in their daily lives generally behaved better to Jews than the ostracism Geras emphasizes. Much of the cause of the ostracism was the fear of the Gestapo. Thus behaving decently in everyday life, together with voting for parties other than the Nazis, went a long way towards mitigating the supposed contract of mutual indifference.
- The duty to bring aid is also rather abstract. One idea of giving aid is by donating money to charities. Does one have at least some level of obligation to check that charities are behaving appropriately? For example, Save the Children was dogged by allegations that the salaries at the top of the organization were excessive. When there are much-publicized incidents such as the devastating bomb in Manchester on 22 May 2017, an assortment of people set up charity giving sites to benefit those affected, and sometimes the sites are fraudulent. This is emphatically not intended to discourage charitable donations, merely to suggest that there is some obligation to check.
- Is there any merit to discriminating between charities? For example, there could be an argument that Amnesty International, if successful in reining back the activities of oppressive governments, can on occasion save the need to help refugees or victims of torture. Is the work of Oxfam both wider in application and somehow more important than that of the Dogs Trust or The Donkey Sanctuary? What about long- and short-term aid?
- Geras does not generally talk in terms of British political parties, but supporters of Jeremy Corbyn and Momentum would argue that a Labour victory in the next election would bring immense benefits to a whole variety of people in need in Britain. It would also lead Britain to more ethical behaviour overseas, although in the light of the discussion in Chap. 11, where I argue that by supporting the invasion of Iraq in 2003 Geras was effectively supporting British and US imperialism, Geras might well have got into arguments with Corbyn supporters over this. Is there any merit to the views of a Corbyn supporter who says that he is going to devote all his spare time, energy and resources to Momentum, on strategic grounds?

My comments are not intended to demonstrate that there is something wrong with the idea of the contract of mutual indifference, or that of a duty to bring aid, merely that both of these are very substantial and wide-ranging ideas, and it is not surprising that problems of this sort, and doubtless many others should be raised.

Finally in this section, two observations should be made, both of which are rather different from the list above. First of all, so far as I can see, the Holocaust victims Geras discusses are all Jewish. This is perfectly appropriate in the sense that the standard estimate of numbers of victims gives 6 million Jews plus 5 million more miscellaneous other victims, and that on the whole the other victims, except gypsies, were 'merely' terribly overworked, maltreated, starved and so on, but were mainly not there pending complete destruction in the final solution. And there is a massive literature, and one person can only do so much. However, the sheer variety of other victims offers more parallels with our own society. Very many of the victims were *Untermenschen*, sub-human people such as Poles, Rumanians, Russians and so forth, who could be exploited for the benefit of the master race. This has parallels with the treatment of immigrants in many European societies—as people who can be expected to tolerate overwork and bad conditions that would be unacceptable to workers who belong to the indigenous population. And when it comes to undocumented migrants, conditions are frequently worse, to the extent that their treatment is often described as modern slavery. People who are not racist and who may well be generally progressive, nonetheless buy fruit and vegetables and poultry products and ready meals without worrying particularly about the conditions in which they are produced.

One group of people on which some of the techniques of the Holocaust were pioneered was the disabled. There are arguably some parallels with modern debates about whether it is better to abort foetuses when it seems likely that there will be a degree of disability, in which some disabled people feel that those favouring abortion in circumstances are uncomfortably close in this respect of those of Nazi eugenicists. Another group to be found in the camps were homosexuals. Britain was a pioneer in the development of the European Convention on Human Rights, and generally had a reasonably good domestic record on human rights, but male homosexual practices were completely illegal up to 1967. Driving a genius and war hero such as Alan Turing to suicide took Britain uncomfortably close to Nazi attitudes. Political opponents of the regime ended up in camps in Nazi Germany, but were simply hounded from their work by anti-Communist legislation and practices in the USA. Gypsies were also swept up in the final solution, and relations between indigenous populations and Roma people remain fraught. Arguably some version of the contract of mutual indifference has enabled most people to live in societies where there are at least some of these various forms of victimization without unduly troubling themselves. Later in this chapter there is a discussion of a book chapter in which Geras discusses whether or not the Holocaust was unique, which bears some relation to the above comments.

The other miscellaneous observation is that there is an argument that Holocaust studies really took off from the 1970s onwards. While it is perfectly legitimate for anybody to study anything at any time, and the Holocaust was an event of such huge importance and massive scope that there is every reason for there to be a multiplicity of theories, case studies, general histories, oral histories from survivors, and so forth, comments have been made about the timing. It is from the 1970s onwards that the state of Israel really moved from being a plucky survivor of massive Arab attacks to being an occupying power in the West Bank and Gaza, suffering accusations of the illegal building of settlements and oppressive treatment of Palestinians. One way of countering such accusations is to emphasize Jewish suffering during the Holocaust, using this as an explanation for the overwhelming need for the state of Israel, perhaps along with accusing critics of being anti-Semitic and, ideally, Holocaust deniers. Geras was emphatically not using his work for purposes of this sort. On the other hand, given a frequent view that the Israeli state originated in the ethnic cleansing of the Palestinians, Geras's attitude to the state of Israel becomes at least a matter of interest, and this issue will be considered at the end of this chapter.

Geras wrote a further four essays on the area of the discussion in this chapter. Three of them are at the end of Geras (1998), and one in a further edited volume. One of the essays in the book concerns Richard Rorty, and adds little to Geras's earlier critique of him, put together with things to do with the contract of mutual indifference. The other three essays in one way or another concern the issue of the uniqueness, or otherwise, of the Holocaust. Of course, this question in turn relates to the question of explaining the Holocaust.

Socialist Hope in the Shadow of Catastrophe

This essay takes as its starting point part of a book by Ralph Miliband (Miliband 1994). In the book Miliband is reflecting on the viability of a socialist project in the light of the collapse of the Soviet Union, and of a variety of other problems, one of which is very much related to Geras's theme. This is the human capacity for massive cruelty, conflict and blood-letting (Geras 1998, p. 83). Basing himself on suggestions from Miliband, and on fairly obvious reflections, Geras ends up with four possible ideas about human nature, namely that it is intrinsically: (a) evil; (b) good; (c) blank; (d) mixed. He says that the first two alternatives do not mean that human beings are exclusively evil or good, just predominately so (Geras 1998, p. 87). He next relates his fourfold classification to the question of the possibility of socialism. Plainly socialism is incompatible with the idea that human nature is intrinsically evil. On the other hand, neither should there be a simplistic assumption that human nature is intrinsically good, and that this will shine forth in the right circumstances. The struggle for socialism must be premised upon assumption (d) above. Geras reinforces this point with several references to the writings of Holocaust survivors; and he also refers to the way in which the Holocaust in particular shook any Enlightenment faith in a teleology of human progress (Geras 1998, pp. 88–92). It should be obvious by this point in the book why Geras completely rejects assumption (c). He gives a lengthy and persuasive set of arguments against the idea that human nature is a blank in Geras (1983), which is discussed in Chap. 6. There is a further discussion of the same issue but in a different context in Chap. 2 of Geras (1995), discussed in Chap. 9 above.

One way of dismissing the experience of the Holocaust would be to say that it is wrong to judge humanity in general on the basis of an individual and extreme episode. Geras regards this as facile. The Holocaust was facilitated by bystanders who did nothing much to stop it, for the variety of reasons already considered in the above discussion of the contract of mutual indifference. The people who actually carried out the Holocaust were generally ordinary and not psychopaths; they could soothe their consciences by remembering that they were one little cog in a big wheel, so that what they did individually made very little difference. Behaviour amongst the victims also varied very considerably, with some seeking to better their lot by collaborating with the guards, and others behaving almost like saints (Geras 1998, pp. 95–101).

The point of the above is that, in considering the prospects for socialism, the Holocaust was in large part carried out, and suffered, by people with a normal range of human emotions and dispositions. Anger and hatred, greed, love, but also overbearing attachment, moral cowardice, disgust and destructiveness, submissiveness, dominance and cruelty and so on can be regarded as features of human nature that are common to a whole range of societies across widely differing historical periods. The idea that under socialism all of these would simply go away is entirely unrealistic (Geras 1998, pp. 104–105).

Miliband thinks that the potential for human beings doing evil things should be very much diminished under socialism. Geras points out that, by saying this, he is acknowledging that the potential for evil does still exist under socialism. Miliband asserts that episodes of mass slaughter do not come from ordinary people but from those at the top. Geras, as we might by now expect, responds that ordinary people can be enthusiastic participants in slaughter, and cheer it on. Moreover, those at the top are generally ordinary people. In other words, the intrinsic nature of human beings includes this evil potential. Socialism, we usually assume, greatly expands human freedom, which must include the possibility of doing evil. He quotes a series of Holocaust survivors who reluctantly learned that there is no limit to human cruelty (Geras 1998, pp. 106–113). We have to think about the struggle for socialism as part, not of uninterrupted, uni-linear progress, but of an 'open process' in which it will be necessary to try to prevent new tyrannies emerging, renewed inequalities, and possibility of the re-emergence of serious evils (Geras 1998, p. 115). The realm of freedom under socialism actually needs to be restricted by the observance of the 'rule of law—of secure, enforceable individual rights, independent judicial processes, the means of redressing injustice, the means of defending the polity and the community against attack' (Geras 1998, p. 118).

I very much concur with Geras's critique of Miliband, which is also an effective critique of Marxist theory from Marx himself onwards. The assumption he is attacking is also found in Lenin's *The State and Revolution* and is that socialism will simply involve the harmonious following of 'copybook maxims' about relations between people (Lenin 1917). Geras could, in fact, have taken his examples from dreadful abuses of human rights that have occurred in communist societies. Consider, for example, the treatment of the kulaks under collectivization, or that of millions of innocent Soviet citizens in the Great Terror of the late 1930s. Or again, the suffering caused in China by the Cultural Revolution, the ten years or so following the eviction of the Americans from Vietnam, in which conditions led to people crowding into boats in an attempt to get to somewhere capitalist. Obviously, all this could be said to be caused by the societies not being genuine communist societies, but it is remarkable that the major attempts at bringing about communism by revolution all produced major abuses. Something else that is implied in Geras's commitment to the continuance of essentially liberal human rights, except for those over property, is that it leaves little scope for revolutionary socialism. In societies with a functioning bourgeois democracy, such as those of Western Europe, the USA, increasing parts of Latin America, India and the white Commonwealth countries, Geras's implied commitment is to some form of evolutionary socialism as recommended by Eduard Bernstein.

Marxists Before the Holocaust

Much the same theme emerges from Geras's critique of Mandel in the final chapter of the book. Geras starts with a quotation from Trotsky. Writing a few weeks after Kristallnacht Trotsky said that the 'next development of world reaction' signifies the physical extermination of the Jews (Geras 1998, p. 138). This, he says, was remarkably prescient. He then goes on to consider Ernest Mandel's views about the Holocaust after the event. Geras lays out a set of alternatives: the Holocaust was comparable to other crimes/singular or unique; can be explained rationally/is beyond understanding; is the product of imperialism/due to other factors. Geras states that his own view is it is not possible to make an adequate assessment by simply accepting one side of each alternative; both sides need to be taken into account. This is very much the set of themes that we will find him exploring in the next section of this chapter. Mandel's starting position is to accept the first half of each alternative (Geras 1998, p. 143). Demonstrating the prescience and power of a Trotskyist analysis, Mandel forecasts that if there is not a proletarian revolution in the USA over the next decade, American Jews will suffer something worse than the Holocaust because of better US technology. Geras says that Mandel never really overcame the weakness of the initial analysis above (Geras 1998, p. 144).

On a much later occasion Mandel explains the Holocaust in terms of racism, encouraged by colonialism, plus capitalist modernity. Mandel compares the Holocaust to such horrors of capitalism as the slave trade, the conquistadors' slaughter of American Indians, Japanese atrocities in Manchuria and the atomic bombing of Japan. Geras is politer than this, but he basically shares my own reaction that this is just getting silly. Just to take the slave trade, the whole point of the slave trade was to get the slaves to the Caribbean, Latin America and the USA. Whilst the treatment of the slaves was atrocious, they could be thought of in the same terms as a piece of machinery or a beast of burden: a sensible owner tries to preserve such things in working condition. The slave trade precisely wasn't about extermination. It would not be difficult to go down the rest of Mandel's list and make similar comments. The Holocaust, says Geras, needs a much more specific explanation. He notes that Mandel subsequently added additional factors in his account of the Holocaust, but the same problem ultimately remains.

After reiterating the unique features of the Holocaust Geras returns to Trotsky and his account of the pogroms in Russia. Trotsky, he says, had seen into the depths of possible human behaviour. The same was very much evident at times during the Holocaust, for example, when German reserve policemen came to treat shooting Jews as a sport. Mandel did recognize this feature of humanity in an essay he wrote in 1980 where he talked of impulses towards tribalism and destructiveness. Yet the flaws basically persist despite this insight (Geras 1998, pp. 116–170). Mingled with these criticisms is much legitimate admiration of Mandel's Marxist scholarship. However, as with Miliband, Geras is identifying basic flaws in a straightforward Marxist attempt to explain the Holocaust.

The essay on Mandel has some limitations that Geras should have at least indicated. To start with, Mandel would be vulnerable to the same set of criticisms that Geras makes when writing about Miliband. That, in turn, would lead on to the same insistence on the necessity for human rights under socialism, with its implied commitment to evolutionary socialism for much of the capitalist world. The other curiosity is that Geras does not seem to have moved on, at least on the evidence of this essay, from the early adherence to Trotsky and Trotskyism, which was criticized in Chap. 3 above. By this stage in his intellectual career there were some big implications about the role of revolution that were discussed at the end of the section on Miliband. Moreover, some of the wild comparisons and predictions of which Mandel was guilty raise serious questions about the validity of the general Trotskyist framework as a way of understanding society.

Was the Holocaust Unique?

It is obvious that Marxists such as Mandel are missing the specific characteristics of the Holocaust by simply attributing it to capitalism and imperialism. On the other hand, others writing about the Holocaust want to stress that it was unique, emphasizing its scale and the sheer horror that it evokes. Something of this dilemma is bound to affect anybody thinking about the Holocaust.

It will be recalled that Geras remarks that there is remarkably little written by political philosophers about the Holocaust. This is remedied to some extent in an excellent collection of articles about philosophy and the Holocaust (Garrard and Scarre 2017). Geras's contribution is a well-considered article that gives good arguments for regarding the Holocaust as unique, but in so doing allowing comparisons to be made with other events of mass slaughter (Geras 2003—this indicates the original date of publication; the text used was in the new, 2017 edition. References will thus take the form: Geras 2003/2017).

Geras starts by considering some claims about uniqueness. Was the Holocaust unique because it involved the mechanized slaughter of a whole people? Another common claim is that it was unique because there is nothing else so horrific, requiring such an extreme moral judgement (Geras 2003/2017, pp. 25–26). A well-known alternative was proposed by Ernst Nolte, who gestures towards uniqueness but then compares what happened under the Third Reich with US intervention in Vietnam, the exodus of the Vietnamese boat people, and, particularly, the liquidation of the kulaks under Stalin. This was hotly debated by other historians including Ian Kershaw and Richard Evans, and philosophers such as Hannah Arendt and Jürgen Habermas, among others, who emphasized that the Holocaust was a singular enormity. Certainly the plight of the Vietnamese boat people, awful though it was, seems slight in comparison. However, another argument is that the uniqueness claim downgrades, for example, the organized slaughter of a million Armenians by the Turks to the status of a second-class genocide. Or what asks David Stannard, about the slaughter of the indigenous peoples of the Americas, comparable in terms of numbers? Finkelstein argues that the Holocaust should open our hearts to the suffering of others, and worries that the uniqueness claim is prone to be linked to the idea of the Jews as the chosen people, and thence to acting as an alibi for the state of Israel. Finally in this part of Geras's exposition he discusses Novick, who regards the uniqueness claim as intellectually empty, a claim that relates to context. Thus it is important for Germans to respect the uniqueness claim so as to accept their nation's historical responsibility (Geras 2003/2017, pp. 26–29).

Geras starts the next section by saying that eventually one might dismiss this whole discussion as tedious. However, he says, this would be premature. For example, even if some of those arguing for uniqueness have an agenda of defending the Israeli state's brutal occupation, most of them cannot remotely be accused of this. Some Israeli historians, who would seem likely candidates for the claim that they are using their assertion of uniqueness as a defence of the Israeli state, reached the conclusion of uniqueness at the end of lengthy empirical study. There is not, he goes on to say, any neat pattern that those advocating the uniqueness claim have in common. Having made this argument at some length, Geras performs the same exercise for those who argue that the Holocaust is not unique. His view is that, though there are some tendentious arguments such as the one by Nolte comparing the Vietnamese boat people to victims of the Holocaust, and assertions on both sides of the argument to the effect that those on the other side are missing something crucial, the majority of the argument on both sides is driven by a study of the facts and by analysis, not by trying to vindicate the Germans or the Israelis, for example (Geras 2003/2017, pp. 30–36).

Geras next, very helpfully, points out that those involved in assertions about the uniqueness of the Holocaust rarely define what they mean by unique. There is a trivial, uninteresting, sense in which any historical event is unique, down to you blowing your nose as you read this—nobody else blows their nose at precisely the same time and in precisely the same place. So the sensible question is: when somebody asserts that the Holocaust is or is not unique, what aspects of it do they think stand apart from, or resemble, other historical events (Geras 2003/2017, p. 36)? Plainly, he continues, there will be some respects in which any historical event is unique, whereas in other respects it is not. Why do we make the distinction, for example, between a chair and a stool? If the distinction is useful to us in daily life we will make it, otherwise not. Similarly, if we are making a study of wars, for some purposes it will be appropriate to distinguish between wars between states and civil wars, but for others not, without any suggestion that something is being swept under the carpet. The question about whether the Holocaust is unique should be treated as a question of classification in the same way, the question therefore arising as to whether a particular difference or similarity is of interest for a particular issue (Geras 2003/2017, pp. 36–38).

Geras then attempts to answer the substantive question. He starts by listing some basic facts and numbers about the Holocaust, about other victims of the Nazis, such as Russian prisoners of war or Roma, about the Armenian genocide, the Rwandan genocide, where 800,000 people were killed in a few weeks, the slave trade, the genocide of indigenous people in the Americas and so forth. He then considers four respects in which the Holocaust has been argued to be unique, constructing a composite account of each.

The first of these is totality of intent. The Holocaust is argued to be unique because the intention was to eliminate Jews from the face of the earth—every man, woman and child, simply on the basis of race. The second is the modernity of the event: the bureaucratic, industrialized, planned slaughter. Third is the aim of crushing out the humanity of the Jews, their dehumanization, the unnecessary suffering inflicted on them. Fourth is the idea that the Holocaust was an end in itself. Many of the other events that Geras lists had a rationale beyond eliminating a people: the acquisition of territory, making a profit and so forth. In contrast, the Holocaust sent potential slave labourers to gas chambers. German railways and personnel were clogged up with trains containing Jews, when they would have been better used for military purposes. The idea was to cleanse the world of a demonic evil.

Geras next considers arguments that have been used to question the above four criteria. Uniqueness of intent has been argued to have limitations because the Nazis failed to eliminate European Jews entirely, let alone world Jewry. Certainly much of the Holocaust was carried out by industrialized methods, but, particularly in Eastern Europe and Russia, the killing was carried out by much more traditional methods. What, one may ask, is the point of asserting modernity? Arguably modern methods were used in Germany because Germany was a modern society. But perhaps the modernity of the method is beside the point, which is to do with, for example, motivation. The third putatively unique aspect of the Holocaust was the dehumanization of the Jews. But perhaps the intention, mainly, was to make life easier for the guards. Again it can be questioned whether, just because the Holocaust was an end in itself, did this make much difference to its victims?

In trying to make sense of the above Geras starts by stating that the interest in the question about the uniqueness of the Holocaust is a normative one. It is not just to do with a simple issue of classification, it is an assertion in some way of the enormity of the event, and this idea can be found smuggled in even with writers who assert that this is not their intention when they claim the Holocaust was unique. It would be possible to have a separate classification for the Rwandan genocide, the Armenian genocide and so forth. Each has unique features, which is what we would expect of historical phenomena. The question is whether there is anything about the Holocaust that makes it a morally unique event.

Geras then notes that a number of writers talk about the degree of suffering inflicted, but comments that it is both difficult and invidious to compare, for example, the long-term horrors of the Atlantic slave trade with the relatively brief annihilation of the Jews. Competitive victimhood is morally ugly. Geras's own proposal is based on Wittgenstein's idea of a family resemblance between concepts, so that for example there is no one single feature that characterizes all games, but each game has something in common with another, so that they constitute a conceptual family. The same idea is true of genocidal events—they have a variety of differences of the kind we have been discussing briefly above, but also family resemblances. Geras then suggests that the four criteria proposed above each have features in common with other events, but taken together constitute the uniqueness of the Holocaust. It is this cluster of features that constitute the moral horror of the Holocaust (Geras 2003/2017, pp. 40–51).

The essay discussed in this section is Geras at his best. He displays a wide- ranging knowledge of his subject and of possible appropriate comparisons. He then engages in a thorough classification and analysis of the theories he is dealing with. His conclusion is both plausible and an excellent attempt at capturing the horror of the Holocaust. It also makes sense of a claim that the Holocaust was unique, but at the same time had common features with other historical events. It might be well worth applying the same set of methods and distinctions to other historical events. What about a comparison, for example, between slavery as traditionally practised in Africa, North American slavery, Brazilian slavery, slavery in the British Caribbean and Cuban slavery? It would be interesting to see whether other historians have experienced similar problems to do with uniqueness and similarity, and the ways in which they have dealt with them.

Feet of Clay? Geras and the Palestinians

One of the striking images that Geras uses to introduce the idea of the contract of mutual indifference is of Warsaw residents going up to the rooftops to watch the clearing of the Warsaw ghetto (Geras 1998, p. 8). The television news showed an image that carried echoes of this. During the Israeli assault on Gaza in 2014, groups of Israelis settled down with a nice picnic to watch the smoke and dust rising from Gaza as it was pounded by Israeli artillery and targeted by rockets fired from jets. Of course, we do not know what either group was thinking, but the parallel is close: both look to be instances of the contract of mutual difference. This is reinforced when one finds at least some Israelis, including leading politicians, describing the Palestinians as 'vermin', 'cockroaches' and so on (see Fisk 2014, pp. 588, 597, and, with a lot of variations, 624).

Geras did not write extensively about the issue of Israel. However, he was supportive of Israel as a democracy and as a state that broadly supported human rights, in contrast to its neighbours almost all of whom engaged in significant human rights abuses, and were not functioning democracies. He also advocated a two-state solution to the problem of Israel and the Palestinians, and was critical of illegal settlements in the West Bank and Israeli excesses in Gaza. So, there is a mixed picture here, but it would not be difficult to construct a picture of Geras defending a state that acquired much of its land through ethnic cleansing, which defies numerous UN resolutions, and which deals with Palestinians shamefully in a whole variety of ways, including not just the two major issues above, but also by using rockets to target senior Hamas leaders, thus killing anybody near them, by blowing up houses on flimsy grounds, by shooting stone throwers and by treating Palestinians taken into custody very badly.

Rather than finding a way out of the contract of mutual indifference, we would appear to have Geras colluding in a version of it. Ideally this issue needs to be approached with the thoroughness that Geras exhibited at his best. There is, as one might expect, an extremely extensive literature on the issues involved. To go into it thoroughly would require something longer than this book, but it is worth spending some time on the crucial issue of the founding of the Israeli state and the departure of the Palestinians. To what extent was this a matter of ethnic cleansing, as the Palestinian description of the event as the Nakba, or disaster, implies?

The full background would involve, at least, a discussion of role of Jews as minority populations in many parts of Europe and the Middle East, the growth of nationalism over the nineteenth century, which tended to trigger off an increased emphasis on the differences between Jews and the majority population. This, in turn, led to the growth of Zionism, and encouraged the settling of Jews in Palestine. Following the Second World War, the full revelations of the horrors of the Holocaust led to increased support for the Jews in Palestine. It also led, of course, to increased practical problems as the impoverished and traumatized survivors of the Holocaust frequently wanted to settle in Palestine, even though the British, who were in charge of the Palestine Protectorate, tried to limit the numbers of Jewish settlers. Even if they did not aspire to go to Palestine themselves, Jews elsewhere naturally became increasingly persuaded by the Zionist argument that Jews needed a safe bolthole and their own state to stand up for them.

In a tense situation in the years following the end of the Second World War, the Jews were generally keen for the British to leave Palestine, and a minority, including some future leaders of the Israeli state, engaged in terrorism, notably the blowing up of British officers in the King David Hotel. The Palestinians rejected UN proposals for the partition of Palestine, the British essentially decided to give up and go home. At that point the Jews under the leadership of Ben Gurion declared the existence of the state of Israel on 14 May 1948. Israel was invaded by the armies of no less than five Arab states, who denied the right of Israel to exist. The assault on the Jews was assisted by at least some of the Palestinians, and more particularly by Arab fighters from outside who based themselves in Palestinian villages. One aspect of this was that some three-quarters of a million Palestinians left their homes in Israel—as it now was—and ended up as refugees in Gaza, on the West Bank of the Jordan, in the Lebanon and in Syria. There they, or their descendants, have largely remained as refugees ever since. The above is intended as a relatively neutral introduction to the really controversial matters following.

Many people on the left today appear to take as a starting point the views of the Israeli historian Ilan Pappe, which are also accepted by Noam Chomsky (see Pappe 2011; Chomsky and Pappe 2010). They see the expulsion of the Palestinians as the implementation of Plan D:

> 10 March 1948, a group of eleven men, veteran Zionist leaders together with young military Jewish officers, put the final touches to a plan for the ethnic cleansing of Palestine. That same evening, military orders were dispatched to the units on the ground to prepare for the systematic expulsion of the Palestinians from vast areas of the country. The orders came with a detailed description of the methods to be employed to forcibly evict the people: large-scale intimidation; laying siege to and bombarding villages and population centres; setting fire to homes, properties and goods; expulsion; demolition; and, finally, planting mines among the rubble to prevent any of the expelled inhabitants from returning. Each unit was issued with its own list of villages and neighbourhoods as the targets of this master plan. Codenamed Plan D (Dalet in Hebrew), this was the fourth and final version [of a series of plans]. (Pappe 2011, locations 202–208)

For Pappe, the declaration of the state of Israel on 24 May 1948, was merely one day in an episode of ethnic cleansing, which had started five months earlier. After a few weeks of ethnic cleansing, the neighbouring Arab states dispatched a small army—small compared to their overall military strength—to try to halt the ethnic cleansing (Pappe 2011, location 289). In the years leading up to the conflict, says Pappe, the Jews built up a network of informers and very detailed information about who had conducted operations against them. When the Jews arrived in an Arab village, they would bring with them an informer whose head was covered by a sack with slits for eyeholes. The men of the village would be lined up and those pointed out by the informer most likely shot (Pappe 2011, location 729). The larger town of Haifa, with its 75,000 Palestinians, was subjected to a savage assault from the Irgun and the Haganah (the former was a relatively undisciplined terrorist gang, the latter were Jewish irregulars who in due course became the core of the Israeli Defence Forces) (Pappe 2011, location 1433). Haifa's middle-class Palestinians left voluntarily; the rest of the Palestinian population left in a panic, particularly as they were intimidated by news of the massacre at Deir Yassin, and encouraged by Arab leaders to think that they could soon return to a Palestine purged of Jews.

Deir Yassin was the most spectacular example of a massacre. The Jews had encountered some opposition from the village, and responded by killing men, women and children (Pappe 2011, location 2063). The death toll was initially believed to be 254, and the horror was amplified by Arab broadcasts. Subsequent research suggests that the total was lower, somewhat over 100.

The cleansing of Jaffa went more smoothly. There were several further lesser massacres. By the time the conflict ended the majority of the Palestinians had been ethnically cleansed. Their villages were typically destroyed then looted. Large numbers of Arab males, mainly from age 10 to age 50, were held in prison camps.

There is much more along these lines in Pappe's book. Very many of the exiled Palestinians continue to live in slums in Jordan and Lebanon. Many Palestinians are crammed into 2% of Israel's land area on the Gaza Strip. Israeli Arabs do get representatives in the Knesset, but are subject to various restrictions. Through a variety of wars the Israelis have expanded the area under their control, and have substantially expanded the number of settlements, in defiance of UN resolutions. The Palestinians thus have substantial and serious grievances.

However, Pappe's book, and the use that Chomsky makes of it, are exaggerated in various respects. This has a very bad effect on the approach taken by many on the left to the state of Israel, meaning that they are starting from unrealistic and exaggerated assumptions about the origins of the state. I will now begin to sketch in some problems about Pappe's book. To start with, for people with such a detailed plan, the Israelis do not seem to have been very good at ethnic cleansing. Their massacres, while totally unacceptable, were really very small compared to those practised by other people engaged in ethnic cleansing, such as Serbs in Bosnia during the wars following the breakup of Yugoslavia. The state of Israel currently has a population of about 8.5 million, of whom about 1.7 million are Palestinian Israelis. Ending up with a fifth of your citizens being people who were supposed to have been ethnically cleansed is quite an oversight!

Another immediate point is that although Israel was decisively victorious over the five Arab armies, which invaded her territory in 1948, it was by no means an easy victory. Israel lost about 1% of the Jewish population in the course of the war, which lasted a few months. This compares with Britain losing just under 1% of her population over the five years of the Second World War, or Belgium, whose Jews were subject to the Holocaust, losing just over 1%. One often feels when watching the television that it would be nice to see something about Germany other than the Second World War, but some of the reason it has sunk into the British national psyche is that it was such a frightening time, when the population suffered real threats.

Another fact that is not generally very much remarked on is that, although 750,000 Palestinians became refugees, Israel took in 350,000 Jews from Arab countries where they were no longer welcome. There are no strident assertions of a right of return, nor are these Jews still living in refugee camps. Once the Arabs had not merely lost the 1948 war, but also one or two further wars, a sensible pragmatic response would have been to make peace with Israel, and then to devote as many resources as possible to making life better for displaced Palestinians. Given the massive military spending on both sides, the potential for peaceful development would have been very considerable. There is certainly the point that the Gaza Strip is now home to 1.85 million Palestinians, who occupy about 2% of the land of Israel, and is the third most densely populated polity in the world. That said, heavily populated areas can be vibrant and desirable places to live—consider capitals such as London or Tokyo. Also, whilst it is undoubtedly true that conditions in the Gaza Strip are extremely bad in several respects, bare percentages of territory in Israel need to be treated with caution—for example, the Negev desert is quite a large percentage of the territory of Israel, but much of it is precisely what it says.

Returning to the crucial issue of ethnic cleansing, there is a much more detailed and plausible account of why the Palestinians left Israel from another Israeli historian, Benny Morris (2004). He documents Ben-Gurion, who became the first Prime Minister of Israel, advocating the compulsory transfer of Arabs to relatively empty Arab lands in 1937 (Morris 2004, p. 40). As the war ended and the scale of the Holocaust became apparent, there was both a growing sympathy for the Zionist project, and an increased obviousness amongst Jews of the need for somewhere in the world where they could feel safe (Morris 2004, p. 45). By the time we get to the 1948 war, which was initiated by the Arab states, the idea of transfer was certainly in the air on the Zionist side, but the war was not entered into specifically with a view to engaging transfer (Morris 2004, p. 51). Indeed, as Nur Masalha (1992) shows, the idea of transfer had featured in the Zionist project more less since its inception, but generally the aim was for voluntary transfer, with the idea that land in neighbouring Arab states was cheaper than that in Israel, so that it would make sense for Arabs to sell their land and move. In 1947 the UN proposed the partition of Palestine. This was generally not acceptable to the Arabs, and the period December 1947 to March 1948 was characterized by sporadic attacks and rioting against the Jews by the Arabs, and the increasing flight of middle-class Arabs to neighbouring countries (Morris 2004, pp. 56, 58). The attacks, however, were largely confined to some urban centres, and, whilst Jewish leaders decided that the Haganah needed to engage in reprisals, there was a concern not to provoke Arabs in the countryside, who had generally been quiescent (Morris 2004, p. 71).

In a generally deteriorating situation, the influence of the Mufti of Jerusalem, Haj Amin al-Husseini, the main acknowledged leader on the Arab side in Palestine, was decidedly unhelpful (e.g. Morris 2004, p. 89). Husseini had played the principal role in fomenting the riots of 1936 to1939, which involved attacks on Jews, and which became known as the Arab Revolt, but which was put down by the British (Morse 2010, p. 43). He was interviewed in 1936 by the Peel Commission, and made it clear that his aspiration was for an Arab/Muslim Palestine, from which 400,000 Jews would be summarily evicted (Morse 2010, p. 44). He had spent the Second World War in Germany, where he had encouraged Adolf Hitler to pursue the final solution. He toured the death camps and encouraged pro-Nazi leaders in Eastern Europe to send their Jews to Poland, which meant sending them for extermination (Morse 2010, location 126, pp. 60–67). A letter in his handwriting was instrumental in getting 4500 Jews sent to Auschwitz, when there had been a chance of them getting sent to Israel (Morse 2010, p. 62). He was responsible for recruiting Muslims to the

Hanzar brigades, units of the SS who operated in the Balkans, implementing the final solution there (Morse 2010, p. 74). He was thus definitely anti-Semitic as opposed to simply anti-Zionist, and encouraged both Arab intransigence and generally hostile relations between Arabs and Jews. During the Second World War he made frequent broadcasts across the Arab world in favour of a Nazi victory (Morse 2010, p. 57).

As it became increasingly clear that the Arab states were going to invade Israel, Husseini and the Arab states advised that Palestinian women and children should leave to allow the men to concentrate on fighting, which actually had the effect of encouraging the general exodus (Morris 2004, p. 94). By March 1948 the town of Haifa set a pattern, which was to be widely repeated: Arab irregulars infiltrated the town, intimidating residents and carrying out attacks on the Jews, which led to much more effective Haganah reprisals, and in April to the panicky evacuation by sea of virtually all of Haifa's Arab population. The British, whose mandate was still in effect, were very surprised at the poor quality of the Arab leadership (Morris 2004, pp. 97–104, 185–190). The pernicious role of Arab irregulars was particularly seen in Nazareth at a later stage. The residents were delighted that the Jews got rid of them, and were happy to settle down under Jewish rule (Morris 2004, p. 410).

In the spring of 1948 the Haganah formulated the notorious Plan D. In Morris's judgement, this was not a plan for general expulsion of Arabs, but it implicitly called for expulsion where Arabs were engaging in hostilities, and particularly where they were threatening transport links. Indeed, Jewish leaders were very surprised at how rapidly the Arabs fled (Morris 2004, pp. 155–157). Part of the reason for the flight was an Arab assumption that refugees would be coming back after a few weeks, hopefully to a land cleared of Jews (Morris 2004, p. 164). Arab evacuations were much accelerated by the widely publicized massacre at Deir Yasin, and another at Nasir al Din, the former of which is described earlier (Morris 2004, p. 174). This massacre, and its frequent retelling in the Arab media, hardened the determination of the Arab states to invade once the British had left (Morris 2004, p. 230). At a later stage the Israelis engaged in further disgraceful conduct in the areas of Lydda, Dawayima and during operation Hiram (Morris 2004, pp. 423, 460, 472). They did, however a display various signs of conscience about these (Morris 2004, p. 481). Indeed, the Deir Yassin massacre was stopped by ultra-Orthodox Jews from a neighbouring village, and was condemned by the leadership of the Haganah, two rabbis who covered the area, which included the village, and the Jewish Agency, which sent a letter of apology to King Abdullah of Jordan. The clearing of villages in the countryside followed very much the same pattern as in Haifa, being initially precipitated by Arab attacks on the Jews, but then followed up with very rapid Arab flight when revenge attacks were mounted (Morris 2004, p. 223). Jewish willingness to engage in expulsion increased as the 15 May deadline for the British withdrawal approached, their concern being to clear potentially hostile villagers from their lines of communication and in places where they might obstruct operations against the invading armies (Morris 2004, p. 256).

The state of Israel was declared as the British left on 14 May 1948, and the Arab armies invaded forthwith. By the time of the truce in June 1948, a consensus was being reached in Israel that the land that Arabs had left should be permanently taken over for Jewish settlers (e.g. Morris 2004, p. 330). By autumn 1948 there was less fear of an Arab return, and the emphasis moved to preserving rather than destroying Arab houses so that they could be used for Jewish immigrants (Morris 2004, p. 348).

Some 750,000 Arabs had become refugees. In December 1948 the United Nations General Assembly passed one of the landmark resolutions on Israel, stating that the refugees had a right of return. However, according to Morris, there was a general international recognition that there was no way the resolution could be fully implemented: the Israelis would not permit the bulk of the refugees back; they would be returning to wrecked villages, or villages now occupied by Jewish immigrants; the Israelis had legitimate security concerns about a fifth column (Morris 2004, p. 540).

Morris concludes that the majority of the refugees left not because of direct Israeli coercion, but because of concern about what would happen as the Israelis conquered their area, and also with the idea that they would be able to return after a few months when the Arab armies had defeated Israel (Morris 2004, location 15955). The Israelis, he reminds readers, suffered 1 in every 100 of population killed and a further one injured, as a result of an onslaught by Palestinian Arabs and irregulars, followed by an invasion by Arab armies. From this perspective, denying any right of return was a reasonable response, particularly given the danger of the Arabs acting as a fifth column (Morris 2004, location 16108).

The point of this rather lengthy story is that the origins of the state of Israel do not lie with a straightforward act of ethnic cleansing, but with a failure on the part both the Palestinians and the neighbouring Arab states to acknowledge the right of the state of Israel to exist. Israel has been involved in a whole series of subsequent wars. In the 1956 Suez episode

Israel acted as a stalking horse for Britain and France. More significant are: the 1967 Six Day War between Israel and her main Arab neighbours, which was a disaster for the Arabs and led to the Israeli occupation of the West Bank, the Golan Heights, the Gaza Strip and Sinai; the limited War of Attrition, 1967–1970; and the Yom Kippur war of October 1973, none of which produced territorial gains for the Arab states. In all of these major episodes from 1967 onwards the Palestinians were used as a reason for attacking Israel. However, there were other major reasons including wounded pride, a continued denial of the right of the state of Israel to exist, and popular sentiment also fuelled by anti-Semitism, including the popularity in Arab countries of the notorious Protocols of the Elders of Zion, so that attacking Israel was a way for Arab dictators to court popularity at home. One would think that at the end of all this unsuccessful bloodshed the Arab states would conclude that the state of Israel was there to stay, and to devote their energies to be ameliorating the condition of the Palestinian refugees. However, in marked contrast to the way that the Israelis have taken in very large numbers of Jewish refugees, many of them in a parlous condition, including 600,000 Jews from Muslim Arab countries by 1972, relatively little has been done to resettle the Palestinians or to develop their economy.

Morris and Pappe belong to a group of revisionist historians, although they have to some extent parted company subsequently. The third eminent member of this group was Avi Shlaim, who wrote an immensely scholarly and detailed account of Israeli foreign policy (Shlaim 2014). He points out that, as well as the mainstream Zionist movement, there was also the New Zionist Organisation led by Jabotinsky, which developed into the Irgun, the most militant of the irregulars on the Zionist side. They were characterized by a belief that the biblical land of Israel, which included the West Bank, was properly part of the land of Israel. Settlers in the West Bank, of whom there are now about half a million, tend to have beliefs similar to his. The Israeli leadership generally has frequently had sympathies with this tendency, and therefore to place first priority on making sure that Israel can defend itself, second priority developing the Israeli economy, and only third priority on peace with the Arabs. They thus arguably bear at least some of the responsibility for the frequent wars in the area, and the fact that peace treaties have only been signed with Egypt and Jordan (Shlaim 2014, p. 11).

Palestinians have ended up in squalid conditions spread across Gaza, Lebanon and Syria. With the Syrian civil war, Palestinians living there have largely become refugees again. Some 400,000 Palestinians were living in the wealthy state of Kuwait, but were expelled either by the Iraqis, or by the returning Kuwaitis, during or after the Iraqi invasion. The best conditions are enjoyed by those in Jordan, who have largely been given Jordanian citizenship, with access to education and healthcare. Although 200,000 Palestinians live in the very wealthy Saudi Arabia, they are not entitled to Saudi citizenship.

The problem has grown somewhat from the 750,000 or so Palestinians displaced in 1948, and there are now almost 5,000,000 registered Palestinian refugees, all notionally with a right of return. Nonetheless, if the resources that go into military spending and corruption in the Middle East were at least partly devoted to the welfare of the Palestinians their plight would surely be much alleviated. It would also bear repeating the comment above: if the Israelis are aiming to inflict a Holocaust on the Palestinians, as some critics of the Israeli state allege, they are doing a really rotten job of it!

So does Geras have feet of clay? Given the criticism in the next chapter, 12, it is important to stress that, where Israel is concerned, his position is fully defensible. He asserts the right of the state of Israel to exist, and that it has a better human-rights record that that of most of its neighbouring states. The above analysis is quite compatible with both of these assertions. He is then critical of the building of illegal settlements in the West Bank, and of excessive retaliation meted out notionally because of Palestinian attacks, but at least partly motivated by electoral considerations. The Jews sitting watching the Palestinians of Gaza getting a pounding in 2014 may have been deriving entertainment from the misery of others, just the same as Poles watching the clearing of the Warsaw ghetto, but they were doing so in a situation where the ancestors of the Palestinians had to some extent brought their miseries on themselves, rather than having racist extermination forced upon them.

Geras and Anti-Semitism

The above comments also relate to some positions that Geras took about anti-Semitism and the unthinking anti-imperialism of much of the left, be they the Marxists of the Socialist Workers Party/Respect, or Guardian reading liberals. Geras is critical, to start with, of people who take the view that any intervention by the USA and Britain, be it in Kosovo, Afghanistan or Iraq, is to be opposed on principle because it is imperialist meddling.

He argues that just because the USA has engaged in actions that involved interventions that massively violated human rights, for example in Chile or Vietnam, it does not follow that every US intervention is automatically a violation of human rights.

Along with this he is concerned that the anti-imperialist left has a skewed set of values when it is a matter of supporting opponents of the USA, whilst overlooking massive human rights violations in, for example, Afghanistan, Iraq or China. For this reason he was entirely out of sympathy with the massive demonstrations against the invasion of Iraq, arguing that instead the demonstrators should have been supporting an invasion on human-rights grounds (see, for example, Cohen and Garrard 2017, pp. 124–129). This issue will be discussed at more length in Chap. 12.

A very similar set of issues applies to criticisms of Israel. Israel, Geras argued, had become an alibi for a new climate of anti-Semitism on the left. For example, Jews outside Israel are seen not as articulating a normal set of opinions and interests, but as a sinister Jewish lobby. He also raises the issue of anti-Semitic tropes. One example is Caryl Churchill, who ascribes to Israeli Jews genocidal attitudes to Palestinian children. This, Geras thinks, carries echoes of the blood libel. Another is Günter Grass, who implies that Israel has genocidal ambitions against Iran, although with no evidence. Both of these defend themselves on the grounds that they are not personally anti-Semitic—but that surely does not resolve the issue! Or again, consider the willingness of Western liberals and leftists to overlook the Hamas charter, which includes deductions from the validity of the Protocols of the Elders of Zion, and which celebrates, with Koranic excerpts, the killing of Jews. Why, says Geras, if Hamas do not really mean what is in their charter do they not alter it? Would people on the left to be similarly indulgent to overtly racist attitudes elsewhere (Cohen and Garrard 2017, pp. 134–139)?

There is much to be said for Geras's comments. However, this is a very fraught area, which has attracted a substantial literature (see, for example, Fine and Spencer 2017; Rich 2016; Roberts 2014; Ornstein 2017).

It seems to me that there are two polar positions that are definitely unacceptable. One of these is to assert that because of the dangers of a repeat of the Holocaust any kind of action by the Israeli state is acceptable. The other is to assert that because the Palestinians are oppressed, any beliefs, for example the Hamas Charter, and any actions, such as the suicide bombing of Israeli cafes, or the random firing of rockets into Israel, are acceptable and understandable. Finding a position somewhere between the two, which is definitely not anti-Semitic, is plainly a significant challenge. One thing that emerges from the literature is that anti-Semitism is rather different from other forms of racism. Many Jews in Britain and the USA have been very successful, so that, whereas racism is often directed at poor immigrants or refugees, in this instance the issue is more to do with Jewish worries about various outrages against Jews themselves, synagogues and shops. This arouses memories of the Holocaust. Although Jeremy Corbyn and the leadership of the Labour Party emphasize anti-racism, they actually fail to recognize the particular worries felt by Jews, which are enhanced by uncritical support for Hamas and Hezbollah.

There is plainly a very great deal more to be said in this area, but Geras's views are on the right lines.

References

Chomsky, N., & Pappe, I. (2010). *Gaza in Crisis: Reflections on Israel's War Against the Palestinians*. London: Hamish Hamilton/Penguin.

Cohen, B., & Garrard, E. (Eds.). (2017). *The Norman Geras Reader 'What's There is There'*. Manchester: Manchester University Press.

Fine, R., & Spencer, P. (2017). *Anti-Semitism and the Left: The Return of the Jewish Question*. Manchester: Manchester University Press.

Finkelstein, N., & Birn, R. B. (2014). *A Nation on Trial: The Goldhagen Thesis and Historical Truth* (Kindle ed.). New York: Metropolitan Books.

Fisk, R. (2014). *The Great War for Civilisation: The Conquest of the Middle East*. London: Fourth Estate, Harper Collins Publishers. (Kindle edition), (first published 2005).

Garrard, E., & Scarre, G. (2017). *Moral Philosophy and the Holocaust*. Oxford: Routledge. (the 2003 version was published by Ashgate).

Geras, N. (1983). *Marx and Human Nature: Refutation of a Legend*. London: Verso.

Geras, N. (1995). *Solidarity in the Conversation of Humankind: The Ungroundable of Liberalism of Richard Rorty*. London: Verso.

Geras, N. (1998). *The Contract of Mutual Indifference*. London: Verso.

Geras, N. (2003). In a Class of Its Own. In E. Garrard & G. Scarre (Eds.), *Moral Philosophy and the Holocaust*. Oxford: Routledge. 2017 (the 2003 version was published by Ashgate pp. 27–56).

Geras, N. (2003/2017). In a Class of Its Own. In E. Garrard & G. Scarre (Eds.), *Moral Philosophy and the Holocaust*. Oxford: Routledge, 2017 (the 2003 version was published by Ashgate pp. 27–56).

Gill, A. (2014). *An Honourable Defeat: A History of German Resistance to Hitler, 1933–45* (Kindle ed.). London: Endeavour Press.

Lenin, V. I. (1917). *The State and Revolution*. Chapter 5. Retrieved from https://www.marxists.org/archive/lenin/works/1917/staterev/ch05.htm.
Masalha, N. (1992). *Expulsion of the Palestinians: The Concept of 'Transfer' in Zionist Thought, 1882–1948*. Beirut: Institute for Palestine Studies.
Miliband, R. (1994). *Socialism for a Sceptical Age*. Cambridge: Polity Press.
Morris, B. (2004). *The Birth of the Palestinian Refugee Problem, Revisited*. Cambridge: Cambridge University Press.
Morse, C. (2010). *The Nazi Connection to Islamic Terrorism: Adolf Hitler and Haj Amin Al-Husseini* (Kindle ed.). Midpoint Trade Books.
Ornstein, J. (Ed.). (2017). *Whitewashed: Anti-Semitism in the Labour Party*. London: Kitty Hawk Press Ltd.
Pappe, I. (2011). *The Ethnic Cleansing of Palestine*. Oxford: Oneworld Publications.
Rawls, J. (1999). *A Theory of Justice*. Boston, MA: Harvard University Press. (This Particular Reference is to a Re-Issue of the First Edition, Which Originally Appeared in 1970).
Rich, D. (2016). *The Left's Jewish Problem: Jeremy Corbyn, Israel and Anti-Semitism*. London: Biteback Publications.
Roberts, A. (2014). *The Modern Swastika: Fighting Today's Anti-Semitism*. A Kindle Single.
Shlaim, A. (2014). *The Iron Wall: Israel and the Arab World*. Harmondsworth: Penguin.
Thatcher, M. (1987, October 31). Interview with Women's Own Magazine. Retrieved from http://briandeer.com/social/thatcher-society.htm.

CHAPTER 12

Crimes Against Humanity

Geras's book *Crimes against Humanity* (Geras 2011) aims at a discussion of the concept drawing on political philosophy. He starts by stating that the 'official birth' of the concept came with the Nuremberg trials at the end of the Second World War (Geras 2011, p. 3). Earlier appearances of the concept were linked to piracy and the slave trade, both of which were seen as crimes against humanity, which it was the duty of all states to suppress (Geras 2011, p. 5).

The Nuremberg principles were adopted by the United Nations General Assembly in 1950, but are linked to war. In 1973 however the United Nations General Assembly declared apartheid to be a crime against humanity on the basis that it was an offence that affected significant numbers of people, but, obviously, was not linked to war (Geras 2011, p. 24). In 1984 the United Nations brought torture into the range of crimes against humanity, accepting the idea of the possibility of prosecuting torture under international law (Geras 2011, p. 26). Geras points out that even a single act of torture is covered by this concept. This then raises the question as to whether there needs to be a threshold requirement for crimes against humanity (Geras 2011, p. 27).

Things were taken a step further with the establishment in 1998 of the International Criminal Court. Under the statute crimes against humanity are deemed to be those that are carried out against a civilian population in a widespread or systematic way and include quite a wide variety of acts, including acts of sexual violence and a catchall clause

M. Cowling, *Norman Geras's Political Thought from Marxism to Human Rights*, https://doi.org/10.1007/978-3-319-74048-5_12

about 'other inhumane acts' (Geras 2011, pp. 29–30). The International Criminal Court was intended to operate only in cases where national courts were unable or unwilling to prosecute (Geras 2011, p. 31).

What is it that makes a crime against humanity specifically a crime *against humanity*? They are subject to universal jurisdiction (Geras 2011, p. 33). As indicated above, piracy and the slave trade were the first crimes in this category because their perpetrators were said to be 'an enemy of all mankind' (Geras 2011, pp. 33–34). What about the idea of a threshold of seriousness in this context? Geras rejects the idea of diminishing mankind, or diminishing everyone in a particular category, because this could apply to relatively trivial examples (Geras 2011, p. 42). Threatening the peace and security of humankind seems to be too all-embracing—one could imagine thoroughly inhumane but individual acts that not do this (Geras 2011, p. 44). Shock and moral offence are likely to be reactions to crimes against humanity, but are not appropriate for defining them because shock and shame 'do not establish the severity of harm' (Geras 2011, p. 49). Geras says that a good criterion is grave and inhuman acts, meaning those above a certain level of seriousness (2011, p. 49). What about the idea of crimes against the human status? Geras does not find this particularly plausible. It does point to the general idea (Geras 2011, p. 54), but some versions of it want to restrict it to acts of genocide, which seems too narrow, but a version that works better is the idea of crimes that terrorize us all (Geras 2011, p. 59) and Geras allows that this can include the cultural meanings of acts (2011, p. 74).

Geras moves on to consider the question of a jurisdictional threshold. He starts by noting that it is very common to link the concept of crimes against humanity to that of human rights (Geras 2011, p. 76). Geras discusses the legal distinction between *mala prohibata* and *mala in se*, the first being acts that are wrong only because they are prohibited, the latter being prohibited because they are wrong. An example of the former might be driving on the right-hand side of the road, which is prohibited in England but is required in France. There is nothing inherently good or bad about driving on the right-hand side of the road as such, but driving on the wrong side of the road is potentially lethal if a country's laws have specified that one should only drive on one side of the road, namely the other side. Crimes that are *mala in se* are wrong in themselves, whether or not they are legally prohibited. An example might be domestic violence, now seen as criminal and frequently very serious, and wrong wherever and whenever it takes place. Obviously in former times it was legally sanctioned, what with ducking stools and 'rule of thumb', but, arguably, was still seriously wrong in former and less enlightened times. Crimes against humanity are manifestly *mala in se*: internationally seen as wrong wherever they occur (Geras 2011, p. 80).

For this reason they are also seen as an appropriate area to be covered by international law. Geras notes that at the time of the Nuremberg trials there was a tendency to respect state sovereignty by restricting the notion of crimes against humanity to crimes committed in the context of war (Geras 2011, p. 81). There has, however, he notes, been a steady movement away from linking crimes of humanity to war, and the link with war did not feature in the Rome Statute of the International Criminal Court (Geras 2011, p. 83).

Parallel with this there has been a move against requiring state action, and a recognition that non-state actors can violate human rights. This may be seen in legislation surrounding the International Criminal Court and the tribunals on Yugoslavia and Rwanda (Geras 2011 p. 86). Also, someone does not have to be treated as a member of a group in order for crimes against humanity to occur (Geras 2011, pp. 88–89). This links to the idea put forward by Sir Hartley Shawcross at Nuremberg that the individual human being is the 'ultimate unit' of all law (Geras 2011, p. 90). The International Criminal Court, however, is restricted to considering violations against a civilian population as part of a 'widespread' or 'systematic' attack (Geras 2011, p. 93). Geras accepts that as a pragmatic matter a restriction of this kind is necessary, but argues that in terms of a 'pure' definition this restriction is not appropriate (Geras 2011, p. 93). In principle, crimes against humanity are properly dealt with by the community of nations, and some day international courts might be able to try all such offences where national courts had failed to deal with such an offence (Geras 2011, p. 95).

Geras then moves on to the controversial issue of humanitarian intervention, which placed him in the relatively isolated position of being a Marxist who argued that international intervention in Iraq was justified. He adopts what he says is a standard definition of humanitarian intervention, namely it:

> (a) involves the use of military force (b) by one state on the territory of another, (c) in order to protect people in danger of grave harm (d) when the state within the jurisdiction of which they reside cannot or will not do so. (Geras 2011, p. 99)

One other thing that will emerge in the historical discussion of humanitarian intervention is that other forms of intervention can also be important, such as diplomatic and economic pressure. Indeed, military intervention without other forms of intervention first must be unusual.

Geras notes that a common view is that, with the creation of the United Nations, intervention is absolutely prohibited except for self-defence or when authorized by the UN (Geras 2011, p. 101). He disagrees with this:

> There *is* a right of humanitarian intervention. For the implication of holding the contrary is that crimes against humanity may be committed on a mass scale, violating the most fundamental human rights ... and no coercive action may be taken to do so nonetheless. (Geras 2011, pp. 101–102, italics in original)

Having asserted this, there is obviously a question about what circumstances might justify such an intervention. He then offers one example of a small intervention directed at carrying out a limited task, namely the Israeli raid on Entebbe in Uganda in 1976 to rescue airline passengers who were being held hostage. The point about this is that it is an example of a limited action well short of all-out war (Geras 2011, p. 104).

What about interventions on a sufficiently large scale to create the risk of war? One view is that the situation must involve mass death or the imminent danger of it. Geras argues that this perhaps sets the bar too low as it would entail that the sovereignty of a regime that had just finished carrying out acts of genocide should be respected. Similarly, a regime that tortured and murdered large numbers of people over an extended period of time but not sufficient to produce a humanitarian crisis would have its sovereignty respected, as would one that presided over people starving to death through its own misrule (Geras 2011, p. 106).

There should be some standard constraints on such intervention:

> (i) the exhaustion of other possible remedies, such as diplomatic and/or economic pressure; (ii) a good prospect of the intervention being successful; (iii) a readiness to withdraw expeditiously when the humanitarian purpose has been accomplished; and (iv) proportionality of the military means to the situation with which they are required to deal ... (v) there is a genuine humanitarian purpose at work and that it be central in guiding the conduct of the intervention. (Geras 2011, p. 107)

He says that this is backed up by the international law on genocide, which has been in force since 1948, and the doctrine that has come to be argued for recently of a responsibility to protect (Geras 2011, p. 108). Whilst such intervention should ideally go through the United Nations Security Council if possible, it must be possible for there to be exceptions (Geras 2011, p. 109). This is because veto-wielding members of the Security Council may block intervention simply for reasons of state (Geras 2011, p. 110).

These proposed philosophical principles for the justification of humanitarian intervention will be revisited below. Before this, more needs to be said about Geras's general exposition of the idea of humanitarian intervention. A major merit of Geras's way of doing political philosophy is his insistence on the use of good historical evidence to back up his own analysis. It would have been desirable to say rather more about the history of the concept. A recent collection of articles traces a recognizable concept of humanitarian intervention back to the immediate aftermath of the Reformation (e.g. Simms and Trim 2011, p. 31).[1] The earliest examples it considers are intervention by Elizabeth I of England in the Netherlands, concerned about the welfare of Dutch Protestants under Spanish oppression, in France, which was close to being a failed state thanks to the Wars of Religion, where she was concerned about the welfare of the Huguenots, and arguably prevented genocide, and of Philip II of Spain, concerned about the welfare of Elizabeth's Catholic subjects. Some of this intervention came in the form of material assistance, and some was military (Simms and Trim 2011, pp. 44, 47, 52). It should also be obvious that these humanitarian interventions also had other motives, for example, an English desire to preserve the Dutch because they were important trading partners, an English worry that France might become a failed state with consequences for England, and Philip II's desire to win England back to Catholicism.

Although Oliver Cromwell's major reputation is hardly for humanitarian intervention, he was widely praised for a genuinely disinterested humanitarian intervention on behalf of Protestants in Savoy (Simms and Trim 2011, p. 61).

One topic that Geras fails to consider, but certainly should have done, is the historical legacy of the Peace of Westphalia. Many political theorists argue that the international order has been historically underpinned by the principles of the Peace of Westphalia (1648). This ended the Thirty Years War, and laid down principles that have been the basis of international relations ever since. A major reason for intervention at the time was religious. To avoid such interventions the principle was established that princes (which meant the sovereign body of a particular state, rather than a prince as such) should be able to lay down the official religion of that country. However, those subscribing to other variants of Christianity should have reasonable freedom of public worship and unrestricted freedom of private worship. There was also a right to leave the country where you are living and move to another country. Within these principles the sovereignty of states should be respected.

The point of this is that there should be no reason for states to interfere in the internal affairs of other states. The experience of the time preceding the Peace was that unrestricted intervention on religious grounds caused greater misery than the evils it was supposed to avoid. Brought up to date the doctrine is basically that most states have some level of human rights violations, and that intervention is prone to cause more misery than it alleviates. A modern example of humanitarian intervention, which could be held to justify the principles of the Peace of Westphalia, is the invasion of Iraq in 2003. This will be discussed later. A powerful argument based on Westphalian principles can be seen in action in Sir James Mackintosh's criticisms of Austrian intervention on humanitarian principles (Simms and Trim 2011, p. 124).

Although Geras should definitely have considered likely objections to his views based on the Westphalian principles, some of the historians in the Simms and Trim collection offer him some ways to argue back. It is possible to argue, indeed, that the Westphalian Treaties were actually a recipe for intervention (Simms and Trim 2011, p. 91). Over the years between the signing of the treaties and the 1990s, there have been many examples of humanitarian intervention. Certainly, humanitarian intervention was a subject of political argument, with Edmund Burke justifying humanitarian intervention in France, and, in an officially non-interventionist period, John Stuart Mill arguing that definite principles for intervention were required, because it was both widely practised and was justifiable in principle (Simms and Trim 2011, pp. 103, 106, 117, 137). One example of such intervention at the time was Palmerston's intervention on behalf of Jews in the Ottoman Empire, which was simply diplomatic, but which was backed by powerful public sentiment (Simms and Trim 2011, p. 145). Multilateral humanitarian intervention on behalf of Christians in the Lebanon in 1860 can be seen as having parallels with multilateral humanitarian interventions in the 1990s—in both cases definite political interests were at stake, but clear humanitarian motives prevailed (Simms and Trim 2011, p. 182). In 1876 the Ottoman Empire was again the subject of public outrage and calls for at least diplomatic intervention, reflected in a pamphlet by Gladstone, and a feeling that Russian humanitarian intervention in the Balkans was justified. A successor to the 1876 episode was further agitation for intervention by the Balkan committee in 1903 (Simms and Trim 2011, pp. 193, 203, 214).

Geras mentions intervention against the slave trade as one of the early forms of humanitarian intervention. The British legislation of 1807, which famously turned Britain from the leading nation of the slave trade to prohibiting the trade in British ships, was a result of a massive public campaign (Simms and Trim 2011, p. 232). From 1839 this turned to strictly illegal intervention against non-British slaving ships. Thinking of modern humanitarian invention, Geras is insistent that, although United Nations backing for humanitarian invention is desirable, it cannot be regarded as essential. He could have cited Britain's actions, in violation of well-established principles of the Freedom of the Seas, meaning that interfering with the ships of other nations was prohibited, as a precedent for the approach he is advocating (Simms and Trim 2011, pp. 253, 254). There were also diplomatic initiatives and attempts to get other nations to cease trading in slaves. Britain's international intervention against the slave trade was against her commercial and territorial interests, and driven by a humanitarian consensus (Simms and Trim 2011, p. 259). However, particularly later in the nineteenth century, the anti-slave cause was used to win support for imperial expansion (Simms and Trim 2011, p. 271). Sudan became a British colony, but this facilitated the activities of British and US missionaries in the south of the country, the part of Sudan from which slaves had been traditionally taken. Christian converts retained a belief in wrongness of attempts from the north to impose Islam on the whole of the Sudan. This subsequently became the basis of a series of civil wars, but on the whole the humanitarian intervention by missionaries continued to be regarded by Southerners with gratitude (Simms and Trim 2011, p. 297).

Geras could have considered a major episode of humanitarian intervention within the communist world, the toppling by Vietnam of the Pol Pot regime in Cambodia (Simms and Trim 2011, p. 343).

A somewhat different, but also historical insight into the question of human rights and humanitarian intervention is offered by Moyn (2017). While Moyn acknowledges to some extent the more distant origins of the concept of human rights, which can be found in Geras (2011) and Simms and Trim (2011), he emphasizes that the concept only really emerges as a live issue in the context of dissidents in Eastern Europe in the 1970s, on the ruins of revolution in the sense of widespread social change promising human liberation on the model of the French, American or Russian revolutions (Moyn 2017, pp. 12, 69, 81, 94, 98, 138). Indeed, he says that human rights have frequently been offered as a justification of imperial expansion, pointing out that even John Stuart Mill was willing to contemplate expansion to benefit backward societies (Moyn 2017, pp. 17, 35). The most appalling case of this sort was Belgium's promise to eliminate slavery in the Congo, followed by the most terrible human rights abuses (Moyn 2017, p. 36). Although the concept of human rights might have appeared to have taken centre stage with the Nuremberg trials and the United Nations Universal Declaration of Human Rights, Moyn argues that human rights were actually marginal during the 1940s, and in particular that what colonial subjects really wanted was national liberation (Moyn 2017, p. 73). We may perhaps see genocide as the worst possible case of human rights violation. We might therefore naturally expect the Holocaust to have had a central role in the Nuremberg trials, but it was scarcely mentioned (Moyn 2017, p. 78). Nor, he asserts, was it mentioned during the diplomatic discussions leading up to the Universal Declaration of Human Rights (Moyn 2017, p. 90). Holocaust memory only came to the fore in the 1970s (Moyn 2017, p. 94). A few NGOs lobbied at the United Nations on behalf of human rights, but secured little traction between the 1940s and the 1970s (Moyn 2017, p. 79). He attributes the success of Amnesty International's campaign to put torture at the centre of the issue of human rights in the 1970s both to the paradigm shift away from socialism and nationalism and to the ending of circumstances in which the Western powers frequently used torture, such as the war in Vietnam or during colonialism (Moyn 2017, p. 104). He offers an alternative paradigm that resonates with Geras's work, namely the idea that nations have duties, for example the duty to alleviate poverty (Moyn 2017, p. 134).

At least one of Moyn's judgements is highly questionable: the word 'Holocaust' may not have been used during the Nuremberg trials, but the concept that one very important atrocity committed by the Nazis was the slaughter of some six million Jews played a major role in the trials. An affidavit that played a considerable role in the prosecution of Goering was sworn by the commandant of Auschwitz, who amongst other things testified that the camp had killed some 2 million Jews. All this is very evident from a straightforward history of the trials, such as Roland (2012)—the references are so frequent, once he gets to the substance of the main, international trial of the leading Nazis, that listing individual references would be unnecessarily tedious. Apart from the very frequent references in the first, main trial, there was a specific trial of leaders of the *Einsatzgruppen*, the death squads that operated in the areas of Russia invaded by the Nazis (Roland 2012, location 2771). That said, much of the rest of his argument looks plausible, if somewhat overstated.

Justifying the Invasion of Iraq

Geras achieved considerable notoriety on the left by supporting the 2003 invasion of Iraq. For example, in a trenchant obituary by Paul Blackledge (2013) he is praised for some of his earlier work, but denounced as an imperialist because of this:

> Norman Geras died an apologist for imperialism and had spent the last decade and more trying to justify Bush's and Blair's drive to war in Afghanistan and Iraq.

This is a singularly harsh judgement, given that Geras was engaged in numerous other activities over the final years of his life! However, it does make the point that his justification of the invasion was, to say the least, extremely controversial. Let us start by going through his arguments. They are all available in normblog, but are also conveniently available in Geras (2005). He starts by saying that he became committed to the left in the 1960s. He was committed to 'an open, multifaceted and pluralist Marxism', and in protesting against the war in Vietnam, Pinochet's coup in Chile, and the role of the USA in both of these (Geras 2005, p. 192). (Geras's Marxism developed from his early Trotskyism, and his protesting against the war in Vietnam. The North Vietnamese and Vietcong guerrillas were extremely ruthless with officials and senior soldiers of the various southern regimes, including deciding that it was not worth expending a bullet on despatching somebody, but that they should simply be buried alive. Both they and Trotsky may have been on the right side in some wider sense, but their human rights record was somewhat lacking.) Geras then talks about the 'massacre of innocents' in New York on 11 September 2001, and his disgust at people on the left and liberals talking of the murders as unfortunate, but describing them as some sort of comeuppance. Why, he wonders, did not the Chilean left resort to the mass murder of civilians in the USA back in 1973?

The comeuppance notion was definitely not appropriate, and Geras is right to emphasize that there was no justification for the slaughter of innocent civilians. The origins of the comeuppance sentiments were perhaps more to do with a feeling that the USA, and the West more generally, had a dismissive attitude to the lives of people in the Arab world. There was also a widespread suspicion of imperialist activities in the Middle East. A great deal more will be said about this later.

Geras then moves on to discuss the massive demonstrations against the invasion of Iraq, which took place in 2003. An important question to discuss here would be the link between the 9/11 attacks and the invasion of Iraq. The majority of the hijackers came from Saudi Arabia, and others came from Pakistan. None of them came from Iraq. Saddam Hussein was certainly an extremely bloody dictator, but he was a secular ruler, not an Islamic fundamentalist. A striking picture of him shows him promoting university education for women. He is sitting at a table surrounded by women who are revealing their faces. This sort of behaviour would be completely unacceptable to Al Qaeda, for whom women should be veiled in public and accompanied by a male relative. Education for women was looked on by them with suspicion. Saddam Hussein's Foreign Minister, Tarik Aziz, was a Christian—again a very strange choice for a supporter of Al Qaeda. There was no evidence of Iraq supplying a base for Al Qaeda, although one Al Qaeda member may have visited Iraq on one occasion. George Bush got round this by talking about an axis of evil, which included Iraq, Iran and North Korea, all of whom he said were state sponsors of terrorism. This looked suspiciously like a justification for attacking any of a variety of states according to choice, particularly when Cuba, Syria, and Libya were added to the list by John Bolton, Undersecretary of State. In the Second World War the Axis powers co-operated with each other. A conspiracy mounted by the countries listed by Bush and Bolton would be extremely odd.

Geras does not address this issue. Instead he stresses the appalling human rights record of Saddam Hussain, asserts, in line with the arguments to be found earlier in this chapter, a '*moral* right of humanitarian intervention' (Geras 2005, p. 194), and notes that both Bush and Blair mentioned a humanitarian case for war more than once. He says that instead of the processions of shame, meaning the marches against the invasion of Iraq, there should have been a popular move in civil society calling for humanitarian invention, and thus sending a message to other dictators as well. He notes that, according to a Human Rights Watch estimate, over the 23 years of Saddam's rule at least 230,000 Iraqis fell victim to regime, the vast majority dying—some 200 people every week. If the marchers had succeeded, this regime would have gone on indefinitely.

He says that just because the invading forces came from states with a bad foreign policy record—Vietnam, Chile, Nicaragua and so forth, it doesn't prevent them from doing good on this occasion. Moreover, their recent record, be it evicting the Iraqis from Kuwait, intervening in Kosovo, intervening in Sierra Leone or getting rid of the Taliban, was a good one (Geras 2005, pp. 195–197). People who relish US setbacks since the fall of Saddam Hussain are failing to align themselves with 'a rapid stabilisation and democratisation of the country, promising its inhabitants an early prospect of national normalisation' (Geras 2005, p. 198). This appears to be presuming that rapid stabilization and so on was a reasonable prospect. He also deals with the argument that to be logically consistent the case for humanitarian intervention in Iraq would also be a case for intervention against large numbers of other dictatorships. He says that the dictatorship of Saddam Hussein was dramatically worse than most of the other obvious possibilities (Geras 2005, p. 199). In the final pages of the chapter Geras considers the argument that although the regime in Iraq had done some really terrible things in the past, it was not currently engaged in a level of mass slaughter sufficient to justify intervention. To this he basically replies that Saddam's record was so awful that there would be every reason to think he would engage in further atrocities in the future (Geras 2005, pp. 200–206).

Geras's humanitarian case for supporting the invasion makes sense as far as it goes, but is a serious case of the abstract application of political philosophy to a situation with other very important dimensions. In particular, he fails to consider the bulk of the case given for the invasion, which was not humanitarian intervention, and most important, fails to consider the long history of intervention by Western imperialists in Iraq and the Middle East more generally.

To avoid the danger of the critical points that follow turning into a book in their own right, a series of bullet points will be used.

- Historically the area that comprises modern day Iraq was extremely fertile and lay on trade routes between the East and the West. For this reason it was invaded on a high number of occasions. As a consequence of this it was very much a cradle of civilization, rivalling ancient Egypt. It generated forms of mathematics, scientific ideas, astronomical observations, medical ideas and treatments and religious ideas, having much to do with the basic ideas of Judaism, Christianity and Islam, all of which have broad similarities with the earlier Zoroastrianism. Scholars from Iraq or who migrated there preserved the major works of ancient Greece, and were the source of the European revival of interest in them in the Renaissance. The point about this is that the Iraqis deserve a degree of respect from us, in the same way as we respect the Greeks. Also, Iraq has a wealth of artefacts and historic sites that need to be preserved as part of world heritage. (This is a very brief and inadequate summary of an astonishing history taking in some 5000 years—see Robertson 2015, Chaps. 1–5).

- The formation of the modern state of Iraq involved squalid manoeuvrings by Britain, largely motivated by the discovery of oil near Mosul, and Britain's purchase of the right to exploit it in 1914—see Robertson 2015, location 3972). There was an aspiration for some form of Arab unity for the area from the Mediterranean to the borders of Iran, which was inspired by the doctrine of national self-determination announced by President Wilson during the First World War. Motivated by this, the Arabs engaged in a revolt against the Ottoman Empire, co-ordinated by T. E. Lawrence. Once victory was secured the British reneged on this, and agreed with the French to divide the area into protectorates. In addition came the Balfour declaration of November 1917, backing the Zionist aspiration of a Jewish homeland in Palestine. The British governed Iraq in such a heavy-handed fashion as to inspire the great revolt of June 1920 in which virtually all the disparate groups in Iraq rose up. The revolt was brutally quelled, with summary executions and the use of air power, and a cost of some 9000 Iraqis killed or wounded. Winston Churchill authorized the use of chemical weapons. Britain then installed Iraqi democracy in a referendum involving the kidnap of the candidate who seemed likely to stand up to them, and a dubious 94% vote in favour of their preferred candidate, King Faisal. He was duly installed, but was heavily dependent on a Sunni elite and authoritarian methods of rule. Thus was established a pattern that, with variations and coups, persisted until the time of Saddam Hussein (Robertson 2015, location 4032–4145).
- The British had established an authoritarian state with simmering tensions between roughly equal numbers of Sunnis and Shias, the

Kurds in the north, and other minorities such as Christians and Turkmen. There was also extreme inequality between wealthy landowners and the rural poor. Iraq was finally declared a republic in 1958, following a coup by army officers inspired by Arab Iraqi nationalism. The same pattern of authoritarian rule and social tensions persisted. This pattern of authoritarian rule reached new heights with the coming to power of the Baath party in 1968, and particularly under Saddam Hussein in 1979. Saddam established the notorious rule by secret police, involving massive surveillance, torture and executions execrated by Geras (Robertson 2015, location 4267–4564).

- By the time Saddam came to power the oil revenues had grown enormously and had been reclaimed by Iraq, so that it was possible to extend the benefits outside the elite. As Robertson puts it:

> By 1980, Iraq's standards and availability of education, health services, electricity production, and large-scale industry were among the most advanced in the Arab world. On the other hand, using oil revenue to augment goods and services effectively bought the public's acquiescence in the rule of an authoritarian, one-party state—which could—and did—crush any dissent (Robertson 2015, location 4681).

- Saddam Hussein calculated that, following the Islamic Revolution in Iran in 1979, the country would be in sufficient disarray that he could claim some of Iran's oilfields. He met with very stiff resistance from Iran, and used chemical weapons, including nerve gas, against both Iranians soldiers and disloyal Kurds—again as charted by Geras. The Americans under President Reagan showed their respect for Iraqi human rights by restoring diplomatic relations with Iraq, sending Donald Rumsfeld on two friendly visits, supplying Saddam with quantities of military equipment and military intelligence. Feeble protests were made about the use of chemical weapons, although a British company supplied equipment to help produce them. The supply of one of the precursors of mustard gas was justified because it was useful for making ballpoint pens (Fisk 2014, p. 870) The Americans supplied Saddam with assistance in producing biological weapons including anthrax and botulinum (Robertson 2015, location 4892). By the time of the war ended, the total dead and wounded, taking both sides together, was over 1 million. A government concerned with human rights would surely have intervened at least to stop the use of chemical weapons, and ideally to stop the war altogether.

- Saddam's next adventure was the notorious invasion of Kuwait in 1990. Shortly before the invasion he met with the US ambassador, April Glaspie, who assured him that the USA had no interest in inter-Arab disputes. As will be well known, President Bush (senior) launched an overwhelming military campaign supported by many Arab nations amongst others which rapidly expelled the Iraqis from Kuwait. The retreating Iraqi army was repeatedly strafed from the air, killing some 20,000 Iraqi soldiers in what US pilots described as a 'turkey shoot'. President Bush then urged the Iraqi people to throw off the dictator Saddam. The Kurds in the north and the Marsh Arabs in the South, particularly, took Bush at his word, assuming that US military assistance would be available. It was not, and Saddam took the dreadful revenge, which Geras rightly charts. Again, Saddam's actions were completely inexcusable, but they were a result of actions triggered by the USA.
- Between 1990 and the fall of Saddam in 2003, Iraq was very seriously affected by a sanctions regime imposed by the United Nations, intended to prevent sale of Iraqi oil, and the import of anything that might help produce weapons. Prohibited items included:

> pencils, pencil-sharpeners, shoe laces, material for shrouds, sanitary towels, shampoo, water purification chemicals, medical swabs, gauze, medical syringes, medical journals, cobalt sources for X-ray machines, disposable surgical gloves, medication for epilepsy, surgical instruments, dialysis equipment, drugs for angina, granite shipments, textile plant equipment, toothpaste, toothbrushes and toilet paper, tennis balls, children's clothes, nail polish and lipstick. (Fisk 2014, p. 870)

- During the 1990s it was widely believed that the sanctions had led to the deaths of half-a-million Iraqi children. President Clinton replaced Bush, but the policy was maintained. Madeleine Albright, the US ambassador to the United Nations, was interviewed about this for a programme entitled 60 Minutes:

> Correspondent Leslie Stahl said to Albright, 'We have heard that a half-million children have died. I mean, that's more children than died in Hiroshima. And—and, you know, is the price worth it?'

Madeleine Albright replied, ‘I think this is a very hard choice, but the price—we think the price is worth it.’

- This is the background to the massive demonstrations against the invasion of Iraq in 2003. Any human rights issues were seen as secondary, partly because the invasion was justified mainly in terms of the Iraqi possession of weapons of mass destruction, but overwhelmingly because the demonstrators did not remotely trust the Americans under President Bush. UN weapons inspectors had failed to find any weapons of mass destruction; the USA had not helped the process of inspection by including CIA spies amongst the inspectors. Bush was known to be an oilman by background, and there were widespread suspicions that a major part of the US motivation was a desire to get access to Iraq’s oil. (In the run-up to the war, the British press and the BBC let the public down very badly. They never seemed to get outside the minutiae of people’s integrity at Westminster, when there were plenty of publicly available sources of information suggesting that Iraq had got rid of its chemical and biological weapons, that it was highly unlikely to possess nuclear weapons, and that if there were any chemical weapons hidden away they would have turned to useless sludge by 2003—for this and plenty more, see a variety of pamphlets and articles by David Morrison at: http://www.david-morrison.org.uk/).
- Lies and half-truths told in order to justify an invasion intended to bring about regime change do not inspire confidence in the humanitarian intervention element in the reasons given by Geras for supporting the war. Given that what was planned was regime change, responsible planning for the aftermath of the war was paramount. The US government’s assumption seems to have been (1) a delighted and united Iraqi people would move rapidly to set up democratic institutions; (2) there would be no real problem in restoring Iraq’s infrastructure because (3) Iraq’s oil would soon be flowing freely, thanks to the assistance provided by US oil companies in return for generous and profitable concessions. Very little attention was paid to the potential for divisions between Sunni and Shia Muslims, and the Kurdish desire for their own state. Administration in Iraq had, obviously, been in the hands of members of the Baath party, but these were now disbarred. This exacerbated problems of disorganization and corruption. If you have democracy but no reliable supplies of

water and electricity, your support for the government is likely to wane. The Iraqi army was disbanded, which meant that unemployed soldiers, perhaps still sympathetic to Saddam, could be a source of resistance and disruption. Iraq's rich cultural heritage in the form of artefacts suffered badly with virtually no protection.

- Al Qaeda had, contrary to President Bush's assertions, not been welcome in Iraq under Saddam Hussein. However, perhaps predictably, in the chaotic situation following the war, they found a welcome amongst Iraq's Sunni population. Despite his Wahhabi background, Osama bin Laden said relatively sympathetic things about Shia Muslims. However, the leader of Al Qaeda in Iraq, Abu Musab al-Zarqawi, was violently antipathetic to Shia Muslims, and inaugurated a campaign of suicide bombings, which included two of the holiest mosques according to the Shia faith, and otherwise specialized in setting off car bombs in markets in Baghdad where poor Shias were doing their shopping. Unsurprisingly this led to Shia retaliation against Sunni targets. Perhaps this latter development and the eventual rise of Islamic State in Iraq was not something that the best of planners could have foreseen, but the possibility of sectarian tensions and of post-invasion chaos was certainly predictable.
- It will be recalled that Geras's justification for humanitarian intervention was that Saddam Hussein had killed a total of some 230,000 Iraqis over his 23 years in power. Household surveys suggest that deaths from the war and subsequent chaos amount to somewhere between 600,000 and over 1 million (for details of several surveys and methods of counting see Wikipedia: http://en.wikipedia.org/wiki/Casualties_of_the_Iraq_War).

Geras is at his best when he combines political philosophy and an analytical approach to Marxism with detailed study of the literature in the area, as can be seen particularly with his study of the Holocaust discussed in the previous chapter, and his demolition of Richard Rorty's ignorant assertions about the motivations of people who saved Jews from the Nazis. However, when it comes to humanitarian intervention, relatively abstract political philosophy seems to have taken over from a detailed case-by-case analysis, and he did indeed effectively become an apologist for imperialism.

He did, subsequently, in normblog acknowledge that things had not gone well in Iraq following the invasion:

> That is, had I been able to foresee, in January and February 2003, that the war would have the results it has actually had in the numbers of Iraqis killed and the numbers now daily dying, with the country (more than three years down the line) on the very threshold of civil war if not already across that threshold, I would not have felt able to support the war and I would not have supported it. Measured, in other words, against the hopes of what it might lead to and the likelihoods as I assessed them, the war has failed. Had I foreseen a failure of this magnitude, I would have withheld my support. Even then, I would not have been able to bring myself to oppose the war. As I have said two or three times before, nothing on earth could have induced me to march or otherwise campaign for a course of action that would have saved the Baathist regime. But I would have stood aside. (Geras 2006: http://normblog.typepad.com/normblog/2006/10/failure_in_iraq.html)

This is particularly clear in the political issue of bombing Syria in 2013. One would expect that a Marxist analysis would cover such matters as potential divisions in Syrian society, the capacity of the Assad regime to defend itself, and so forth. In a brief normblog entry of 27 August 2013, Geras starts by asserting that there is a duty of humanitarian intervention in a situation of the kind obtaining in Syria, where the government was using chemical weapons on its own people; that such an intervention is warranted in international law, and that a UN mandate is not required. He then says, in essence, that he is completely uncertain as to whether intervention would actually do any good. In which case, is there really any point in the preceding arguments (Cohen and Garrard 2017, pp. 201–202)? There is, in fact, a series of previous posts about Syria, but in essence they all chart very serious iniquities of the Assad regime, and assert the justifications for humanitarian intervention that derive from the arguments in his book about crimes against humanity. In one of them he asserts, in spite of the problems that arose in Iraq in the years following the 2003 invasion that it was nonetheless better than leaving Saddam Hussein in place.

Overall, Geras has a rather gung-ho approach to humanitarian intervention and, indeed, to intervention intended to bring about regime change. The lack of an attempt at a careful analysis of, for example, Syrian society and history, while definitely signalling a liberal rather than a Marxist approach, is part of a view in the background of Geras's thinking, which was that if a consensus developed in favour of humanitarian intervention that could be triggered off by relatively limited crimes against humanity, then it might not actually be needed very often. Regimes that contemplated inflicting widespread torture or murder on their populations would know that there was a very strong likelihood of retribution, and therefore refrain. The domestic criminal law of well-run states has something of this effect: because individuals know that if they commit serious offences there is a good chance of being prosecuted and imprisoned, they tend to refrain. Obviously, they do not always refrain, criminal laws may be unjust, they are not applied equally to different sections of the population, but the overall effect is nonetheless better than in their absence. There would be very little support for the decriminalization of murder and grievous bodily harm, even though most of us refrain from these acts on moral grounds rather than for fear of being caught.

Most of Geras's arguments fit straightforwardly into the idea of developing international law and institutions to more closely resemble the domestic law of states that respect human rights. His argument that intervention should not require a UN mandate, while understandable in the sense that the UN Security Council reflects a series of political interests, and may not, therefore, support humanitarian intervention when it would be thoroughly warranted, is open to criticism on the grounds that simply ignoring UN institutions is undermining rather than supporting the development of a framework of international law and of effective intervention mechanisms.

Other examples where humanitarian intervention that might have been justified on the Geras criteria could include the Irish potato famine of the 1840s, in which about 1,000,000 out of 8,000,000 Irish people died and another million emigrated in extremely impoverished circumstances. The only problem being that the state, which was allowing Irish people to die as a result of neglect (the government of the day subscribed to an early version of Thatcherism, with an excessive emphasis on self-reliance), was the government of the United Kingdom, overwhelmingly the most powerful state in the world at that time. The worry I am expressing about incautious and widespread humanitarian intervention was put somewhat frivolously by the jurist Sir James Mackintosh in 1826, commenting on Austrian proposals for humanitarian intervention, that there might be similar (and dubious) grounds for other states monitoring British activities in Ireland, so that we might end up with Cossacks camped in Hyde Park (see Simms and Trim 2011, p. 124).

Another example could be the US intervention in Vietnam, which probably cost the lives of some 2 million Vietnamese people out of a total population of 50 million. Dropping liberal quantities of high explosives, napalm and the defoliant Agent Orange on large areas of Vietnam was arguably a serious crime against humanity, and would warrant outside intervention. However, the only power that could seriously have intervened was the Soviet Union. Whilst the USSR helped to provide the materials of war for the North Vietnamese, a more serious intervention would have risked nuclear warfare, which would plainly be much worse than anything happening in Vietnam. The various South Vietnamese regimes, the USA, the North Vietnamese and the Vietcong all engaged in serious human rights abuses. Those by the USA and South Vietnamese are sickening and well documented, but the other side was ruthless and indiscriminate in eliminating collaborators with the South. Geras plainly sided with the left at the time, but one wonders where his eventual humanitarian intervention above all else approach would have left him.

The above considerations may be linked to an argument that Geras considers in the final chapter in the book, 'Utopia into Law'. This is that international law is too feeble to be taken seriously. An obvious example might be the failure of the USA to ratify the Rome Statute of the International Criminal Court. George Bush is therefore not likely to end up imprisoned in The Hague charged with being a war criminal (Geras 2011, pp. 116–117: he does not use the argument about George Bush, given his views about Iraq, but it is plainly the sort of argument he has in mind). Geras argues that we should work towards a more effective system of international law: 'an imperfect system can be better than the absence of all law, and selective prosecution can be better than no prosecutions at all' (Geras 2011, p. 119). He accepts an argument put forward by D. H. N. Johnson that codes of international criminal law can be seen as part of the process of building an international community that might enforce them (Geras 2011, p. 121). For the same reason he applauds Geoffrey Robertson's idea that a vast global audience is now starting to think like global citizens (Geras 2011, p. 122). Geras acknowledges that there is something in the argument that liberals do not pay sufficient attention to social and economic rights, for example adequate nourishment, healthcare and education. Deliberate deprivation of these rights by a political agency should be thought of as crimes against humanity, as should apartheid and systematic gender oppression (Geras 2011, pp. 123–125). Whilst it is certainly good to see gender oppression included in crimes against humanity, there is definitely an argument for proceeding with considerable caution given that even the best of states in gender terms remain patriarchal, so that intervention would be legitimate virtually anywhere and anytime. At this point something that looks initially like an attractive approach reaches its reductio ad absurdum. The violations of human rights that Geras considers are all well-chosen and thoughtful, but, together with his strong emphasis on the potential legitimacy of humanitarian intervention lead to an excessive justification of intervention.

This relates to a final point. Geras is realistic in that one of the criteria he provides as to whether humanitarian intervention should actually be attempted is that it should have a realistic prospect of success. This criterion offers a good reason for restraint in the examples where intervention would be justified anywhere and at any time. More worryingly, military forms of intervention would appear to be ruled out against states possessing nuclear weapons, on the grounds that nuclear war would be worse than any of the human rights abuses considered above. Thus states with nuclear weapons may be subject to moral obloquy or economic sanctions, but may abuse human rights with impunity from any sort of military sanction.

Notes

1. Although the book referred to is an edited collection, the articles it contains are very much on a common theme, namely the contribution to the study of humanitarian intervention made by looking at the practice in history, rather than simply considering it from the standpoint of political theory. For this reason I have simply referred to the book as a whole rather than distinguishing the individual articles.

References

Blackledge, P. (2013, November). Norman Geras, 1943–2013. *Socialist Review*. Issue 385. Retrieved from http://socialistreview.org.uk/385/norman-geras-1943-2013.

Cohen, B., & Garrard, E. (Eds.). (2017). *The Norman Geras Reader 'What's There is There'*. Manchester: Manchester University Press.

Fisk, R. (2014). *The Great War for Civilisation: The Conquest of the Middle East*. London: Fourth Estate, Harper Collins Publishers. (Kindle edition), (first published 2005).

Geras, N. (2005). Pages from a Daily Journal of Argument. In T. Cushman (Ed.), *A Matter of Principal: Humanitarian Arguments for War in Iraq* (pp. 191–206). Berkeley and Los Angeles, CA: University of California Press.

Geras, N. (2011). *Crimes Against Humanity*. Manchester: Manchester University Press.

Moyn, S. (2017). *Human Rights and the Uses of History, (expanded edition)*. London: Verso.

Robertson, J. (2015). *Iraq: A History*. London: Oneworld Publications.

Roland, P. (2012). *The Nuremberg Trials: The Nazis and Their Crimes against Humanity*. London: Arcturus.

Simms, B., & Trim, D. J. B. (Eds.). (2011). *Humanitarian Intervention: A History*. Cambridge: Cambridge University Press.

CHAPTER 13

Conclusion

What an amazing lifetime's achievement! And what a shame that Geras's voice was silenced in 2013 at the relatively young age of 70. His main works are characterized by the way that they unite a thorough study of the issues in question with intense analytical rigour. Also awe-inspiring is the very wide range of areas he covered, including Rosa Luxemburg, the issue of human nature in Marx, an intelligent critique of Althusser, a superb analysis of the major issues concerned with whether or not Marx had a theory of justice, followed by Geras's own attempts to develop and elaborate a Marxist theory of justice. Then there is his trenchant critique of the trendy postmodernism of Laclau and Mouffe, and the better thought out, but still deeply flawed pragmatism of Richard Rorty. Then there is his excellent edited book on the Enlightenment, and his willingness to confront the horrors of the Holocaust, and his account of human rights. All of the above have been discussed in the course of the book, but there has not been room for a systematic discussion of the intense energy that Geras put into writing normblog for ten years, nor of his two jointly authored books about test matches.

I have indicated some criticisms and also have appreciated Geras's work by adding some supporting argument.

By way of conclusion I shall raise some issues about his work that I regard as flawed, puzzling, or not really resolved. The first of these is its relationship with Trotsky and Trotskyism. Then there is the question of democratic routes to socialism. In Britain this would normally involve a

M. Cowling, *Norman Geras's Political Thought from Marxism to Human Rights*, https://doi.org/10.1007/978-3-319-74048-5_13

discussion of the possible role of the Labour party; alternatively one could look at a European model of Social Democracy, involving a development of the European Union. Finally, given the amount of Marxist analysis that Geras actually rejects, there is the issue of the endpoint of his relationship with Marxism.

Starting, then, with Geras's views about Trotsky. In Chap. 2 I indicated various reasons to suggest that the youthful Geras, who was a member of the Fourth International, should have had more reservations about Trotsky. Even at this early stage in his intellectual development, Geras was keen to advocate genuine democracy. Trotsky, however, when in power, engaged in, and, indeed, developed various forms of state terror. He went along with the ban on factions in the Bolshevik Party. Subsequently, when out of power, he did not make a thorough criticism of his conduct when in power. It is therefore open to question whether, if he had had the good fortune to be restored to the leadership of the Bolshevik Party, he would have conducted himself any differently. He also had unrealistic expectations of human perfectibility under socialism.

All of these should have led Geras to be more critical of Trotsky at an early stage. But even later in his career, when discussing Ernest Mandel and the Holocaust (see Chap. 11), there is little to suggest that his admiration of Trotsky had abated, even though he is critical of the way that Mandel, in a manner reminiscent of Trotsky, lists a series of evils attributable to capitalism. Particularly by the time of the Euston Manifesto, or his book on crimes against humanity, Geras was placing human rights at the centre of his politics. It would have been useful at this stage if he had attempted to settle accounts with his youthful Trotskyism in a systematic way.

I made an additional criticism of Trotsky and Trotskyists, which serves as a link to my second line of criticism and questioning. This was that Trotskyists have never actually managed to carry out a revolution. Trotsky himself lost the power struggle within the Soviet Union. He attributed this to contingent factors, such as getting ill at the wrong time, or failing to make enough of the possibility of criticizing Stalin over the Georgian question. He failed to consider the way in which the Bolsheviks looked to the precedent of the French revolution, worrying about which of them might turn into Napoleon, and seeing Trotsky as the most likely candidate. Also, Trotsky had only joined the Bolsheviks in 1917, whereas other Bolsheviks leaders, notably Stalin, had spent long years working underground. The broadly Stalinist form of politics was responsible for all of the communist revolutions that were successful up to about 1975. They may have been bringing into being a flawed version of socialism, but it did actually work for many years.

This relates, then, to the second line of questioning and criticism that I want to pursue. Geras says remarkably little about practical ways of bringing about socialist change. By the time of the Euston Manifesto, with its very strong commitment to human rights and to the central features of liberal democracy other than the preservation of property rights, he had clearly abandoned any idea of violent revolution, at least in the advanced capitalist countries of Western Europe, the USA and so forth. The Euston Manifesto is basically a charter for online activists, aiming to alter some of the major guiding ideas on the left. It potentially relates to a variety of different capitalist states, and therefore says nothing specific about political parties.

So what about, in Britain, the Labour Party? Given the democratic commitments of the Euston Manifesto, the Labour Party would seem to be the natural vehicle for attempting to introduce socialist change in Britain. Under Blair Labour abandoned its Clause 4 commitment to nationalization and achieved victory in a succession of three general elections. It disappointed many people, me included, by failing to make the social advances that we thought should have been possible. On the other hand, it did achieve substantially increased spending on NHS and education. The only prominent comments from Geras concerning the Blair government are his support for the invasion of Iraq, which is generally seen as a major reason why Labour lost popularity. Apart from this and a more general commitment to humanitarian intervention, together with a generalized worldwide commitment to minimum decent living standards and political freedoms for all, there is nothing on the possible merits or otherwise of the left or right in the Labour Party, policy priorities within Britain or electoral strategies. One of the features of Marxism that Geras was keen to maintain was the avoidance of empty moralizing, and yet with such an extreme lack of reflection about the exigencies of practical politics he is running rather close to that.

Again, I have not come across any comments from him about the European Union. Given the very substantial powers of multinational companies, a union of 28 states (going down to 27 with Britain leaving), stands much more chance of successful socialist change than any one state in isolation. In particular, the German model of *Mitbestimmung*, in which trade unions have representatives on company boards, might offer an interesting way forward. Overall, then, for somebody with a Marxist background and a commitment to socialist change achieved through democratic politics, there is a singular lack of comment about practical politics.

The final critical area concerns Geras's commitment to Marxism. He continued in the last years of his life to describe himself as a liberal Marxist. One has only to read the Euston Manifesto to see the very strong commitment to liberal values. What about the Marxism? I would agree with Geras's distaste for laying down one straightforward criterion for deciding whether or not somebody is a Marxist. In the final part of Chap. 7 there was an account of a late, jointly written article in which it is clear that Geras had abandoned the labour theory of value, and together with that the central propositions that Marx derived from it. So he had abandoned Marxist economics, without espousing any obvious replacement. Another central proposition of Marxism is the materialist conception of history, involving the idea that, in some way, the mode of production determines the other features of society (there are several versions of what this involves—for a brief discussion of some of them, see Cowling and Manners 1992). Harvey and Geras provide a constructive and interesting account of a whole variety of ways in which the purchase and use of labour power is different from the straightforward confrontation between a capitalist and a labourer, which Marx considers in *Capital*.

The other major area that is considered in the Harvey and Geras paper as their contribution to historical materialism is the forms in which labour is carried out. A major example that Marx underestimated was the role of slavery as a major source of capitalist profit. But there are also a wide variety of both preconditions of working and situations in work that need to be considered.

Harvey and Geras definitely identify a range of important issues that need to be considered as part of an egalitarian politics, and that might thus increase the purchase and popularity of left-wing politics. However, what they have provided is a set of extensions to the set of issues that need to be considered by egalitarians beyond the relatively simplistic reappropriation and redirection of surplus labour, which was at the centre of Marx's conception of the move from capitalist to communist society. This is a valuable set of insights in its own right. However, a central feature of historical materialism was the idea that it helped its adherents to understand how societies, particularly capitalist societies, function. What is likely to happen? What forms of strategic intervention might be particularly successful? What, for example, would be appropriate class alliances for the working class to make in particular situations? This seems to have basically disappeared in the Harvey and Geras reinterpretation. It may well be that they think it is beyond salvaging, but it would be useful to make this explicit.

The series of issues considered in the critical part of this conclusion suggest that Geras essentially ended up as an egalitarian liberal. There is nothing wrong with being an egalitarian liberal, but there is a much greater distance between this and his youthful Trotskyism than Geras perhaps realized.

Overall, though, in a lifetime of major achievement over a wide range of fields, consistency is not to be fully expected. The reader is bound to be more impressed with some aspects of Geras's achievements than others. Different readers will definitely carry away different ideas that they find stimulating and important. It is a tribute to Geras that there is so much there to argue about—which is surely exactly what he would have wanted.

Reference

Cowling, M., & Manners, J. (1992). Pre-History: The Debate Before Cohen. In P. Wetherly (Ed.), *Marx's Theory of History: The Contemporary Debate* (pp. 9–29). Aldershot: Avebury.

Index[1]

[1] Note: Page number followed by 'n' refer to notes.

M. Cowling, *Norman Geras's Political Thought from Marxism to Human Rights*, https://doi.org/10.1007/978-3-319-74048-5

The manufacturer's authorised representative in the EU is Springer Nature Customer Service Centre GmbH, Europaplatz 3, 69115 Heidelberg, Germany. If you have any concerns regarding our products, please contact ProductSafety@springernature.com

Printed and bound by CPI Group (UK) Ltd, Croydon, CR0 4YY
05/10/2026
02228128-0002